THE ENGLISH
PARISH CHURCH

1. OAKHAM, RUTLAND, FROM THE SOUTH-EAST

THE ENGLISH PARISH CHURCH

AN ACCOUNT OF THE CHIEF BUILDING
TYPES & OF THEIR MATERIALS DURING
NINE CENTURIES

By
J CHARLES COX, L.L.D., F.S.A

CLASSIC EDITIONS

This edition digitally re-mastered and
published by JM Classic Editions © 2008
Original text © J Charles Cox 1914

ISBN 978-1-905217-95-3

All rights reserved. No part of this book subject
to copyright may be reproduced in any form or
by any means without prior permission in writing
from the publisher.

CONTENTS

Chapter I : INTRODUCTION

PAGE

The Parish Church : Great number and antiquity : Succession of styles : Contrasting types in country and city : Origin and rise of the parochial system : Clergy and laity : The fabric—its construction and repair : The church as the centre of social life : Varying situations and contrasting local types : The effect of local industrial progress : Surrounding landscapes : The municipal church : Customs and practices in the use of the church : The maintenance of the fabric : The study of churches as repositories of art and craftsmanship : Harmony of design and situation 1

Chapter II : THE PLAN OF THE PARISH CHURCH

Summary of development : The three fundamental types : The influence of ritual and ceremonies on the plan : THE NAVE AND SANCTUARY TYPE : Continental influences : The square end and the Italian apse : THE NAVE, CHANCEL, AND SANCTUARY TYPE : Limitations due to roofing : Addition of aisles : Lighting problems and the CLERESTORY : Aisle lighting : Examples of Norman and later clerestories : Window development : Clerestories in unaisled churches : CHANCEL CHAPELS and their development : The final "parallelogram" plan : The great development of the rood screen : THE CRUCIFORM OR TRANSEPTAL TYPE and its widespread occurrence : The central tower in various periods : Changes and development in transeptal examples—aisles to tran-

CONTENTS

PAGE

septs: THE TOWER: Dwelling rooms in towers: Detached belfry towers and their peculiarities: THE PORCH: The western porch: Upper chambers, their occurrence and uses: Smaller porches or portals: THE VESTRY: Crypts: eastern extensions: THE AMBULATORY 57

CHAPTER III: ARCHITECTURAL STYLES

Introductory note on variations of style and terminology: Pre-Saxon remains: SAXON CHURCHES and their features: NORMAN BUILDING and its characteristics: Richness of Late Norman masonry: TRANSITION to Early English: The appearance of the pointed arch: EARLY ENGLISH: Its windows: Groined vaultings: Conventional floral carving: "Dog-tooth" ornament: Towers and spires: The dawn and progress of GEOMETRICAL building—general character: Examples of the DECORATED style: Curvilinear and flamboyant tracery; "Net" tracery: Profusion of Decorated detail: Retarding influence of the Black Death: Transition to Perpendicular: PERPENDICULAR or Fifteenth Century building: Typical arcades: Window tracery and painted glass: Western towers: Clerestories, roofs, and parapets: Waning of the style, RENAISSANCE INFLUENCE: Brickwork examples: Georgian work: Eighteenth century "Gothic": Restorations: Churches of composite periods 132

CHAPTER IV: MATERIALS

STONE: Saxon construction: Examples of Oolitic limestone churches: Norman importation of stone: Belgian and Purbeck marble: Doulting oolite and Bath stone: Other inferior stones: Cornish granite: Stone roofing: Vaultings of the different periods 215

FLINT: Its sources and qualities: Extensively used in East Anglia: Flush panel and diaper work: Various applications of flint: Chequer work—variety and effectiveness 234

CONTENTS

	PAGE
BRICK: Mediæval brickwork: Decadence of brickmaking: Revival by Flemings: Local usage: Extent of East Anglian productions: Brick mouldings: Picturesque repairs in brick: Brick linings: Various examples	243
PLASTER: Early internal and external plastering—paintings in distemper: Later work	252
WHITEWASHING: Its early practice and continuance	255
MORTAR: Width of joints and composition as identifying dates: Mortar of Roman work	256
TIMBER: The church at Greenstead: Saxon examples: Timber belfries: Timber framing of the nave: Arcades in timber: Tracery: Timber-built towers and porches: Varied occurrence	256
TIMBER ROOFS: Construction of Norman roofs: Steep roofs of Early English period: Extant examples: Later developments: Decorated roofs: Perpendicular roofs: Examples of flatter pitch aisle roofs: Decorative features: The hammer-beam	271
ROOFING: Thatched roofs, lead roofs, tiles, pantiles, slates, stone slates, shingled roofs	282
DOORS: Wooden doors and accompanying IRONWORK: Norman work: Early English scroll-work: Inscriptions: Handles and escutcheons	291

CHAPTER V: WHAT TO NOTE IN AN OLD PARISH CHURCH

Examination of the EXTERIOR: Review of constructive features and details: Where to look for evidences of early features and demolished work: Their likely positions, significance, and interest: The INTERIOR: Items of interest in Construction, Furniture, and Decoration; also Tombs, Brasses, etc.—references to existing examples	301
INDEX to Illustrations arranged under Counties	319

ERRATA

Page 199, Fig. 171 : for "HAYLEY" read "HANLEY"
,, 227 ,, 190 ,, "STOWE" read "STOW"
,, 248 ,, 211 ,, "*J. L. Griggs*" read "*F. L. Griggs*"
,, 296, line 2 from bottom, for "Sussex" read "Surrey"

PREFACE

It seems necessary to write a few words as to the aim and object of this book. It is an endeavour, however imperfectly accomplished, to put into plain language the origin, development, and aims of the old English Parish Church, more especially in the country districts. Notwithstanding the wear of time, the ravages of civil war, the fierce flames of religious bigotry, the devastating consequences of contemptuous neglect, or the ill-judged zeal of reconstruction, our ancient churches remain the envy of other parts of Christendom for their frequency, their innate beauty, their marvellous adaptability to surroundings, and more especially for the way they reflect the life and devotion of successive generations of our forefathers.

The study and examination of the story of our progenitors, as evidenced in the fabrics they have left behind them, is a fascinating pursuit, and it is nowadays being followed up after a more intelligent fashion and by increasing numbers. It is hoped that these pages will prove to be of some real assistance to those desirous of gaining knowledge as to the central and most important old building of the vast majority of England's innumerable parishes. Where there is one old castle, or even fragments of its component parts left standing, or the remains of a single ancient manor-house, there are scores of extant churches, whose very walls breathe of the spirit and hopes that animated our forefathers for a thousand and odd years. Doubtless, as time goes on, we are immeasurably their superiors in general taste and refinement, as well as in our science and our application of science to mechanical arts. But the shame still, in some measure, rests upon us that we, with all our

PREFACE

advantages, are their inferiors in the application of architecture to its highest purpose. A sentence from an ardent writer on ecclesiastical architecture some seventy years ago, when England was in the dawn of her recovery from a prolonged period of lethargy as to the history and condition of her churches, will always dwell in my memory, it was at that time only too true : " *They* dwelt in hovels and worshipped in houses exceedingly magnificent ; *we* dwell in cedar and worship in meagre or dilapidated churches."

An endeavour too is made in these pages to set forth, after a succinct fashion, the undoubted but often forgotten fact that our ancestors, whilst regarding the church as primarily devoted to the worship of God and to the continuous round of the expression of their highest Faith, considered that the soul and body were so intimately connected that they habitually used the nave for purposes which we call secular or civil. All this tended in the direction of every class uniting in the maintenance and development of the parish church.

More than usual attention is herein given to the Materials rom which our churches were constructed, and how their shape and size so largely depended upon the nature of the stone by which they were surrounded, or by its absence and the frequency of flint or timber. It had been intended to follow this up by a chapter or section on Local Types, mapping out England into more or less definite divisions ; but it was found, after some progress had been made, that the subject was too big for inclusion in a book of limited size, that it had as yet been scarcely sufficiently studied, and that it was better on the whole to give more attention to planning and to the successive periods of architecture.

It should also be remembered that this book makes no profession to be in any sense a glossary of architecture. There are many good manuals, as well as larger and more expensive works, which deal with details after a technical fashion ; they sometimes repel the general reader by specializing on the component parts of a church fabric, whether it be a vault, a

PREFACE

pier, or a buttress. My endeavour, on the contrary, has been to take a broader grasp of the church fabric as a whole in all its different aspects.

As to periods of architectural development, it is necessary to have some landmarks for guidance, at all events of elementary students, and, after many fluctuations, I have ventured to explain the reasons why it seems best to adhere to a sevenfold division, namely, Saxon, Norman, Transition, Early English, Geometrical, Decorated, and Perpendicular. At the same time it cannot be too often insisted upon that all these periods considerably overlap, and that the approximate date of the change differed not a little in various parts of the country.

No space could be found for the discussion or illustration of church furniture or fittings; useful manuals on such subjects can be readily found. The subject is, however, just lightly touched upon in the last chapter, wherein the points of interest in the average church are briefly summarised. In this connection I cannot but hope that I have done something towards the suppression of foolish fables which are still current, about our old churches, such as "leper windows" or "sanctuary rings," and also towards the right understanding of such a subject as consecration crosses.

With regard to the important question of plans, no attempt has of course been made to treat this subject with any approach to exhaustiveness or comprehensiveness. The aim kept consistently in view has been to supply illustrations of the chief types and varieties in a manner not too complex or difficult for non-technical readers. Most old churches are in themselves an epitome of Gothic Architecture, and the subject of the Parish Church Plan in England is one which still awaits a full and exact record.

The plans have been represented as far as possible to a uniform scale of 25 feet to the inch, though in the case of some larger examples the exigencies of the page area have rendered it necessary in reproduction to halve that scale and employ 50 feet per inch. A uniform system of hatching has been

PREFACE

adopted to differentiate the various building periods through mediæval times.

The editor of the "Victoria Counties History" has very kindly permitted the reproduction of several examples from that splendid series.

Although these plans have, as far as possible, been founded upon the best authorities, it is too much to expect that absolute exactitude in detail has been attained in the representation of the different periods, yet it is felt that the purpose in view will have been served if the reader can gain some idea of the patchwork of additions and reconstruction which may be found in most old parish churches.

Mr. Geoffry Lucas, F.R.I.B.A., must be heartily thanked for the unflagging service he has rendered in the preparation of this chapter; he has contributed the illustrations (Fig. 43) and description of the series of development plans illustrating the growth of a typical Parish Church, and, in addition, has made numerous valuable criticisms and suggestions.

My indebtedness to my friend and cousin Mr. Aymer Vallance is also considerable, both by way of suggestions and by definite illustrations (Figs. 221, 224, 248, and 263).

To my publishers Mr. Herbert and Mr. Harry Batsford I owe far more than I can say for their continued kindness and patience throughout the long period during which this book has been in gestation. To the latter I am particularly indebted for a variety of helpful suggestions, and for his unwearying trouble in the selection and arranging of illustrations. I should like also to include in my grateful acknowledgments the name of Mr. Haggis (of Messrs. Batsford) for the care he has taken over the planning chapter.

It is simple justice to say that if this book meets with any degree of success or appreciation that it will be at least as much due to the beautiful pictures, chiefly from unhackneyed sources, as to the nature of the letterpress. Particulars of the authorship of these illustrations will be found in the Note of Acknowledgment which follows.

PREFACE

It may be egotistical to add, but I should like to do so, that I have personally visited every church, with one exception, herein illustrated, and many of them repeatedly. I know comparatively little of the Continent, for I have, for upwards of half a century, found such an abundance of interest in my own country. If there is anything of the nature of a blunder or misconception in this rapid survey of England's old parish churches, it will not be caused from any lack of acquaintanceship with these fabrics. With thousands of them I seem to be on terms of friendship, and in at least ten counties I know them all.

I pray God to grant that these pages may induce others to appreciate these ancient fabrics with a better and a purer love than my own ; for :

> Could we but read it right,
> There's not a furrow in these time-worn walls
> But has its history.

J. CHARLES COX

SYDENHAM,
October 1914

NOTE OF ILLUSTRATION ACKNOWLEDGMENT

In addition to those already mentioned in the Preface I take this opportunity of acknowledging my indebtedness to several gentlemen who have very kindly lent material for illustrations. My thanks are due to Professor Baldwin Brown for permission to reproduce the plan of Escomb from his admirable work "The Arts in Early England." In addition I am indebted to Mrs. Godman for allowing me to reproduce Figs. 40 and 217 from her late husband's works. For Figs. 39 and 77 my thanks are dne to Mr. P. M. Johnston, and to Mr. F. E. Howard for Fig. 42; Mr. E. M. Beloe has kindly advised about Fig. 44, while Mr. Roland Paul has contributed Figs. 89 and 90, and Mr. W. P. D. Stebbing Fig. 47.

I have also to thank Mr. F. L. Griggs, whose drawings of Figs. 14, 93, 217, and 225 were specially executed for this work. Mr. A. E. Newcombe has also kindly permitted me to reproduce eight subjects (Figs. 26, 35, 50, 72, 165, 181, 256, and 257) from his excellent pencil drawings.

For photographs I must acknowledge my indebtedness in many quarters, but I feel particularly grateful for having had access to the very fine series taken by Dr. G. Granville Buckley, Mr. F. H. Crossley, and Messrs. F. Frith & Co. Mr. H. W. Bennett has kindly supplied Fig. 54; Dr. G. Granville Buckley, Figs. 1, 41, 63, 64, 111, 117, 121, 129 (three), 133, 134, 136, 137, 142, 143, 148, 151, 152, 153, 154, 161, 169, 185, 200, 201, 202, 204, 215, 234, 239, 242, 243, 245, 253, 262, 270; Mr. F. H. Crossley, Figs. 8, 19, 31, 74, 97, 114, 126, 127, 138, 139, 141, 144, 155, 166, 172, 190, 196, 203, 205, 238, 240, 241, 251, 254, 255, 256, 265, 267, 269, 271, 272, 273; Mr.

NOTE OF ACKNOWLEDGMENT

S. A. Driver, Fig. 170; Messrs. F. Frith & Co., Figs. 2, 4, 5, 7, 11, 12, 13, 15, 16, 17, 18, 22, 23, 24, 28, 29, 30, 32, 34, 45, 60, 61, 62, 65, 67, 71, 86, 96, 106, 107, 108, 109, 115, 122, 124, 130, 156, 157, 158, 159, 163, 164, 173, 178, 180, 183, 187, 188, 189, 193, 194, 209, 212, 214, 219, 227, 236, 237, 244, 246, 247, 249; Mr. H. N. King, Fig. 36; the Photochrom Co., Figs. 3, 27, 80, 81, 85; Messrs. W. H. Smith & Son, Fig. 25; and the Rev. F. Sumner, Figs. 6, 78, 82, 120, 123, 160, 167, 174.

My thanks are also due to Mr. G. E. Kruger for his design for the cover.

J. C. C.

2. CHURCH AND COTTAGES, GODSHILL, ISLE OF WIGHT

CHAPTER I

THE PARISH CHURCH & ITS SURROUNDINGS IN TOWN AND COUNTRY

THE parish church is England's finest and most characteristic contribution to mediæval art. These old churches form a vast series of grand monuments of English vernacular craftsmanship at times when the capacity to produce works of great artistic value was far more widely spread than at later periods. Parish churches, especially those of country districts, were centres, during the Middle Ages, not only of those religious devotions for which they were consecrated, but also of English community life in its various aspects ; they served the purposes now supplied by the clubroom or the church institute, and were regarded with pride and affection by all classes of the community.

Notwithstanding the melancholy fact that the study of ancient churches is bound to convince the inquirer of the truth of the old proverb, *Tempus edax, homo edacior*, a noble heritage

3. ST. MARY MAGDALENE, TAUNTON, FROM THE SOUTH-EAST

yet remains to us of these hallowed walls. For the most part these buildings tell the tale of their evolution with greater clearness in the country than in the town. In the latter case they have often disappeared in favour of successors, as population increased and commerce thrived, or, when they were spared, alterations and additions were effected on wholesale lines.

There can be little or no doubt that England stands first in all Christendom in the number and antiquity of her churches. Their frequency is astonishing in certain districts, and testifies in a remarkable fashion to the genuineness of the Faith of early days. England was broken up after the Conquest into a variety of small manors and tenures, considerably surpassing, so students of economic history assure us, any like dispositions on the Continent; the very smallest hamlet had its chapel, if not its church, and though a large number have disappeared, a far larger number yet remain. It is not a little remarkable to note how well, in many respects, these fabrics have withstood the strenuous changes in religious expression both of the sixteenth and seventeenth centuries. In fact, those very changes, repressing with more or less vehemence the beautifying of sanctuaries in accordance with prevailing tastes, tended towards the preservation of the actual fabrics. For in England all church adornment, with the exception of a very few Elizabethan and Jacobean screens, ceased with the Reformation, until what is termed the "Catholic revival" of the middle of last century.

4. CULBONE CHURCH, SOMERSET

The most that was usually done during that long period was to keep the roofs in tolerable repair. But on the Continent the outward expression of the Faith remained practically the same, and the churches were used for a continuous round of services as of yore. The generosity of church folk was but little checked, and hence it came about, especially in France,

5. A GREAT TOWN CHURCH: HOLY TRINITY, COVENTRY

that repairs and extensions were directed into the newer architectural channels of the Renaissance. In the country districts but little taste was shown in the introduction of the new style, and it soon became apparent that there was a complete lack of harmony between the remains of the florid and somewhat degraded Flamboyant and the imitation Classic, with the result that the old work, in many a case, gave way to a complete rebuilding after the new fashion, and in other instances was almost overwhelmed and degraded by the contrast. In no other country, too, but our own was there that happy intervention of a dignified and simple development of later Gothic, termed Perpendicular, which formed so successful and conservative an interregnum between the beautiful work of the thirteenth and fourteenth centuries and the

6. A HAMLET INTERIOR: PUXTON, SOMERSET

upheavals in both art and religious expression which heralded the dawn of the sixteenth century.

That the parish churches of England form such a fascinating study arises, in no small measure, from their strong contrasts. There is no monotonous reiteration. Sometimes they are great and splendid, at other times lowly and almost diminutive. Illustrations already given have shown the great contrast, in the selfsame county of Somerset, of the noble church and glorious tower of St. Mary Magdalene, Taunton (Fig. 3), and the humble little church of Culbone (Fig. 4). Or, again, Godshill village church (Fig. 2), nestling amid thatched cottages on a hill-top in the Isle of Wight, awakens pleasurable thoughts and old-

6 THE ENGLISH PARISH CHURCH

world memories of a different nature from those aroused by a Northamptonshire village spire or a country tower of East Anglia. These are exteriors, but the contrasts are just as vivid with regard to interiors, if the city is compared with the country, or if early and rude examples are placed in juxtaposition with those of later and more finished work. Look, for instance, at

7. AN EARLY INTERIOR : MORWENSTOW, CORNWALL.

the pictures of, or, still better, recall reminiscences of, the interiors of Holy Trinity, Coventry (Fig. 5), and the village church of Puxton, Somerset (Fig. 6). Or, again, contrast the early interior of Morwenstow, Cornwall (Fig. 7), with that of the later great church of Hull (Fig. 8).

And here, before pursuing the subject further, a brief pause must be made to ask what is meant by a parish church? The division of a country into parishes does not go back into remote antiquity. So far as England is concerned, the parochial divisions, as distinct from manorial, began to be established in the tenth century under Anglo Saxon rule, but they did not assume their complete form until the several

8. A LATE TOWN INTERIOR : HOLY TRINITY, HULL

Councils of London and Westminster in the twelfth century. The English parish priest had his origin as the chaplain of a landowner, to serve not only the lord but his tenants or retainers; but by degrees he acquired the position of an ecclesiastical freeholder. He was appointed in the first instance by the patron, but received his office and spiritual faculties at the hands of the bishop, and could only be removed for grave offences by the canon law. Early in the ninth century the Council of Mainz forbade laymen to deprive priests of churches which they served, or to appoint them without episcopal sanction.

The parish was the district within reasonable distance of a church served by a duly appointed secular priest, and its bounds were laid down by the bishop, and not by a manorial lord. It differed entirely from such limits as those of town, hamlet, or manor. There might be several hamlets in one manor, and several manors in one parish. On the other hand, there might be several parishes within one town, whilst various towns and boroughs grew up in early days without a parish church within their bounds. The parish, with its church and priest, was an arrangement specially devised to meet the needs of the country rather than the city.

Yet another point requires to be remembered, as in part explanatory of the wonderful hold that the parish church of the olden days had upon the affections of the whole countryside. The religious duty of paying tithe became enforceable at law, in this country at least, as early as the tenth century. "God's portion," as the tithe was sometimes happily termed, was intended to be applied, as a first charge, to the maintenance of the poor or for the exercise of hospitality. This intention, though somewhat obscured as time went on, was unceasingly upheld throughout the pre-Reformation period—a fact, though often forgotten, which is abundantly witnessed by episcopal registers and by a great variety of other documentary evidence. In the recent words of a most careful ecclesiological writer:

"It must always be remembered that, in the view of the Church, first-fruits and tithes of increase were destined, not to provide a maintenance for the clergy, but for the relief and support of the poor; and the rector, whether of a religious house or parochial incumbent, was supposed to administer them for those purposes, he being only a ruler or administrator of them. During the whole of the time that the English Church was ruled as an integral part of the Western Patriarchate this view of the destination of tithes, and of the rector or administrator's duty in respect of them, was never lost sight of."

The same writer ably sums up the idea of an English parish as a unit for the collection and disbursement of tithes and offerings, and at the same time as a unit of spiritual administration. He also points out that after the Norman Conquest private oratories were readily converted into churches with burial and baptismal privileges.*

Moreover, it has to be borne in mind that the parish, and hence the parish church, was entirely divorced from the power or authority of the lord or lords of the manor, or of any State officials or personages. If the lord's steward held court in the nave of the church, or if the court rolls were stored there, it was only by permission of the parish. The parish was organized for Church purposes, subject only to Church authority. Within its area every resident was a parishioner, and the wardens were their chosen representatives, elected by the whole people of both sexes, not by the parson, nor by any select vestry, still less by the squire. The contrast between a manor court and a parish meeting has been ably set forth by Bishop Hobhouse in his citations from numerous extant records. Manor court rolls show the condition of the community as divided up into sharply defined classes: the lord of the soil and his tenants, and the tenants themselves into bond and free, and the villeins again, in their turn, according to the

* "The Rise of the Parochial System in England," by the Rev. O. J. Reichel; an essay reprinted in 1905 from the "Transactions of the Devonshire Association."

size of their holdings. Contrariwise, all such distinctions vanished when the parishioners assembled in the church to pass the wardens' accounts, to elect their successors, to listen to the annual roll of gifts and bequests, or to learn the details of the gatherings by the youths or the maidens, by the wives or the husbandmen, or of the profits from the church ales, the plays, or the games. In the eyes of the Church all were on an equal footing at the parish meeting, as they were when they knelt before the altar—lord, tenant, villein, or serf.*

Nevertheless, both in town and country the actual fabric of the church was, as a rule, in close juxtaposition with the public and private buildings of the community. This is well illustrated by the accompanying Elizabethan plan of the town of Kingsbridge, Devon (Fig. 9).

The fabric of the English parish church, broadly speaking, consisted of the chancel and the nave, with or without contributary aisles or chapels. The care of the chancel and its maintenance belonged to the rector, or to his deputy as impropriator of the great tithes, whilst the nave was maintained by the parishioners. This was the general custom, with but few exceptions. On this point various synodal directions are quite explicit. It is sufficient to cite a single example. Bishop Brentingham of Exeter (1370-94) laid it down, as the old rule in his diocese, that:

"The work of constructing and repairing the chancels of all mother churches belongs to the rectors of the parishes; but that of the naves pertains to the parishioners, without regard to any contrary custom. In the case of chapels, which have their distinct parochial district, the entire duty of maintenance belongs to the parishioners of the chapel, as it is for their

* See Bishop Hobhouse's Introduction to "Churchwardens' Accounts," Somerset Record Society, 1890; Abbot Gasquet's "Parish Life in Mediæval England," 1906; and Dr. Cox's "Old Churchwardens' Accounts," 1913. It is necessary to be clear and definite on such points, for some strange and confusing theories have recently been put forth by Mr Addy in "Church and Manor," 1912.

convenience such chapels were built, and, moreover, they may be obliged to assist, in case of need, the mother church."

Although it is true that the building of the church in early days was not infrequently the work of the lord, who hence

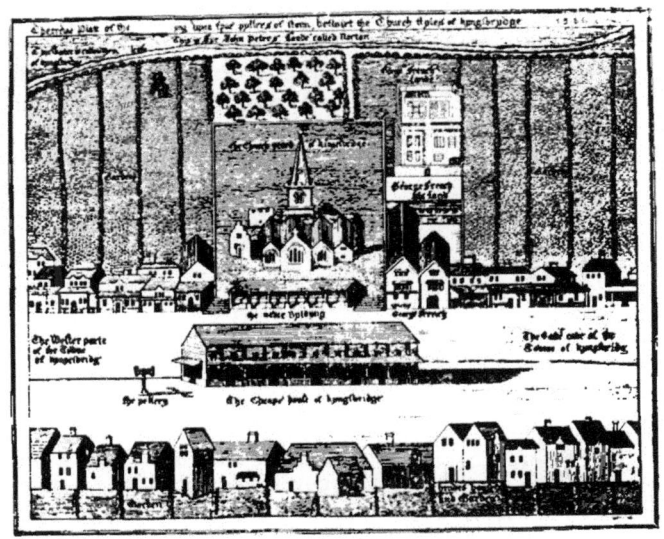

9. THE CHURCH AND THE TOWN SURROUNDINGS, KINGSBRIDGE, DEVON, FROM AN ENGRAVING AFTER A SURVEY OF 1586

became the patron, and that in later times important wealthy residents occasionally contributed the whole cost of an aisle, chapel, or tower, it is equally true that substantial repairs, additions, or rebuildings were generally accomplished by the united devotion of the parishioners as a whole, or by special gilds or gatherings. Notable examples of these united efforts occur in the rebuilding of the whole of the large church of St. Petrock, Bodmin; of the Lady Chapel of St. Michael, Bath; and of the fine towers of Ludlow, St. Laurence; Reading, St. Mary; Sandwich; Great St. Mary, Cambridge, and

All Saints, Derby (Fig 10).* The oldest parish accounts of St. Andrew, Holborn, have long since vanished; but one John Bentley, who was warden in 1584, left behind him an interesting MS. book, still preserved in the church, entitled "Some Monuments of Antiquities Worthy Memory." In this book he states that the steeple of the church was begun in 1446, and finished in 1468; the north and south aisles were rebuilt about the same period. He adds:

"And note that all this, as many things else in the church in those days, even when the church had most lands, were nevertheless builded by money given of devotion of good people, then used to be gathered by the men and women of the parish in boxes, at ales, shootings, etc., for the only purpose, through the parish weekly, during the time of these works as by their accounts, yet remaining, may and doth appear."

These pages are not concerned with the internal fittings or ornaments of the churches

10. ALL SAINTS, DERBY

* See Dr. Cox's "Old Churchwardens' Accounts" (1913), chap. vi.

in any detail, but it is well to note, in a single sentence, how the old accounts of our parish churches invariably contain abundant evidence, even in the poorest of country parishes, of the lavish generosity of all classes of the community. As Dr. Jessopp has admirably written :

"The immense treasures in the churches were the joy and boast of every man and woman and child in England, who, day by day and week by week, assembled to worship in the old Houses of God which they and their fathers had built, and whose every vestment and chalice, candlestick and banner, organ and bells, pictures and images, and altar and shrine, they looked upon as their own, and part of their birthright."

In the face of all these facts, in the days when there was but one common faith, when the Holy Day of the Church was the holiday of the people, when the religious life and the secular life were so closely interwoven, is it to be wondered at that the parish church, especially the country parish church, became a centre of English community life, played an important part in the everyday events as well as in the devotions of the people, and was looked upon with pride and affection by all classes of the villagers? In short, the fabric served in many respects, as has been already stated, the purposes for which a clubroom or institute is nowadays used, as well as for the Divine Offices for which it was primarily built and hallowed.

In the later pre-Reformation days the church house, as a usual adjunct to the parish church, served for church ales and such-like entertainments, together with the baking and brewing which were their inseparable accompaniments ; but right on through much of Elizabeth's reign the parish churches continued to serve for a variety of uses, which seem curious and unsuitable to the present generation. Prominent amongst those which were difficult to eradicate were the mystery plays. They continued to be occasionally acted within churches down to the very last years of the sixteenth century.

The holding of fairs and the sale of merchandise within or around churchyards occasionally encroached, in the large parishes, on the porches and other parts of the actual churches; but such proceedings were always regarded as illicit and duly prohibited by the ecclesiastical authorities. Dancing undoubtedly took place in the naves of certain churches at festival seasons; the wardens' accounts of St. Edmund's, Salisbury, testify to the children dancing therein round a maypole in the fifteenth century. Within the village church, under the tower or at the west end, it was usual to find a plough. This was kept there ready for use on Plough Monday, the Monday after the Epiphany, which was the season when ploughing and other rustic toil began. In old days the Church made this the occasion of blessing the tilling of the fields. The plough was solemnly blessed before the procession started. In many a country parish the labourers maintained a Plough Light burning in the church before the patron saint. In troublous times, or when fires occurred, the parishioners were allowed to store wool and grain, or chests containing valuables, or household goods within the church, paying for this privilege to the wardens' common fund. Deeds, too, which had no concern with Church lands, but related to leases or transfers within the parish, were not infrequently permitted to be placed within the parish chest for safe custody. Such covenants were often signed within the church porch, and, if they related to the fabric or to the parish generally, on the very altar itself. If a dead body was found within the parish, or did a parishioner die a violent or mysterious death, the corpse was placed in the church's porch, and there the coroner held his inquest.

These are but a few of the almost numberless uses for which the old parish churches of mediæval England habitually served, without any thought of irreverence. In this connexion it is well to remember that the rood-screen, with its doors or gates, at the entrance of the chancel, shut off the high altar, and that the altars of the nave or its aisles were also encompassed by their own screens or parcloses. The whole was strongly safeguarded from anything savouring of actual profanity or violence by heavy penalties and penances imposed by the ecclesiastical authorities not only on the delinquents themselves, but in a certain very real way on the parish at large. For in such cases the church was placed under an interdict, and the priest dare not exercise any of the religious ministrations until it had been purified, by the costly process of formal " reconciliation," at the hands of the diocesan or his suffragan, the expense being borne by the whole parish.

Nor should it be forgotten that in the fierce days when limbs were lopped and lives taken for comparatively trivial offences by a cruelly severe State, the Church, on the contrary, bore perpetual witness to the spirit of mercy by insisting on all her consecrated churches and churchyards being regarded as safe sanctuaries, under strictly defined limits, for all wrongdoers. There was probably not a single parish church in the whole length and breadth of England which had not exercised, at some time or another in its history, its blessed privilege of sheltering a fugitive, and eventually substituting banishment from the realm in the place of loss of life or limb.*

Notwithstanding the infinite number and variety of our parish churches—and they show great differences in size, design, construction, and plan, which it is the object of this work to consider—yet distinctly national types were evolved, characteristic of the English temperament and enshrining many of its best qualities, such as sturdiness, practical utility, and above all adaptability to circumstances. For instance, English parish churches usually harmonize with the older village buildings of which they form the centre, and are in striking accord with their natural surroundings. The infinite value of the church in the average English village landscape can be best appreciated by endeavouring to realize what its condition would be if that central fabric was removed.

The lovely village of Godshill (Fig. 2), commanding a beautiful prospect on an abrupt hill in the Isle of Wight, clusters thickly round the parish church, the picturesque thatched

* See Dr. Cox's "Sanctuaries and Sanctuary Seekers," 1911.

cottages striving, as it were, to gain the nearest place beneath its shelter. The fine cruciform Sussex church of Harting (Fig. 11), close to the Hampshire border, rears its slate-covered spire with some dignity above the well-built houses by which it is surrounded. The great striking tower and spire of the well-

11. SOUTH HARTING, BY THE SOUTH DOWNS

ordered Salop church of Worfield, near Bridgnorth (Fig. 12), rises amid the quiet scenery, as though in stately protection of the many-gabled half-timbered house, the quaint round pigeon-house, and various comely cottages ranged about the churchyard.

Many a village church, by its close proximity to the manor-house, testifies to the intimate connexion in days of yore between the lord and the rector, reminiscent of the time in the dim distance when the priest was but the chaplain of the manorial oratory. An instance of such a survival is here pictured from one of the most attractive of Oxfordshire villages, Asthall, not far from Witney. Here the fine early Elizabethan manor-house lies immediately to the west of the parish church. The most usual position for the English village manor-house was within a short stone's-throw of the porch or principal entrance on the south side; but this arrangement varied with a fair degree of frequency. There is a remarkable instance of propinquity to the church on the north side at Brympton, near Yeovil, in South Somerset (Fig. 13). To the north transept of this

12. WORFIELD, SHROPSHIRE

cruciform church—a church distinguished by the top-heavy bell-cote on the west gable—is attached a two-storied building known as the "chantry-house," whilst immediately adjoining this building is the valuable example of fifteenth and sixteenth century domestic architecture known as Brympton Hall, the seat of the Ponsonby-Fanes.

Occasionally, too, the lord had covered access from his manor-house into the church. The ancient manor-house of the celebrated Fitzherbert family stood close to the west end of the parish church of Norbury, Derbyshire; a fair amount of fourteenth-century work is still standing, and there are traces of a covered gallery which used to lead directly into the church. At Morley, in the same county, the mansion of the Stathams and Sacheverells stood on land almost adjoining the north-west angle of the church; a passage from the house communicated with the entrance into a gallery at the west end of the north aisle; the built-up doorway can still be seen in

13. BRYMPTON MANOR-HOUSE AND CHURCH, SOMERSET

the interior of the church, as well as the place on the outer wall where the beams supporting the passage rested. When Tollerton Hall, Notts, was rebuilt in 1794 a kind of cloister was thrown out for covered communication with the south side of the church, in pursuance, it is said, of a similar previous plan.

Almost every county affords one or more examples of a parish church shut up in a park, close to the big house, and more or less difficult of access. Instances of this may be noted at Kedleston and Wingerworth, Derbyshire; Overstone, Northamptonshire; Edenhall, Cumberland; Lullingstone, Kent; and Babraham, Cambridgeshire. In all these cases, and probably in every like example, comparatively modern selfishness or love of privacy has deprived the church of the village by which it used to be surrounded. Derbyshire, too, affords a further monstrous case of a parish church encroached upon by a great house. About 1740 Nicholas Earl of Scarsdale rebuilt Sutton Hall a few feet to the north of the church

14. CHURCH STRETTON, LOOKING TO CARADOC, SHROPSHIRE
[*Drawn by F. L. Griggs*

of Sutton-in-the-Dale, actually using the north side of the tower and the west end of the north aisle as supports for outbuildings. At Winkburn, Notts, though there is no park, the church has been so hidden away immediately behind the hall and so smothered in trees that it is quite difficult to find it.

It is a pleasanter matter to revert to the often remarkable

20   THE ENGLISH PARISH CHURCH

adaptability of the fabrics of England's old churches to the scenery by which they are surrounded. The finest churches are usually in districts where the neighbourhood is monotonously flat or destitute of striking features, as in most of Norfolk or Suffolk, or in the fens of the counties of Lincoln

15. BRANSCOMBE, SOUTH DEVON

or Cambridge. True, there are striking and interesting churches to be found amidst delightful scenery, but not of the same uplifting and monumental scale that characterizes not a few of those on duller levels. Lovers of scenery delight in the South Shropshire village of Church Stretton, which lies in a valley 600 feet or more above the sea-level, in the midst of fine ranges of wild and heather-clad hills. Now here, as will be seen from the picture (Fig. 14), is a good cruciform church, which lends a distinct and leading feature to the houses around it. But the designers and successive builders, as they gazed on the Caradoc range to the east, or on Longmynd on the west, were unwittingly restrained from any competition with Nature in the matter of elevation. Or, again, to turn to a very different part of England, namely, to the beautiful combes near the

16. THE CHURCH ON BRENT TOR, DARTMOOR

22 THE ENGLISH PARISH CHURCH

coast of the south-east of Devon, the striking and highly interesting church of Branscombe (Fig. 15), halfway between Seaton and Sidmouth, is well worthy of close consideration. But though the Normans added a nobly substantial tower to a Saxon foundation, and though the north-west turret was subsequently raised, together with various costly improvements at

17. ROLVENDEN, KENT

the charge of the Dean and Chapter of Exeter, the structure retained quiet lines and made no attempt to vie with the beauties of Nature.

Perhaps the most striking English example of a church on a height occurs at Brent Tor, near Tavistock (Fig. 16), where the church of St. Michael crowns the volcanic cone of rock 1130 feet above the sea-level, from whence there are noble widespread views. Here the Early English church has a low, humble tower; aught else would have been a bathos.

This acquiescence in circumstances which they could not change seems to have generally affected our mediæval church builders, though doubtlessly, for the most part, after an unconscious fashion. Though in the few instances that occur in Kent, where churches have been planted on the comparatively lofty ranges of the Weald, humble proportions, so far as height is concerned, are to be noted ; the Kent church builders of the lower levels of the south of the county were experts in producing, from the native ragstone, lofty characteristic towers, with a yet loftier angle turret. A striking instance is the celebrated " Tenterden Steeple "; Cranbrook, too, has a good west tower, and so also have Biddenden and Rolvenden (Fig. 17) ; whilst Ashford soars above the town with its four great pinnacles, and Frittenden is graced with a lofty crocketed spire. Only a little further south, and the dead level of Romney Marsh is relieved by the uplifting of the tower of Lydd to a height of 132 feet. Surely it cannot be mere accidents that reduce some towers to insignificant proportions in the midst of splendid prospects, whilst others soar upwards with a noble ambition. Were not such coincidences brought about, at least in part, by the obvious vanity of striving to aim skyward when at a considerable elevation ?

Convinced as we are of the subtle, and perchance almost unconscious, influence of scenery on the church builders and designers of mediæval England, it is only fair to remember that the wealth of the wool-growing and wool-weaving districts, as contrasted with the comparative poverty of mountainous regions, has also to be taken into account.

The true lover of England's parish churches, in their infinite variety and marvellous adaptation to the surroundings and requirements of the site, will not hasten to expend his admiration on the mere size or height of the fabrics. There is often something winning and attractive about those of diminutive proportions. Is there not something charming in the quiet little village church of Heyshott, in West Sussex, a little to the south of Midhurst (Fig. 18) ? It is of Early English origin, with windows of Decorated and Perpendicular insertion ; it possesses a timber porch of fairly simple design, and the western bay is adorned with a wooden belfry and low spire. The interior has a curious

24 THE ENGLISH PARISH CHURCH

old font and other attractions; but it is as a whole, without any thought of details, as it stands in modest simplicity, enfringed in trees, that we feel its loveliness and its exact suitability to the very site that it occupies.

Or, again, to find a church tiny and remote, but eminently lovable, it might be well to visit Yelford (Fig. 19), a little out-of-the-world parish, with nothing to call a road leading to it. It lies

18. HEYSHOTT, SUSSEX

twelve miles to the west of Oxford, on the further side of the little river Windrush, and only contains three or four houses, one of which is the old manor-house, now a farmstead, of much interest. But the charm of it all is the delightful little Perpendicular church, with its properly proportioned chancel, nave, south porch, and double-bell gable. It would have been strange to have found in this scene of quiet sylvan aloofness aught that was big or imposing. There, as it stands, with large trees growing up within the very graveyard as an overshadowing shelter, with the simplest of rail-and-post fences, and with mere field-gates for admission, this tiny church of St. Nicholas forms an ideal shrine for country worship. Where else in all Christendom could such another be found save in the very heart of England?

But there remains yet another diminutive parish church to be mentioned, now fairly well known to discriminating tourists

19. YELFORD, OXFORDSHIRE

to the West of England, namely, that of Culbone, by Porlock, Somerset, near the bottom of a most lovely wooded combe running down into the Bristol Channel (Fig. 4). Its claim to be the smallest perfect parish church in England cannot by any possibility be controverted, notwithstanding the continued assertions of its rivals.* It is not only absolutely unrivalled in

* I have known Culbone from boyhood upwards, and have several times taken its exact measurements. The total length is 35 feet, the width of chancel 10 feet, width of nave 12 feet 8 inches, length of nave 21 feet 5 inches, width of chancel arch 2 feet 6 inches. Lullington, on the Sussex Downs, is only 16 feet square, but then it is merely a chancel; the outlines of the ruined nave can still be traced. St. Lawrence, Isle of Wight, once the smallest, has been enlarged some years ago by the addition of a chancel. Wythburn and Wastdale, Cumberland, are out of the running, as they are mere chapelries.

the beauty and picturesqueness of its situation, but it has distinct architectural attractions. It consists of chancel, nave, south porch, and an octagonal slated spire rising from a tower within the west bay of the nave. In the churchyard are the considerable remains of a churchyard cross, of Ham stone, which must have been brought here all that distance on pack-horses. The walling on the north side of the chancel is indubitably early Saxon, with a remarkable little window of two diminutive lights cut out of the solid (Fig. 20). It is even possible that the tradition as to this being part of the cell of St. Culbone may be true. He crossed over the Channel from Wales in the sixth century with St. Dubricius to Porlock Bay, and eventually retired to this sea-girt glen to end his days as a hermit. In Norman days, and possibly earlier, the cell became a parish church, with baptismal rights; the font is of that period. There was some reconstruction in the fifteenth century. The frame of the two-light, square-headed window on the south of the nave is of Ham stone; it has an exact counterpart of timber in the north wall (Fig. 21). The chief point of interest in the interior is the early Perpendicular rood-screen. This tiny church is amply sufficient for its modern needs, for the parish population is about thirty. The immediate "village" consists of but two small cottages; higher up the combe are three small farmhouses. It is difficult to imagine anything more

20. AN EARLY WINDOW, CULBONE, SOMERSET

AND ITS SURROUNDINGS

absolutely akin to its fascinating surroundings than the parish church of Culbone, complete in every point, yet most meet for the worship of the Most High, for in its ancient parts it is destitute of every trace of assertive vulgarity.

The overpowering size and occasional sublimity of the mountains of Lakeland have had the broad result of dwarfing much of the efforts of the church builders of Cumberland and Westmorland, though by no means to the extent that is sometimes supposed. Wythburn, on the verge of the high road, immediately under the shadow of "the mighty Helvellyn," and Wastdale (Fig. 22), in equally solemn

21. OAK XV. CENTURY WINDOW, CULBONE, SOMERSET

22. WASTDALE, WESTMORLAND

and majestic scenery, are obviously crushed by their surroundings; notwithstanding enlargements, both continue to assert that they are the smallest of England's *churches*, but in neither case was this ever true, for the first was one of the several chapels of Crosthwaite, and the second a chapel of the far-

23. CROSTHWAITE, NEAR KESWICK

distant St. Bees. Crosthwaite itself, though of fair size, is low and unaspiring (Fig. 23).

Since these thoughts were penned the writer's attention has been drawn to similar reflections made by the Rev. J. J. Petit in 1841, in his "Remarks on Church Architecture," when visiting Switzerland :

"We are now among the 'palaces of Nature,' and do not look for many traces of the hand of man. The rough course of the Lutschine, the precipitous faces of the Wengern Alp, the distant peaks of the Wetterhorn, the golden Staubbach crossing the dark road like a downward stream of fire, the majestic Jungfrau closing the view in front, leave us but little inclination to think of the nice arrangements and elaborate workings of the Gothic cathedral. If we met with one here we should condemn the art for ever. Yet even in the solitudes of these wild regions

24. THE VALE OF DEDHAM [*J. Constable, R.A.*

we do not altogether lose the objects of our pursuit. The cottage-like chapel of Guttanen harmonizes as well with the bare granite rocks and fir-covered slopes that cradle the Aar, as the minster of Strasburg or Milan with the vast levels of Alsace and Lombardy. The little gabled turret of Grindelwald does not distract our eye from the gigantic buttresses of the Eiger and Wetterhorn. We could not willingly miss these humble places of worship; we cannot wish them to be more pretending. A slight token now suffices to remind us of the presence of our Creator among His sublimest works."

On the other hand, John Constable, the great landscape painter, was much impressed by the dignity given by fine churches to comparatively level views in that part of England which he knew the best. He was born at East Bergholt, on the Suffolk side of the river Stour, which here forms a boundary-line between that county and Essex. He first arrived at real fame by his memorable picture of the Vale of Dedham (Fig. 24), which was painted from the summit of the church tower of Langham, Essex. The fine tower of Dedham appeared in several of his other landscapes, but he was also much attracted by the stateliness of the tower of Stoke-by-Nayland, on the Suffolk side of the Stour, which rises to a height of 120 feet, and has excellent and characteristic panelling on both plinth and battlements. Of this church Constable wrote:

"Stoke Nayland, though by no means one of the largest, certainly ranks with the great churches of the eastern counties. The length of the nave, with its continuous line of embattled parapet and its finely proportioned chancel, may challenge the admiration of the architect, as well as its majestic tower, which from its commanding height may be said to impart a portion of its own dignity to the surrounding country."

Attention will be subsequently drawn to the East Anglian towers and to the general beauty of the flint and freestone combination, usually termed flushwork; but here, where we are taking a general survey of the part played by our parish churches on broad lines, attention may be very briefly drawn to the majestic superiority of so many of the churches and their

AND ITS SURROUNDINGS

steeples over the rest of the buildings of either town or village in this part of England. Such is especially the case with the lofty spire-crowned Essex tower of Thaxted, or such stately Suffolk towers as Eye (Fig. 201), Lavenham (Fig. 165), or Woodbridge, and many equally noteworthy Norfolk towers, as Cawston, Sall, or Wymondham. The small picture of Southwold brings out well the pre-eminence of that grand church over

25. SOUTHWOLD FROM THE LIGHTHOUSE

both town and district (Fig. 25). Or what could be more delightful as a typical East Anglian village church than the charming drawing of Great Bromley church, near Colchester (Fig. 26)?

A very different part of England, namely Cornwall, possesses the like feature in a marked degree, especially in its towers, as typical of the power of the Church in days of yore. The transcendent importance of the parish church, as marked by its lofty towers, is distinctly notable at the village of Probus with an elevation of 150 feet, at the port of Fowey rising to 124 feet, and approximating 100 feet in about twenty other instances. Among these may be cited St. Columb Major, Egloshayle, St. Ives, Launceston, and Week St. Mary. But prominent among them all in dominance though only styled "about 100 feet"

32   THE ENGLISH PARISH CHURCH

in actual height, stands forth the lofty well-proportioned tower of St. Columb Minor (Fig. 27) amid comparatively bleak

26. AN EAST ANGLIAN VILLAGE CHURCH: GT. BROMLEY, COLCHESTER
[*Drawn by A. E. Newcombe*

surroundings, after a fashion which is almost startling in its proud superiority.

Our old parish churches, especially in the small towns and larger villages, usually stand about the centre of the streets or houses. This is the case with all save one of the finer churches of Derbyshire. Thus the famous twisted spire of Chesterfield

27. ST. COLUMB MINOR, CORNWALL

rises proudly amidst the older streets; the fine church of Tideswell stands in the centre of the town; the lofty spire of Bakewell springs from the very midst of the houses; and the substantial large Norman church of Melbourn occupies a fairly central position. The ancient market town of Ashbourne (Fig. 28) forms, however, a notable exception. The beautiful cruciform church of St. Oswald, with its graceful octagonal spire, 212 feet high, stands quite clear of the old town at its west end, surrounded by a wide graveyard; its situation has the advantage of enabling its general features and attractive outlines to be the more readily grasped and appreciated.

It may here be parenthetically remarked that in England it was usual to attach a yard, both in town and country, to the parish church for burial purposes, a custom contrary to the ancient Roman use of a cemetery outside the town walls, and by no means invariably followed on the Continent. Though in towns, and in country sites adjoining an important highway, such a yard would only be placed on one or two sides, its occurrence always added dignity to the fabric. The Sunday procession round the church, of English obligation, had to be confined to consecrated ground. Hence where the yard failed to embrace the church fully, such devices as tunnelling a passage at either end to admit the procession—at the east end, as at Hythe, or St. Gregory, Norwich, or through open arches of the west tower, as at Wrotham, Kent, Wollaton, Notts, and several other instances might be cited.

Another partial exception of a remarkable character as to situation is also worth notice. The large village of Combe Martin (Fig. 29), on the North Devon coast, runs down a combe until it reaches the sea for nearly a mile in length. The church stands separately at the extreme head of the village, beautifully situated among a group of trees, but there is no majesty or grace about the higher hills above it. The very fine tower, upwards of 100 feet high, with a singular series of double angular buttresses, springs up like a great sentinel in charge of the long range of houses that straggle downwards to the sea.

28. ASHBOURNE, DERBYSHIRE

Of all the grand examples of a great church dominating, from a central position, one of our larger towns or cities, the parish church of St. Michael, Coventry (Fig. 30), undoubtedly holds the palm. It lays claim, with some right on its side, to be the finest parochial church in the kingdom. The great characteristic of the body of the fabric is the number of chapels formerly built, screened off, and lavishly furnished by the various wealthy trade guilds of the city. The unparalleled tower, 136 feet high, is of four stages, each of them highly enriched with window openings and sculptured canopies; the niches of the upper stories retain their saintly statues. The eight flying buttresses support an octagonal lantern which rises 30 feet higher. Above the lantern is a slender graceful spire of 130 feet, thus attaining a total height of nearly 300 feet.

Among the more striking of the splendid churches with fine towers or spires springing up amidst our towns, and holding them as it were in thraldom (chiefly in low-lying districts), may be mentioned those of Newark, Notts; the grand Lincolnshire series of Grantham, Heckington, and Sleaford in the western district; the exquisite steeple of Louth, the crown of the Marshland, and the celebrated Boston "stump" of the Holland division (Fig. 183); and the Northamptonshire towers of Kettering, Oundle, and Higham Ferrers.

The affection of the townsfolk of England for their parish churches, so far as boroughs were concerned, usually centred in a particular municipal church. Within its walls not only were mayors, bailiffs, and other town officials elected, but the actual assemblies for the making and carrying out of by-laws were constantly held. The old civic buildings of England were very few in number, and of a meagre character where they did exist. Such splendid old municipal fabrics, both town halls and guild halls, as are found in all the cities of Belgium, and occasionally in Italy and France, were unknown in England. Even the Guildhall of the City of London only came into existence in the fifteenth century, and was of no imposing proportions. Coventry

29. COMBE MARTIN, NORTH DEVON

stood alone in the possession of a fine old building for the meeting of its guilds, which dates back to the fourteenth century. The old municipal buildings of the highly important borough of Northampton were mean in size and of meagre architectural merit.* But what did the burgesses want with a town hall? Up to 1488 they elected their mayor and held assemblies in the spacious nave of the church of St. Giles. The mayor of Salisbury was elected in the church of St. Edmund. Among the ancient churches wherein mayors or bailiffs are known to have been elected may be mentioned the principal churches of Grantham (Fig. 135), Sandwich, Dover, New Romney (Fig. 72), Lydd, Folkestone, Ipswich, Fordwich, Totnes, Plymouth, and Derby.

Mrs. A. S. Green is curiously silent as to definite instances of the election of mayors in churches in her "Town Life in the Fifteenth Century" (1894), but there is a finely comprehensive passage as to the use by the townsfolk of their municipal church or churches. No wonder that they so often were generously grateful in rebuilding the towers, in recasting the bells, or in lavishly providing church ornaments and fittings for their guild chapels or altars.

"All the multitudinous activities and accidents of this common life were summed up for the people in the parish church that stood in the market-place. This was the fortress of the borough against its enemies, its place of safety where the treasure of the commons was stored in dangerous times, the arms in the steeple, the wealth of corn or wood or precious goods in the church itself, guarded by a sentence of excommunication against all who should violate so sacred a protection. Its shrines were hung with the strange new things which English sailors had begun to bring across the great seas—with 'horns of unicorns,' ostrich eggs, or walrus tusks, or the rib of a whale given by Sebastian Cabot. From the church tower the bell rang out which called the people to arm for the common defence, or summoned a general assembly, or proclaimed the opening of the market. Burghers had their seats in the church apportioned to them by the corporation in the same rank and

* Dr. Cox's "Northampton Borough Records" (1898), ii. 170-74 and plate.

30. THE CHURCH AND THE CITY: ST. MICHAEL'S, COVENTRY

order as the stalls which it had already assigned to them in the market-place. The city officers and their wives sat in the chief places of honour ; next to them came tradesmen according to their degree, with their families. . . . There on Sundays and feast-days the people came to hear any news of importance to the community, whether it was a list of strayed sheep, or a proclamation by the bailiff of the penalties which had been decreed in the manor court against offenders. The church was their Common Hall, where the commonalty met for all kinds of business—to audit the town accounts, to divide the common lands, to make grants of property, to hire soldiers, or to elect a mayor."

When considering the secular or ordinary uses to which our parish churches both in town and country were applied, it is well clearly to understand that the standard of reverence for holy places was of a different nature in days of yore from what it has been for several generations. We should be quite false to history and to the story of our country's social evolution, if we imagined that customs within consecrated walls which would now be regarded as acts of impiety were proofs of our ancestors' lack of devotion or of religious convictions. The serious and divine uses for which churches were built were probably just as keenly felt and positively more frequently practised by our forefathers than by ourselves. The most devout would have been far more scandalized and amazed at the notion of the parish church of the people being locked up from week's end to week's end, or only occasionally opened, than at anything done within its walls not in accordance with modern ideas of decorum. As was well remarked by a writer who was full of knowledge on this subject, and who treated it in a bold, earnest spirit some forty years ago :

"From the commencement of the parochial system till its completion each new church was fashioned and ordained for the creature's comfort as well as the Creator's honour. The same spirit animated our ecclesiastical rulers in later times, who, far from thinking that a church was desecrated by arrangements which made it a scene of social diversion and a place for the transaction of honest affairs by secular business, were of opinion that its sacred purpose was observed, and its spiritual usefulness enhanced, by every homely and not absolutely irreverent usage that encouraged people to enter its walls gladly and leave them gratefully—every custom that stimulated the ordinary citizen's gratitude for the existence of the Lord's houses—every practice that led him to regard his parish church as an institution no less convenient or beneficial to his worldly concerns than advantageous to his eternal interests." *

The higher uses of the buildings were, as a rule, assiduously and constantly maintained throughout the days of yore. The Canons of Edgar of the tenth century, made under the reforming influence of Archbishop Dunstan, enjoin that at the right times the bell be rung and the priest say his Hours in the church, and there pray and intercede for all men; priests misdirecting the people as to fasts or festivals were subject, as also provided by the laws of Alfred and Guthrum, to a heavy penalty; they were to preach and duly expound every Sunday. The Canons which are known as those of Elfric, of the end of the tenth century, are most explicit. They direct that the priests and inferior clergy were to be at church for the seven canonical Hours, namely, at *Uhtsang* or Prime, about 4 A.M.; at *Primesang* or Mattins, at 6 A.M.; at *Undersang* or Terce, at 9 A.M.; at *Middaysang* or Sext, at noon; at *Nonsang* or Nones, at 3 P.M.; at *Efensang* or Vespers; and also at *Nightsang* or Nocturns. Hundreds of our parish churches (500 in Somerset alone) have incised upon their walls dials of pre-Conquest and Norman times, with the lines duly indicated for the right observance of the day-hours of the Church. And here, too, it may be remarked, with regard to later days, that in every single set of Churchwardens' Accounts of the fourteenth and fifteenth centuries, both in country and town, which are yet extant, mention is made of the repairs of the church clock, or the providing of a new time-keeper.

It came about by degrees that the open saying of the

Jeaffreson's "A Book about the Clergy" (1870), i. 337.

canonical Hours was restricted to the religious houses or monasteries, and that the public services of the parish church were mostly restricted to Mattins, Mass, and Evensong. The first and third of these consisted of an accumulation, after a somewhat abbreviated form, of the regular Hours; the reformed use of these two offices, as now current in the Church of England, merely accentuates their further reduction. As to the times when the churches were used for these three invariable services, they differed somewhat at various periods and places. Mattins, usually in combination with Prime, was always said before Mass, and the normal hour for the latter was 9 o'clock; no celebration might be held after the hour of noon. The usual hour for Evensong was 3 in the afternoon.

In every town church, and probably in the majority of the greater country parish churches, there was more than one daily Mass, in addition to the parochial high or sung Mass at 9 o'clock. Special benefactors founded chantries for memorial Masses at varying hours and at specific altars; it is an utter mistake to imagine that these chantry ministers were mere "Mass priests," as is usually supposed; it was their bounden duty to assist their incumbent in what were termed "sacraments and sacramentals," and also to take part in the hour offices. Then, too, in country as well as in towns there was a large number of guilds or fraternities, the first charge on whose funds was the maintenance of a chaplain, one of whose duties was a daily Mass at a specified hour. Nothing proves the general spirit of devotion amongst all classes of the community more than the study of these guilds, whether they were composed of the soil-tillers of a country village or the skilled craftsmen of a town.

The exceeding veneration for the mysteries of the Faith, as exemplified in the Holy Eucharist, shown by the English people in our mediæval days is notably exhibited by their voluntary establishment of "morrow-mass priests" for the churches of town parishes and of the larger villages. Such priests were as a rule supported out of the common church funds of the parish as collected and administered by the wardens. The "morrow-mass" was an early Eucharist chiefly maintained to enable travellers and those engaged in early morning duties to attend divine worship. Such Masses were sometimes ordered to be celebrated at sunrise, or, as in a Nottingham parish, "every morning before sune rysing." At Grantham and Newark the morrow-mass was said at 4 A.M. all the year round; but the more usual hour was 5 in the summer and 6 in the winter. At St. Edmund's, Salisbury, the wardens paid for a torch and six pounds of tallow candles "for the Morrow Masse press in Wynter." The multitude of wardens' accounts, of pre-Reformation days, yet extant of the City of London churches abound in references to these extra and popularly supported Masses.[*] In the appointment of a morrow-mass priest at St. Mary-at-Hill, City of London, in 1472, it was provided that "the said Priest say every workeday in the said Church his Mattins pryme and hours, evensong and compline, and all his other prayers and services, by himself or with his felowes priests of the same church." The accounts of this church also show, at another period, that the wardens paid one of the priests an extra fee of 5s. a quarter for taking the "Morrow Masse." At St. Peter Cheap the wardens not only paid the stipend of £6 13s. 4d. to a priest for a 6 o'clock daily Mass, but also the wages of a clerk to serve him.

It was for the use of the celebrants of these early Masses that chambers over porches and elsewhere in church fabrics were often utilized or specially constructed. Evidence, too, of various kinds is also abundant to establish the fact that church attendance on the part of the laity at week-day services, as well as those on festivals and Sundays, was at least fairly good and of general custom. Not only did the majority of the people readily cease work and attend to their religious duties on Sundays and saints' days, but the proceedings of ecclesiastical courts show that delinquents of the fourteenth

[*] See Dr. Cox's " Early Churchwarden Accounts," 1913.

and fifteenth centuries who flagrantly neglected their obligations were presented by the wardens, and fined or put to public penance. But this is not the place to follow up such matters.* It seemed good, however, to set forth sufficient to show the continuous round of services for which our parish churches provided, as well as to point out that such services were keenly appreciated.

Recently so much learning and diligence have been expended in putting together all that was ever done within consecrated walls by way of business or entertainment, as well as occasional illicit matters deplored by all, that it seemed well that the other and brighter side of the shield should be presented. Moreover, the antiquary or archæologist who attempted to study the ancient shrines of Egypt or the further East, the temples of Athens and of Rome, or even the mosques of the Mussulman without any elementary idea of the rites practised therein, or of the myths and traditions that brought them into being, would fail to understand them or to grasp the reasons for their architectural developments. In like manner the student of the English parish church, if he would understand its architectural significance and development of plan, must be prepared to know, at least in outline, the uses to which its component parts were put, to remember that it was in some measure the reflection of the highest of human aspirations—the worship of the Most High— and that its story is based on matters far more momentous than the adjustment of shaft and vault, the refinement of a moulding, or the general effect and construction of a graceful arcade.

Not only was the obligation of all to contribute to God's House, to the maintenance of the fabric, and to the splendour of its appointments generally grasped and practised by the laity, but it was enforced in various popular books of instruction in the vernacular.

A favourite among these was " Dives and Pauper," a book

* See Dr. Cutts's "Parish Priests and their People," 1893, and more especially Abbot Gasquet's "Parish Life in Mediæval England," 1906.

perhaps written in the first half of the fifteenth century, and of much repute among early printed books. It takes the form of a dialogue between a rich man and a poor man, wherein the latter assumes the *rôle* of the teacher and gives the rationale of a number of practices then current. " Dives," in a striking passage, is made to declare that " many say God is in no land so well served in Holy Church nor so much worshipped in Holy Church, as He is in this land of England. For so many fair churches, and so good array in churches, and so fair service, as many say is in none other land as it is in this land." " Pauper " cannot deny this, but suggests that it is perhaps done in a spirit of pomp, " to have name and worship thereby in the country, or for envy that one town hath against another." This suggests to " Dives " that it might be better if the money spent " in high churches, in rich vestments, in curious windows, and in great bells " were given to the poor. But " Pauper " at once rejoins that this is but the argument of Judas, and declares that it is the common business of all, whether rich or poor, to look to the beautifying of God's House.

Churches are usually studied in a variety of manners, good, bad, and indifferent, but generally by detail, or feature by feature. This may be all very well in a monograph on a particular church, but it is a mistake, and not a little bewildering in its results, if such a method is followed when dealing with churches on general lines. Contrariwise, in this work an attempt is made to regard churches as complete buildings and to consider their design as a whole, laying particular stress upon the materials of which they are composed, an important elementary feature hitherto much neglected.

It will be found that parish churches, in these pages, are treated more with regard to varieties than period and date. The treatment is intended to be analytical rather than antiquarian. There are various architectural text-books which set forth with general accuracy, and after a technical fashion, the rise and development of successive styles usually known as Saxon, Norman, Early English, Decorated, and Perpendicular, together with certain intervening periods of transition. A short chapter is given to summarize these conclusions, which have fairly held their own from the days of Rickman onwards. It is found, however, that the very considerable overlapping of one style with its successor materially interferes with the old-fashioned belief in the value of very precise classification by such terms. No harm, however, results from the new conception of Gothic art which has grown up of recent years. In fact, it considerably expands the broader interest in the parish church as a whole, which may be regarded as the record in stone of a gradual growth in architectural effort extending over centuries, in an endeavour to accommodate itself to the ritual developments of ecclesiastics on the one hand, and the growth of social or economic changes on the other.

The conciseness with which this side of the question is treated leaves the more space for the consideration of the different main types of plans, with their variations; later followed by a review of the chief constructive materials employed in mediæval times, and their influence on the fabric of the parish church.

The churches of England have also throughout their history been the repositories of splendid works of art, illustrative of the best efforts achieved by successive generations of craftsmen in freestone, in monumental sculpture, in Purbeck marble, or in Derbyshire alabaster, in the encaustic tiling or contrasting marbles of the pavement, and in the lavish yet chastened application of colour-schemes and gilding to the salient points of stonework: moreover they abounded in every form of carpentry and carving in wood, as well as the woodwork of roofs, screens, and pulpits; in precious metals and enamels, in brass and ironwork, in costly fabrics for hangings or vestments of home-weaving and from every known quarter of the globe, and in all the refinements of skilled embroidery. All this in addition to the abundant pictorial paintings in glazed windows and on the walls, the masterpieces of contemporary art, breathed throughout the spirit of religious instruction.

Numberless instances of the exuberance of craftsmanship, usually local, in adorning the House of God, even in country

31. THE CHURCH AND ITS CRAFTSMANSHIP : EWELME, OXFORDSHIRE

parish churches, might be adduced; but we must be content with two examples: Ewelme, Oxfordshire (Fig. 31), and Swimbridge, North Devon (Fig. 32). Notwithstanding the gross pillage of the days of Edward VI, renewed in the early years of Elizabeth, and brought to a climax by the Puritan barbarities of the next century, our parish churches still retain many a relic of the days when all that was magnifical adorned the sanctuaries of the Faith. But alas! in these pages of wide reflection and of strictly defined space, all such details as pertain to the fittings and furniture of the church must be strictly limited.

The average parish church of our country districts usually advances by a series of fresh developments or reconstruction at intervals of about half a century, from the time of the Conqueror's arrival down to the death of Henry VIII. It is, however, quite obvious that there were great ages of church building and extension, notably in Norman days, during the reign of Henry III, and throughout certain periods of the fifteenth century.

The Normans brought with them their national architectural style, which is generally termed Romanesque. The advent of this type, to some slight extent, preceded the actual date of the Conquest, being intentionally employed by Edward the Confessor at the Royal Abbey of Westminster, and through the influence of the Court in other cases. The new Norman landholders, as soon as the Conquest was an established fact, set to work after a vigorous fashion to build or reconstruct churches, small and great, in accordance with the style of their own importation. Their remarkable zeal in this direction was probably fanned by a desire to show their superiority to the conquered race. They speedily rebuilt the great majority of churches, both monastic and parochial, throughout the land. In such drastic methods they fortunately differed, so far as English church history in stone is concerned, from those who came after them. It seems, however, that, though thus destructive for the most part of the work of their predecessors, the Normans were content occasionally to follow Saxon methods, more especially in the masonry of the western towers. In such instances the probability is strong that they employed Saxon masons. This is especially the case with regard to a number of towers in the northern part of Lincolnshire, which, though they retain the primitive unbuttressed style, and windows

32. A DEVONSHIRE INTERIOR: SWIMBRIDGE, BARNSTAPLE

possessing mid-wall shafts, are generally considered to have been built shortly after the Conquest.

The dawn of English Gothic art coincided fairly closely with the close of the reign of Richard Cœur de Lion. John's evil reign, however, productive as it was of both foreign invasion and civil strife, accompanied by his quarrel with the Papacy, put for a time almost as severe a check on church building and architectural enterprise as came about a century and a half later through the awful ravages of the Black Death. The Interdict left England at one time with only a single bishop in all her dioceses, whilst John continued to absorb the revenues of the Church. But on the accession of Henry III, in 1216, this spoliation ceased, and the stream of architectural art burst forth in marvellous vigour, gaining all the greater strength after the removal of this temporary obstruction to its progress. Bishop Stubbs has called the thirteenth the "golden century of English churchmanship." Under Stephen Langton the Church, at once potent and popular, stepped to the front, victorious over both feudal and papal aggressions, and strong enough to check the undue claims of monastic orders of foreign origin. One of the results of its supremacy was that the reign of Henry III became the Golden Age of English Gothic art. Architecture, fostered by the King as his artistic tastes matured, chiefly owed its beautiful development to episcopal influence. The names of such prelates as Bishop Jocelyn of Wells, Bishop Grostete of Lincoln, and Bishop Poore of Salisbury and afterwards of Durham, will ever be closely associated with the splendid architectural efforts of this reign as manifested in their own cathedrals, and reflected in many a parish church throughout the sees over which they presided.

The fourteenth century also must not be passed over without a word of recognition as one of the great periods of mediæval church building, a time when a school of highly trained craftsmen was available to produce work of magnificent, though occasionally excessive, elaboration.

An extraordinary fervour of church building and extension passed over England in the fifteenth century, from one end to the other, manifesting itself with much emphasis even in remote Cornwall, of which Kilkhampton (Fig. 188) may be taken as a typical interior. The work of this period, usually known as Perpendicular, had no reflection in its dignified simplicity on the Continent, where architectural taste had evolved the elaborate decoration and profuse exuberance of the Flamboyant style. Professor Prior, in his "Gothic Art," has well pointed out that the influence on parish church building of the twelfth century was mainly monastic, of the thirteenth century episcopal, and of the fourteenth century aristocratic; and if one word is to be applied to the fifteenth-century building and upkeep of our churches, it must be "democratic." The old nobility was giving way to one of newer origin. The French wars had killed off many of the ancient feudal families and impoverished their estates, while the later Wars of the Roses brought about still further reductions in the former ruling classes. Meanwhile the middle classes were surely advancing, boroughs were establishing still further their freedom and their trades, the gentlefolk were growing more independent of their lords, and the labouring classes in the country were shaking off the bonds of manorial customs. The extravagances of the fourteenth century were happily passing away; there was a higher morality and a deeper sense of religion among the people at large. Wherever the wool trade and the consequent weaving prospered, whether in the eastern counties or the West, the fabrics of the churches were the first to profit from an increased wealth, and the parish church came to be more and more considered the great house of the parish, built to a large extent and almost entirely furnished by the local efforts of the parishioners.

And just as there were great periods of church building, so it will be found that there were wide districts where the finest building prevailed, such as East Anglia, with the fens of Lincolnshire and Cambridgeshire, where there was a brave determination to rise superior to the monotonous level of Nature, and the fertile stretches of Somersetshire, or of Northamptonshire, where the grand building stone of Barnack and the facilities of water carriage caused such splendid parish churches to spring into being along the banks of the Nen.

The influence of situation and the landscape on the elevation and comparative beauty of parish churches comes out strongly in the case of the fine towers for which Somerset is so justly renowned. By far the noblest of these towers, both in height and decorative though dignified treatment, are to be found in the immediate neighbourhood of Taunton, as at Bishop's Lydiard (Fig. 33), or a little further to the east, where a group of towers, such as those of Ile Abbots, Huish Episcopi, or Kingsbury Episcopi, stand forth in all their stateliness. There are no fine hills or splendid scenery in their neighbourhood; turn to an orthographical map, and it will be found that these towers spring up in all their beauty from level districts ranging from 100 to 200 feet above the sea-level. The foremost writers on the towers of this county, the best of whom are Messrs. Allen and Brereton, are struck by the fact that the towers west of the Quantocks are distinctly inferior both in height and enrichment, though they would be considered good in other parts of England. It has been suggested that this comparative inferiority has been brought about by a lower quality and less abundant supply of stone. But this is not the case. The grandeur of the scenery and the height of the hills or mountains, as Exmoor is approached, almost unconsciously influenced the mediæval builders and designers of parish churches. Where Nature asserted herself in rising majesty, it best became them to make no supreme efforts. The central tower of Dunster and the western tower of Minehead are fine in themselves, but humble as compared with St. Mary Magdalene, Taunton, or St. Cuthbert, Wells, and their compeers. Or take the lovely village of Luccombe

33. BISHOP'S LYDIARD, SOMERSET

54 THE ENGLISH PARISH CHURCH

(Fig. 34), surrounded by hills—or, as the name implies, locked up in a veritable maze of combes—and stretching towards the lofty summit of Dunkery Beacon. Here there is a tower some 96 feet high, guarding with a certain assertive

34. WEST LUCCOMBE, SOMERSET

dignity the cottages at its feet, but entirely devoid of any soaring vanity, nay, almost severe in its comely plainness.

The thought as to the situation of the parish church adds much to the zest of their study. Such consideration appealed to Mr. Billing, that able architectural draughtsman and writer of the middle of last century. In his remarkable work on the ancient architecture of Durham County, when commenting on the little weather-beaten church of Medomsley, on a lofty situation near Elchester, he remarks:

"No one knew better than the ancient architects how to

suit their designs to one intended site. While the lofty spire of Chester-le-Street is applicable to the protected valley, the stunted spire at Boldon may be mentioned as an adaptation to an exposed locality, and the position of Medomsley has

35. GREAT COXWELL, BERKSHIRE
[*Drawn by A. E. Newcombe*

been equally studied. It stands on the summit of the unsheltered lofty hills on the confines of Durham and Northumberland, and consists of a low, almost flat-roofed nave and chancel, a porch, and a vestry, all lower even than the modern cottages which surround it."

And yet these low roofs shelter the interior of a little Early English gem in the chancel.

Instances might be almost indefinitely multiplied of the adaptability of the fabric to its surroundings. Just one other example of a different character may be adduced. In the north-west of Berkshire there is some good stone for the churches, but the towers are anything but lofty, as shown in the drawing of Great Coxwell (Fig. 35), a church abounding in interest, and eminently suited to the village which it serves. But why should its tower be lofty, when, close at hand, the prominent rounded hill of Badbury Camp rises to a height of 500 feet?

In considering these types of parish churches, it must be remembered that they all occurred within five centuries, and that those centuries were not, *a priori*, a period wherein naturally to expect a series of bold conceptions coupled with great mechanical and almost scientific requirements. In a word, the very best of these successive periods was undoubtedly given, in England most emphatically and generally throughout Christendom, to the development and beautifying of the parish church.

CHAPTER II

THE PLAN OF THE ENGLISH PARISH CHURCH

The plans in this chapter have been reproduced to a uniform scale of 25 feet to the inch, except where the page area would not permit, when half the scale— 50 feet to the inch—has been adopted; this occurs in the cases of Figs. 42, 44, 92 and 100. The series of development plans (Fig. 43) has been reproduced to a special scale. A uniform system of hatching has been adopted on the plans to indicate the different building periods, and this is made clear by the key attached to each plan. A later building period in the same century is shown by the use of the same hatching of that century, but more closely spaced. In cases where an analytical division into periods was not to be ascertained a uniform cross-hatching has been adopted

It is perhaps as well to begin this chapter with a few introductory remarks designed to show, in a summarized form, the trend of parish-church plan development in the Middle Ages. Although a subject of the greatest importance to a right understanding of mediæval work, which can on no account be neglected, it has not as yet been thoroughly elucidated, but in recent years considerable progress has been made in its study.

For many years attention was chiefly devoted to subsidiary details of mediæval architecture, such as arcades, windows, doors, mouldings, ornament, etc. And yet the whole appearance, external and interior, of a parish church depends upon its plan. As features and detail advanced and developed, so

58   THE ENGLISH PARISH CHURCH

did the lines on which the church was laid out, as indicated by
ground-plans, and the method of its construction and building,
as shown by sections.

Although the variations in church plans are innumerable,
yet, if the main body of the structure be analysed, every case

36. THE ROUND PORTION, ST. SEPULCHRE'S, NORTHAMPTON

may ultimately be traced back to one of three fundamental
types in use in the twelfth century. These are:

1. THE NAVE AND SANCTUARY.
2. THE NAVE, CHANCEL AND SANCTUARY.
3. THE CROSS CHURCH WITH NAVE, TRANSEPTS SANCTUARY, AND CENTRAL LANTERN-TOWER.

If the Parish Church plan seems much too complex for this
classification, it must be remembered that the variations are
caused in some degree by the occurrence of hybrids or blends

THE PLAN

of the above types, but chiefly by the different combinations and positions of such features as Tower, Aisles, Porches, Chapels, etc., which admit of an infinite variety in plan and grouping.

In England a fourth type, the circular plan, need scarcely be considered, for of it only three parish examples remain, at St. Sepulchre's, Northampton (Fig. 36), Cambridge, and Little Maplestead, while the Templars' church in London, a well-known example which belonged to a military order, and the domestic chapel at Ludlow Castle complete the list of extant examples.

The second type also did not continue as a permanent form. Many more examples of it, however, can be found, either as at Kilpeck (Figs. 37, 38), without a tower, or with the

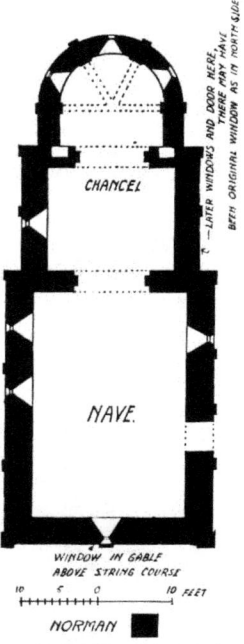

37. KILPECK, HEREFORDSHIRE (TYPE II)

38. KILPECK, HEREFORDSHIRE

chancel carried up as a middle tower, of which Iffley and Stewkley (Figs. 49-51) are instances. Several of these churches have received the subsequent addition of aisles, chapels, etc., during the course of their existence, as illustrated at Newhaven (Fig. 48).

The reason for referring these types back to the twelfth century is that after the Norman invasion, upon the settlement of the conquerors in England, there was a great impulse of church-building all over the country. Almost all the pre-Conquest churches, especially those built of wood, were reconstructed, and many churches of fresh ecclesiastical foundation, and of one of these three types, were erected on their manors by the new Norman lords.

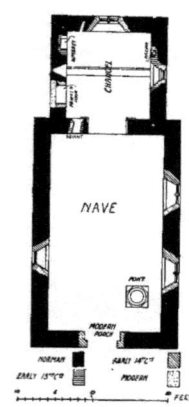

39. CHITHURST, SUSSEX
TYPE I, SQUARE-ENDED

It is true that there are numerous examples of pre-Conquest work in England, but the plans, though reducible to the foregoing forms, are generally of so tentative and experimental a character that it is difficult to specify types which can be said to be peculiarly Saxon. Towards the end of the Saxon period churches approximate more closely to contemporary Continental work, owing to increasing intercourse with foreign countries. It is obvious there must have been from the outset various grades of churches, according to the size or importance of the place where they were erected. It is, however, an open question how far these various distinctions were formulated in the twelfth century. It is clear that an aisleless nave could not be built with a timber roof of unlimited size, particularly with the constructive skill then available, though a larger one might be erected in good building stone than in flint rubble. Nor would the rudeness of the carpentry be without its influence on the size of the building. Possibly, therefore, in the

THE PLAN

twelfth century, the grade of church was marked by multiplication of parts and differences of form; thus, for example, the occurrence of a cross church would denote a more important foundation. With the introduction of aisles and increased skill on the part of the mason and the carpenter, the *raison d'être* for this radical and costly difference disappeared. So it is found that important parish churches, in their later rebuildings, assume much increased size in elemental features, such as aisled nave and chancel. These, through mere magnitude, place such churches above their humbler fellows, and thus it comes about that so many mediæval churches are at present of nave and chancel form.

The simplest form of twelfth-century plan is that of type 1, the nave and sanctuary, the latter either square-ended, as at Chithurst (Fig. 39), or with an apse, as at Little Braxted (Fig. 40). Type 1 may

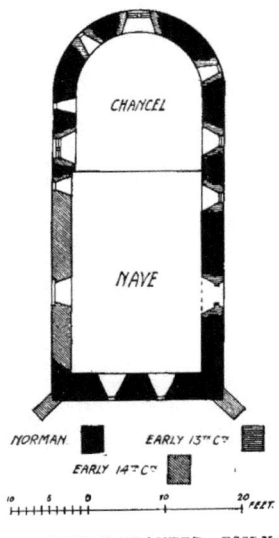

40. LITTLE BRAXTED, ESSEX
TYPE I, APSIDAL

be further elaborated by having a western tower in place of a bell-cote, or small bell-turret erected over the west end of the nave, or it may be without the tower and have aisles to the nave. It is not very common to find a twelfth-century church of this type planned, in the first instance, with both aisles and west tower, for this well-known arrangement among English parish churches seems in many instances to be the result of additions, however early in date, to the original building. This became so usual a procedure that in later times practically complete rebuildings might be erected on old sites upon these lines.

The simplest form of type 3 is a church with aisleless nave, plain square planned transept, and simple sanctuary, with a lantern-tower over the crossing, as at Old Shoreham (Figs. 77, 78). Parish churches but seldom sought to rival the great cathedral and monastic foundations in the multiplication of their parts, but a cross church with an aisleless nave might often have a square or apsidal chapel on the east side of each arm of the transept. Uffington, Berkshire, a thirteenth-century cruciform example, retains twin charming embryo chapels of slight projection in the north transept (Fig. 41), and one on the south; the piscinas show they once contained altars. Sometimes the nave has aisles; twelfth-century churches seldom had large projecting porches. The origin of the transept is a fruitful subject for speculation, but it is outside the scope of this work, since its investigation might go back to the first days of Christianity, and probably to the places of its early sway in Eastern lands. Again, its consideration is intimately bound up with that of the central tower, another wide and important subject. It is enough for the present purpose that transepts and central towers are well established among twelfth-century types.

41. UFFINGTON, BERKS, FROM THE NORTH-EAST

The cruciform plan is attended with obvious disadvantages; the large piers indispensable for carrying a central tower obstruct space, view, and sound in the very heart of the building, while the aisleless cross type has the further drawback that the transepts are entirely secluded from the main body of the church. The chief merits of the transeptal plan

THE PLAN

are æsthetic, and consist in the undeniable picturesqueness of the grouping of the central tower with surrounding parts, and in aisled interiors the charming cross vistas which result. But even on the ground of appearance it has this defect, that there is a decided apparent reduction in the height of the tower, which is necessarily not visible down to the ground. The practical disadvantages probably induced mediæval builders in later times to depart from the cruciform plan, and inclined them to develop the resources of the aisled nave and west tower, a form economical in labour and material, and of great excellence for congregational purposes.

It is from these two types (1 and 3) that the more complex plan of later times has evolved. Naves have received the addition of aisles, clerestories, and porches, the latter often having upper chambers, while the chancel has been lengthened or rebuilt with the addition of chapels, and in many cases with clerestories as well. Large chapels in the case of cross churches often replace the early transeptal chapels, mentioned on p. 62. New towers have been added, existing ones heightened; or in cross churches, a central tower may have been replaced by one erected in a fresh position, generally at the west end. The transepts themselves have disappeared, merged into aisles, or on the other hand have been extended or rebuilt, or in a few cases furnished with aisles. Transept-like chapels have also sometimes been erected; while other additions in well-developed churches are sacristies, crypts, or charnel-houses, and small chantry chapels in convenient though abnormal positions. The plan of Witney, in Oxfordshire (Fig. 42), illustrates many of these features or additions.

Many of these changes might occur in a single church, till it arrived at its full development, and would occupy centuries in the happening. Some churches, always fulfilling the requirements of the parish, have undergone but slight change, perhaps only alteration of door, window, or arch, while others have shown steady growth all through the mediæval period, though still bearing evidences of a simple origin.

Some, again, have only partly developed, throwing out for example an aisle or chapel; while others, which began their evolution later, in times of great prosperity, may have been almost totally rebuilt, with but slight remaining evidence of

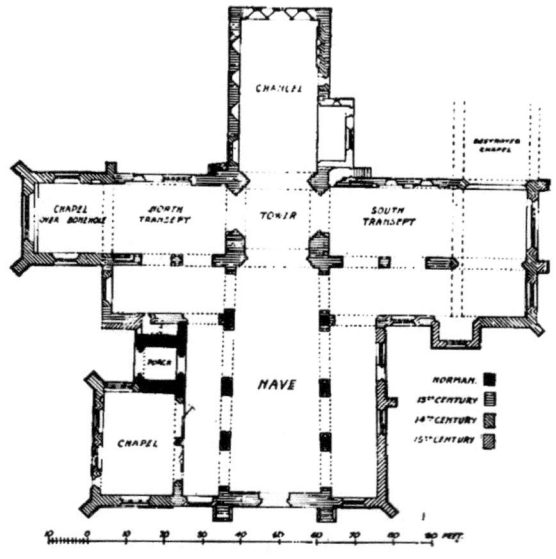

42. WITNEY, OXFORDSHIRE

their original form. It must be borne in mind, however, that in such rebuildings, even if all comprised under one scheme for enlargement, these modifications would be usually undertaken on a piecemeal method, so that the church might always be in use. The result of this system of procedure is that nearly always evidence of the form of the early church still exists, at least in some slight degree, and that the plan of the original church can be traced.

In explanation of this an illustration is here shown, consisting of plans and sections (Fig. 43). The illustration is not of any particular church, and does not profess to show every

THE PLAN

variety of addition, but is designed to illustrate the more natural and usual changes and transformations which the parish church of a prosperous mediæval town might pass through during its history from the twelfth century to the close of the mediæval period.

The various features denoted are paralleled by actual examples, and the diagrams follow a sequence in which necessity and requirements result in a natural extension of the structure.

The first diagrams (*No. 1*) delineate in plan and section the church as it would be built, or rebuilt, in the twelfth century, and in the following diagrams the outline of this church is dotted so that its extension is clearly shown.

At various times during the thirteenth century additions would be made to this small church, at first consisting of aisleless nave and apsidal sanctuary; a south aisle being added for the accommodation of a growing population, the apse removed and sanctuary lengthened to form a chancel in order to meet ritual requirements, while on the north side of the nave a wealthy benefactor endowed and built a chantry chapel in connexion with which a guild might be formed (*No. 2*).

In the fourteenth century, the guild becoming more important, this chapel was extended into an aisle, while the south aisle was widened not only to accommodate more worshippers, but to afford additional altar room. A south porch would be built with this aisle, a sacristy added to the chancel, and the old twelfth-century chancel arch replaced with a wider one (*No. 3*).

During the fifteenth century the early guild still increased in opulence and importance and undertook the rebuilding of the north aisle, adding a porch with a chamber over it and rebuilding the north arcade. A guild of later foundation built a south chapel on to the chancel, while a rich donor erected a screen with loft and rood, altering the chancel arch for the purpose, and building the rood staircase. The parish undertook the erection of the west tower, built in such a way as not to interfere with the use of the nave, and which when carried high enough to roof-in was opened up to the church by the removal of the original twelfth-century west wall (*No. 4*).

Towards the end of the fifteenth century yet another guild undertook the addition of a north chapel to the chancel, a small private chantry chapel being built at its north-east corner, while along with this building operation might go the addition of clerestory to the chancel. A wealthy merchant of the town enriched the church by the addition of an elaborate south porch with chamber over it; the thirteenth-century arcade wall, being faulty from age and possibly leaning outwards from roof thrust, was rebuilt in the latest fashion, and with this would go the addition of clerestory to the nave. While all this was going on the tower would be raised to its full height and receive its peal of bells (*No. 5*).

Such is the history in brief which a parish church of this character might pass through till it arrived at its full development, and it is typical in its various stages of the history of thousands of others, though they have only partially attained to its development.

It must be noted that, throughout its history, the external width and length of the original nave, the width of the chancel, and, till the latest period of growth, the height of the walls, have been dominating factors in the development. The nave and chancel have only been widened by the piercing of their side walls with arcades opening into aisles, the nave has been lengthened only by the method of adding the west tower, and the building heightened by the addition of clerestories in the case of both nave and chancel. At the very last but little of the original structure remains above ground, only the south-east angle quoin may be traced under the plaster of the south chapel, the rood staircase having necessitated the destruction of the north-east one, and the west ones being buried in the masonry of the west tower. But, for all this, it is obvious that the original church has to some extent dictated the form of the building all through its history, and also that the earlier additions have influenced those of later date.

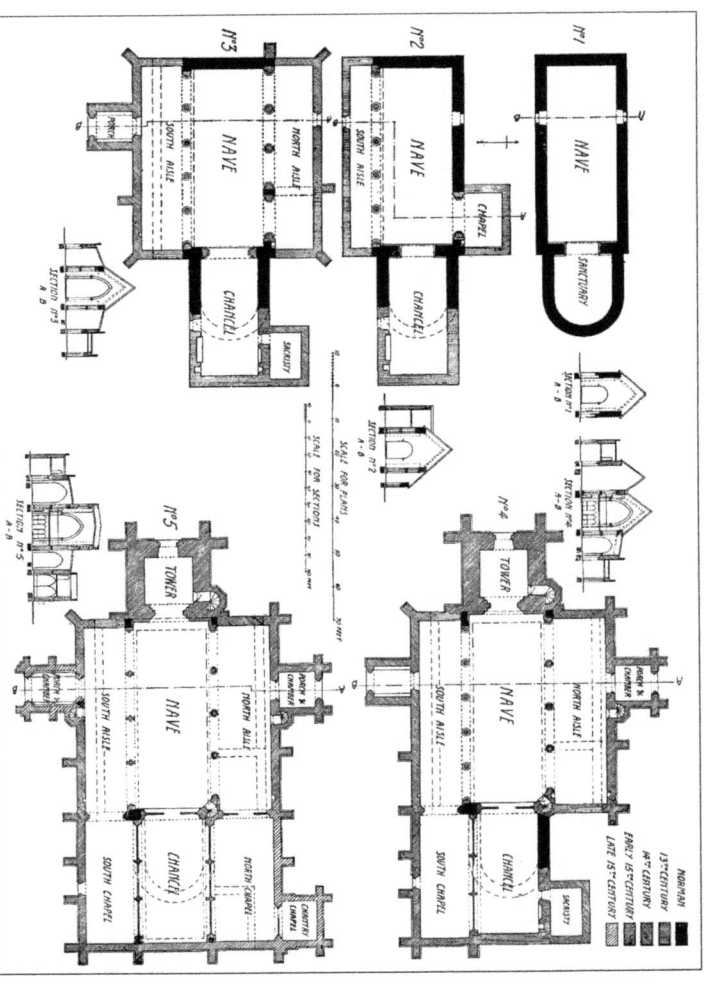

43 SERIES OF PLANS SHOWING TYPICAL CHANGES IN A NORMAL PARISH CHURCH FROM THE TWELFTH TO THE END OF THE FIFTEENTH CENTURY

The life-history of a parish church is of great interest, and to work out the problems of only one plan is in itself an education.

After a church of early foundation has developed in obedience to the requirements of successive centuries, it has attained historically the interest of an ancient document, and in aspect it has undergone a complete transformation. Such a church may have lost all trace of its first confined and dimly-lit aspect, caused by narrow openings, small windows, and generally heavy treatment, and with its large window area and slender supports now gives an effect of space, light, and airiness. The whole conception of the building has undergone a change—the plan has been simplified, while obstructions have been cleared away, walls and supports reduced to the minimum for stability, and the interior area opened out to the fullest advantage. Yet all these changes have been effected without loss of dignity, mystery, or appropriateness to its sacred uses. Throughout the Middle Ages may be traced the tendency to open up the interior, until the parish church acquired an effect

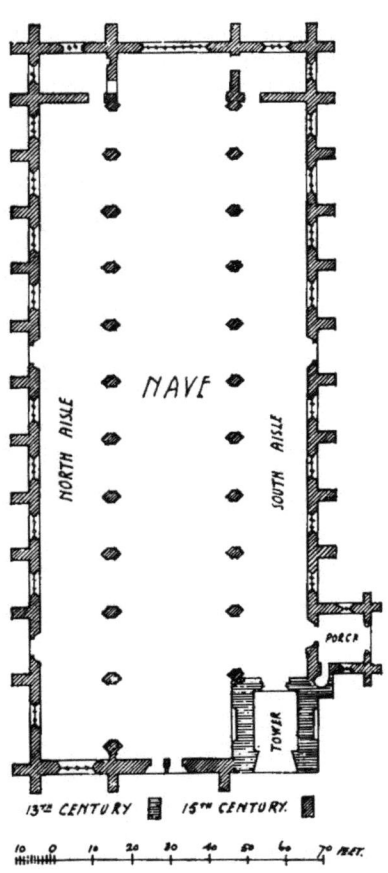

44. ST. NICHOLAS, KING'S LYNN

68 THE ENGLISH PARISH CHURCH

of unencumbered spaciousness. Towards this the English builder tended steadfastly, if but yet half-unconsciously. This purpose is exemplified in the case of many churches where the chancel arch has been considerably enlarged, or has altogether disappeared; of this many instances are to be found, but chiefly

45. ST. NICHOLAS, KING'S LYNN

in the South-West and Eastern counties. The later churches, notably in East Anglia, became huge glass lanterns, the solid wall surface being largely sacrificed for the glories of stained and painted glass. Of this type of building St. Nicholas, King's Lynn, is perhaps the best instance which can be cited (Fig. 44).*

Upon superficial observation of the interior it appears to be all of one date, but careful investigation reveals evidences

* St. Nicholas is only a chapel-of-ease in status, but it has long been for all intents and purposes a parochial church.

of stages of development, while the thirteenth-century tower at the south-west at once shows the existence of an earlier fabric. As it stands to-day the building has developed into a three-aisled parallelogram, about 162 feet long by 70 feet wide within the walls (Fig. 45). The division of the interior into its various parts was effected by screen-work extended right across the church, and probably between the arches of the chancel and its chapels. It is unfortunate that this work has now completely disappeared, and therefore no little imagination is required to picture the church in its full beauty and mystery, which could scarcely have been surpassed by anything in England, though founded on the utmost simplicity of plan.

The architecture of this church belongs to a period which it pleased the arbitrary fancy of the Gothic revivalists to pronounce debased; nevertheless its plan, as the expression of the accumulated tradition and wisdom of the mediæval time, is more suitable for adaptation to modern requirements than any of earlier form, which at best were of the nature of expedients due to the necessity of adding to an existing structure in uninterrupted use.

The foregoing summary of the subject aims at indicating the broad lines on which development proceeded. In the more detailed consideration of parish-church planning, the method pursued, for the sake of clearness, is to deal with the nave and sanctuary plan, with its additions and extensions of aisles, tower, etc., and next, regarding it as a parallel development, to consider the forms of transeptal churches. Then mention is made of such features as towers, porches, and vestries in their differing forms. It is felt that an attempt to keep to strict chronological order or to deal simultaneously with the rectangular and cross plans would have resulted in some confusion owing to the many variations and counter-developments involved.

Here it may be well to mention that in considering mediæval planning one must not forget that in these islands, as well as throughout Christendom, the fundamental doctrines of the Faith and the outward expression of them in worship remained the same during the whole of the mediæval period, though elaborated by the introduction of accessories in the ritual observances. Everything remained centred at the altar at which the priest celebrated.

"Such changes as were made," as has been well remarked by an American writer, Mr. Barr Ferree, "were due to an elaboration of ritual, not to the introduction of new forms of worship or to the addition of new dogmas to the Christian faith. The choirs were enlarged to give more room to those who had place within them."

In the early days of the conversion of Saxon England, after the members of the Romano-British Church had been driven to the extremities of the land, Christian churches followed as a rule two plans, according to the source of the missionary enterprise, either Roman or Celtic, which necessitated their building. In both cases they assumed the form of small buildings with a nave and sanctuary, the latter as a rule, if its origin was from Roman influence, having apsidal termination, and being square-ended if it came from a returning wave of Celtic fervour. As to this highly interesting subject but very little must here be said, for all this was prior to the introduction of even the germ of parish life, the churches of that early period being monastic or missionary settlements.

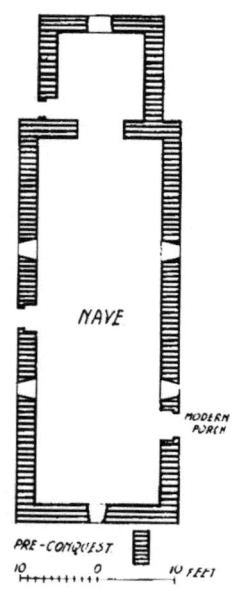

46. ESCOMB, DURHAM
(*For a view of this church see Fig.* 109)

In considering the whole question of Saxon architecture, a third influence is usually overlooked which had a great effect on the development of the late pre-Conquest churches. It was in those days that this country, mainly through Norman influence, came into immediate contact with the monastic developments of Western Europe. Among the monastic bodies the art of building was well developed, and their intercourse with England tended to spread a rudimentary cruciform plan, while in some cases the true cross form of church was actually adopted.

To enumerate one or two factors which may have contributed to the prevalence of the square-ended type, it may be mentioned that little groups of oblong chapels or oratories dating from the sixth to the eleventh century remain in Ireland, as at Glendalough and Cashel. This square-ended type followed the Irish into Scotland, and its plan is still extant in two cases in Cornwall, namely in the oratories of St. Piran and St. Gwithian. A good example of such an early square-ended church is at Escomb, Durham (Figs. 46 and 109), while Worth, Sussex, better illustrates the embryo cruciform plan (Fig. 47). Both are of early date, and show the vigour of these types in two totally different parts of the kingdom. St. Mary-in-the-Castle, Dover, shows a fully developed cross and central tower church of pre-Conquest date.

The second variety of early church, introduced by St. Augustine, is obviously of Roman origin. Eadmer, writing in the eleventh century, says that Augustine's great church at Canterbury was planned by him "in imitation of the Great Basilica of the Blessed Peter." The Saxon cathedral there, until the rebuilding by Archbishop Lanfranc, had apses both west and east, a rare form of which a parochial example existed at Langford, Essex. This little church has a western apse of pre-Norman date, whilst the foundations of the eastern apse can still be traced, though the actual apse itself disappeared during an early extension of the church. Brixworth is one of the most noted examples of an Italian apse, and others, almost equally noteworthy, occur at Wing, in the Vale of Aylesbury, and at Worth, Sussex. The first of these examples is of late seventh-century origin, and the two others later and different

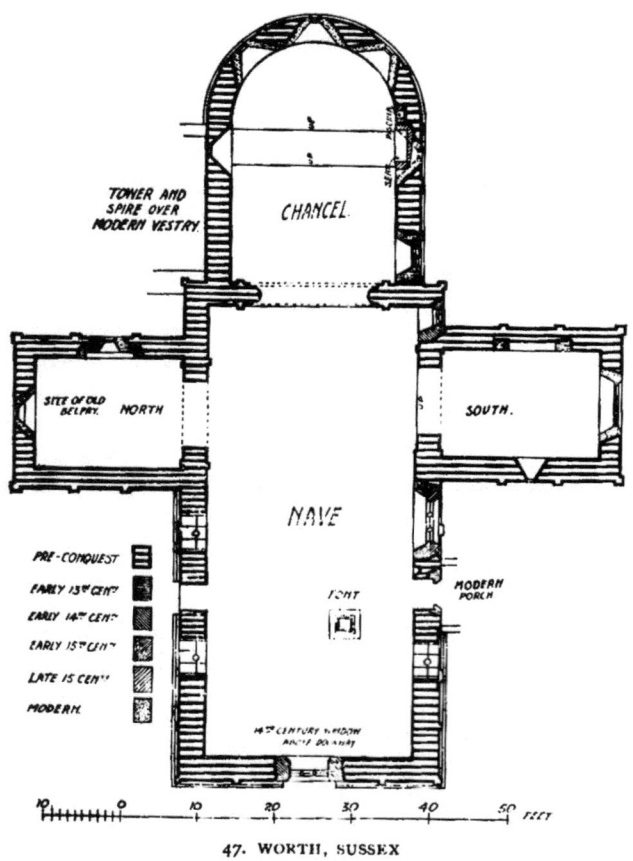

47. WORTH, SUSSEX

developments of apses. The basilican plans of Reculver and of the Canterbury churches of St. Pancras and St. Martin are now allowed by experts to be of seventh century, and not to date from the time of the Roman occupation. Two other interesting little apsidal seventh century churches are those of St. Peter-on-the-Wall, Essex (Fig. 105), built by St. Cedd, Bishop

THE PLAN

of the East Saxons, and South Elmham, Suffolk, built by St. Felix, the first Bishop of East Anglia.

In the energy shown by the Norman landowners in church-building which rapidly followed the Conquest, there came about, as might naturally be expected, a recrudescence of the apse, chiefly in South-Eastern England. Among the most beautiful examples of Norman apses to small country churches are those of Steetley, Derbyshire; Nately Scures, Hants; Kilpeck, Herefordshire; and Fritton, Suffolk. Sussex possesses an interesting example of an Early Norman apse at Newhaven, where it projects from a central Norman tower (Fig. 48). Nevertheless, the firmly rooted Celtic tradition maintained itself in flat contradiction to the rest of Western Christendom, and ultimately resulted in the general removal of apses, and the erection of square-ended chancels. This process applies not only to small parish churches but to cathedrals and monastic churches, and is a feature particularly English.

48. THE EAST END, NEWHAVEN, SUSSEX

In some Norman churches, as already mentioned, there is a threefold division into nave, chancel, and sanctuary. The Norman chancel is often vaulted, and may be formed by the space under a central tower, as at Stewkley, Buckinghamshire (Figs. 49-51). The sanctuary is frequently an apse; of this the interior of Kilpeck affords an excellent example. See chap. iii (Fig. 113). Newhaven is an instance of the rather uncommon treatment of central tower as chancel, in connexion with a short apsidal sanctuary (Fig. 48). At East Ham an apsidal example occurs together with a western tower. In this type the north and south walls of the middle tower form part of the exterior walls of the church. The tower is often as wide as the chancel, or even wider, as at Coln St. Denis, but in other instances, as at Bredon, Worcestershire, and Radnage, Bucks, it is actually narrower than either the nave or chancel between which it stands. This type has sometimes had the addition of aisles, the sloping roofs of which rest against the tower walls when they are carried so far, as at Great Tey, Essex. It is unlikely that many instances of this plan have been developed into the true cruciform type by the addition of transepts, and though the side tower walls may have subsequently been pierced for transept chapels, this does not constitute a cross

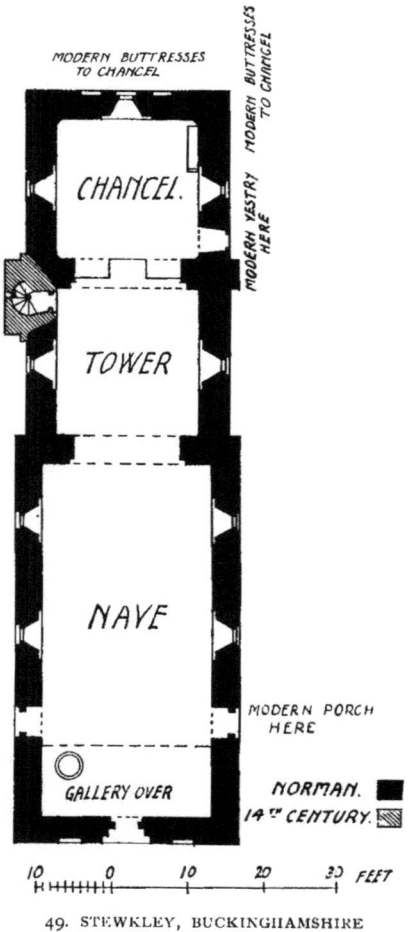

49. STEWKLEY, BUCKINGHAMSHIRE

plan, but only an approximation to its cross form. It is probable that the majority of existing twelfth-century cross

50. STEWKLEY FROM THE NORTH-EAST
[*Drawn by A. E. Newcombe*

churches have been transeptal from their first building. The apsidal sanctuary commonly had a vaulted stone roof, and the rectangular chancel, as a rule, a roof of wood. But to this there are exceptions, as in the vaulted square-ended chancels of Elkstone and Hampnett amid the Gloucestershire Cotswolds, where such a wealth of Norman work survives.

The small Norman churches of the Yorkshire Wolds and elsewhere were often constructed on a plan which gave the

76   THE ENGLISH PARISH CHURCH

nave exactly double the length of the sanctuary, whilst the height of the walls almost precisely equalled the width. In many cases the rectangular sanctuaries, as well as those of apse construction, were found too small for the ritual of the thirteenth century, and were therefore lengthened to form chancels. Before, however, the middle of the twelfth century

51. STEWKLEY FROM THE NORTH-WEST
[*Drawn by Rev. J. L. Petit*

was reached, a few oblong chancels of considerable length in proportion to their width had been built. Good examples of this occur at Earl's Barton, Northants, Stow, Lincolnshire, and another at Moor Monkton, Yorks, while there is a vaulted example at Hemel Hempstead, Herts.

Aisleless churches survived for a considerable time in the sparsely populated and wilder districts, and were now and again even rebuilt on that simple plan in the fourteenth and fifteenth centuries. In these instances, however, the proportions of an aisleless church reveal at a glance its later date. It is usually much broader in the nave, as well as being decidedly larger, than the earlier buildings. Elsing, Norfolk, is an instance of a late aisleless church (Figs. 52, 53).

The number and beauty of Norman arcades in our parish churches bear witness to the early use by the Normans of the aisled nave, a plan not unknown to pre-Conquest architecture.

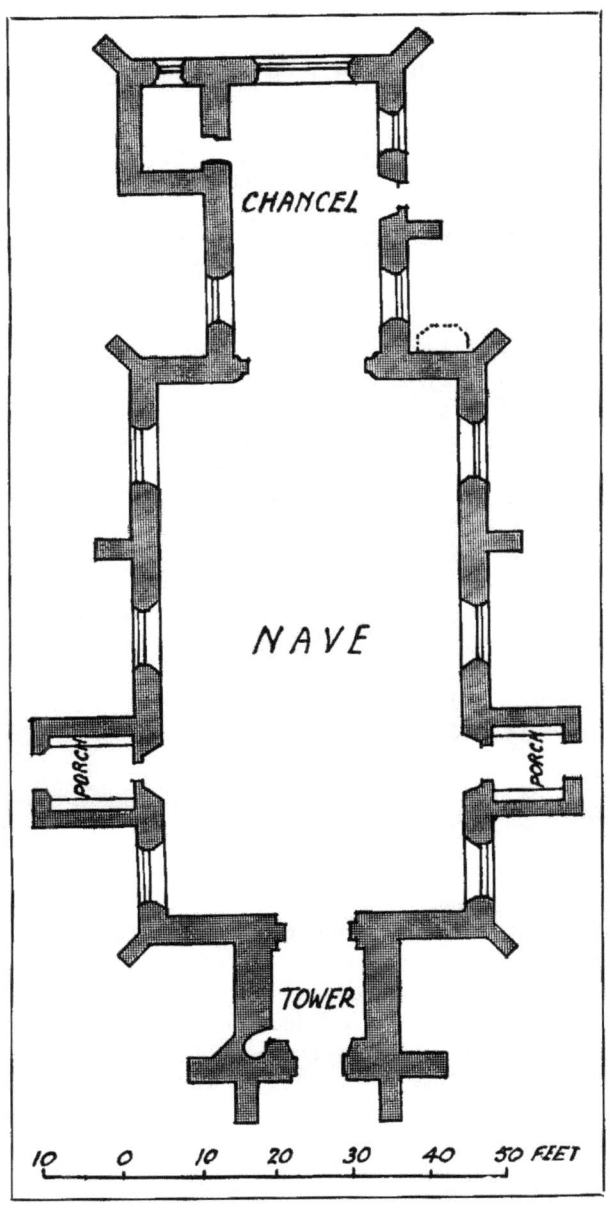

52. ELSING, NORFOLK (CHIEFLY FOURTEENTH CENTURY)

Aisled twelfth-century naves on a grand scale may be seen at Melbourne, Derbyshire; Sherburn-in Elmet, Yorks; Norham, Northumberland; and Tilney All Saints, Norfolk (Fig. 54).

If a church had originally an aisleless nave, and more accommodation was required, it was usually procured by

53. ELSING, NORFOLK

throwing out an aisle on the north side, an addition sometimes found as early as the twelfth century. The reason for the choice of the north side was fairly obvious. The Normans, as a rule, made the chief entrance on the south side of the nave, and it was frequently considerably enriched and occasionally had a shallow porch. Thus it was natural that graves should accumulate on that side, and hence it came about that the north side was preferred for extension, though afterwards there usually followed a south aisle. Little Munden, Hertford-

THE PLAN 79

shire (Fig. 55), is one of many examples where the north aisle alone has been added. It should be remembered, however,

54. TILNEY ALL SAINTS, NORFOLK

that it is not uncommon to find a south aisle alone added, or for it to have been added first.

The arcades were constructed in such a way that the old walling above the piers and arches is often left untouched, and from this circumstance it comes about that during restoration involving the stripping of the wall plaster interesting discoveries have been made of Saxon or other early windows. There is a good instance of this at Gretton,

Northamptonshire, and another of interest occurs at Terrington, Yorks. The only justification which can be pleaded for the otherwise wholly evil custom of robbing the ancient walls of their plaster is the occasional archæological or historic discoveries which are thereby accidentally made, and which might not be shown without this baring of the roughly built masonry.

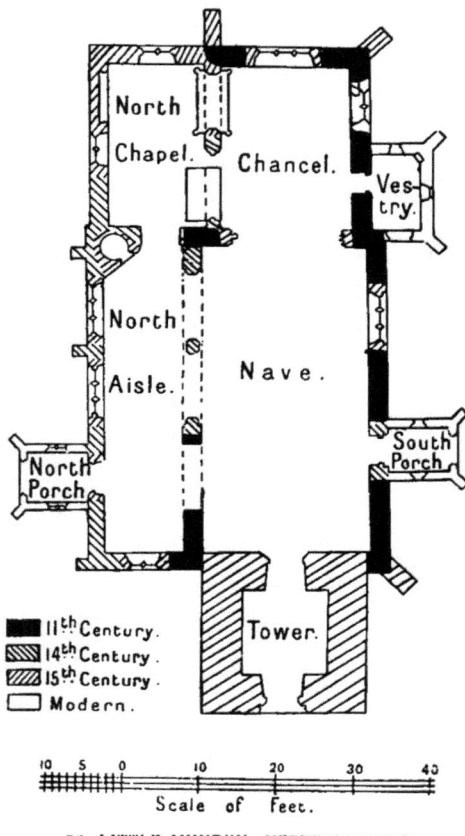

55. LITTLE MUNDEN, HERTFORDSHIRE

THE CLERESTORY.—Immediately the builders started to throw out aisles from the nave, they were faced with problems of lighting, which had to be grappled with during the whole of the mediæval period, with the satisfying results indicated earlier in this chapter (p. 67).

The solution of these lighting problems was often found in the insertion of the clerestory. It may therefore be well to deal by anticipation with this feature and its place in the mediæval church fabric.

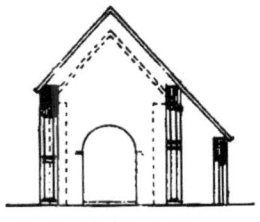
56. EARLY AISLE ADDITION

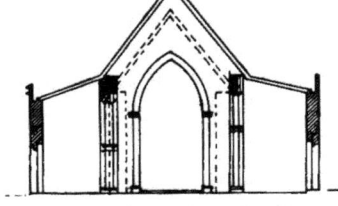
57. LATER FORM OF AISLES

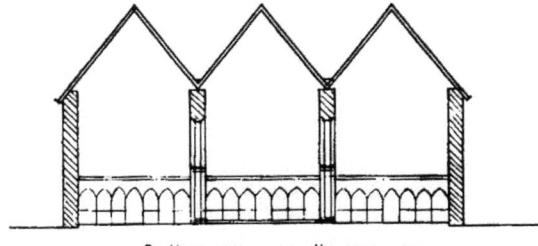
58. "THREE GABLE" EAST END

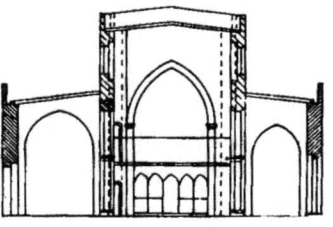
59. CLERESTORIED INTERIOR

The simplest method of roofing an aisle, after converting the nave wall into an arcade, was to continue the slope of the nave roof, as is often found in Sussex (Fig. 56). In a certain type of aisle very characteristic of the fourteenth century, the roof was given a flat pitch (Fig. 57). This, while it precluded a nave clerestory, provided ample window space in the comparatively lofty side walls or, as an alternative, efficient lighting would be obtained by gabling the end walls of the aisles and bringing the ridge of their roofs to the same level as that of the nave. The result at the east end is to form a row of three gables, at often equal height (Fig. 58). This "three-gable" arrangement was followed extensively in the fourteenth and fifteenth centuries in Devon and Cornwall, and is also very common in Kent. However, the most satisfactory system of all was to raise the wall above the nave arcades and pierce it with windows; in a word, to form a clerestory. When this took place early a steep-pitch nave roof was generally em-

60. ST. PETER MANCROFT, NORWICH

ployed, but in the fifteenth century, from which most clerestories date, a roof of flat pitch behind a parapet was customary (Fig. 59).

Where a clerestory followed after the erection of a west tower, the flat-pitched roof may have arisen from a desire not to interfere with the tower or its effect by unduly raising the level of the ridge, or to have too marked a difference in level between the skylines of the nave and chancel by placing a steep-pitched roof on the nave at a much higher level than the earlier one.

Not only have clerestories been erected over naves, but chancels with extensive chapels have also had clerestories and flat-pitched roofs, perhaps not later than those of the nave. In many large, well-developed churches of the Eastern counties,

THE PLAN

the clerestory is continuous over nave and chancel in one unbroken line, as at St. Peter Mancroft, Norwich (Fig. 60), and Long Melford. In very many cases, however, the nave alone is clerestoried, while the chancel retains a roof of steep pitch, the development not having been carried to completion.

There are various instances in our parish churches wherein

61. ST. MARGARET-AT-CLIFFE. KENT

the clerestory of the Norman and of the earlier Gothic styles is an original feature; but Norman clerestories, except in cathedral or minster churches, are very rare. Instances occur at Filey, Yorks; Goring, Oxon; and St. Margaret-at-Cliffe, Kent (Fig. 61). Clerestories became somewhat more frequent in the thirteenth century, and there are good Early English examples at Elm, Cambridgeshire (Fig. 62); Aymestry, Herefordshire; Darlington, Horsham, and elsewhere. In the Geometrical and Decorated periods clerestories became fairly frequent, and although the windows were of small size, usually a quatrefoil within a circle, they are often of much elegance. There are many excellent instances in Northamptonshire churches, as at

Warmington and Hargrave. At Bosham, Firle, and Playden, Sussex, the clerestory lights are plain circular openings; at Felpham, in the same county, the openings are trefoil-headed, at Beddingham ogee quatrefoils, and at Arundel quatrefoils under hood mouldings. Bourn, Cambs, and Preston Bisset,

62. ELM, CAMBRIDGESHIRE

Bucks, may also be named; in the latter the eight-cusped circles are set within square mouldings (Fig. 63). At Trumpington, Cambs, the windows are alternately single light and circular, and they present the peculiarity of being immediately over the nave piers instead of in the centre of the arch. This peculiarity also occurs at the Cornish churches of Fowey and Lostwithiel.

Amid the various beautiful clerestories over Norfolk naves there are many with quatrefoil windows, some of which are undoubtedly fourteenth century, whilst others are of advanced Perpendicular date. At Sheringham quatrefoil windows, and at Cley cinquefoil windows, alternate with pointed lights

63. PRESTON BISSETT, BUCKINGHAMSHIRE

64. CLEY, NORFOLK

86 THE ENGLISH PARISH CHURCH

(Fig. 64). They may be specially noticed at East Bradenham, Heacham, and elsewhere. When a clerestory has been added to a nave it often considerably overtops the chancel, and in most instances a window, usually of three lights, is found above the chancel arch. This latter plan is exceptional outside East

65. CIRENCESTER

Anglia, but it occurs at Chipping Norton, Deddington, and Great Milton, Oxon; Tickhill, Yorks; Chipping Campden, Northleach, and Winchcombe, Gloucestershire; and after a most striking fashion at Cirencester, where the window is of seven lights (Fig. 65).

The development of stained glass, and the desire to find extra room for memorials in that medium, brought about, towards the close of the fifteenth century, such a development in clerestory windows that it is quite common to find the side walls presenting a far greater surface of glass than stone. Instances of this occur throughout England, as at Chipping Norton, Oxon; Boston and Holbeach, Lincolnshire; St. Stephen and St. Peter Mancroft, Norwich (Fig. 60); Leighton Buzzard, Beds; Southam, Warwickshire; and St. Michael's, Coventry (Fig. 66). Occasionally clerestories have been built on to unaisled churches, and form a second tier of windows above the earlier ones of the nave, as at Sandiacre and Wilne, Derbyshire; Halford and Ilmington, Warwickshire; and Madingley, Cambridgeshire (Fig. 67). It is almost certain that

66. THE NAVE AND CHANCEL CLERESTORIES, ST. MICHAEL'S, COVENTRY

in such cases an aisle or aisles were in contemplation but never erected. These instances would seem to indicate a practice, beginning by raising the nave walls and piercing them for clerestories, to provide for lighting the nave during the construction of the aisle walls and the nave arcades. A very curious arrangement is to find a second tier of windows in the aisle walls, as at Broughton, Oxon.

AISLES AND CHAPELS.—In the latter part of the thirteenth century the plan of the normal village parish church, with fairly long aisleless chancel, aisled nave, south porch, and west tower had come into general use, and was current almost everywhere early in the following century. It was, however, but seldom that a church arrived at this stage

88   THE ENGLISH PARISH CHURCH

of development in a single building; first the early sanctuary would probably be lengthened, and then the aisles added at different times, the north aisle usually first, for reasons that have been already set forth, and then would follow the west tower. The east end of the aisles provided con-

67. MADINGLEY, CAMBRIDGESHIRE

venient space for altars, and that even the narrow aisles of the end of the twelfth and beginning of the thirteenth century were thus used can be abundantly shown by the frequent remains of piscinas, almeries, and image brackets in such situations. To provide altar accommodation at the east end was often the first intention of aisles, and instances can be mentioned in which they have never been completed for the full length of the nave, or have been so continued at a later period.

Ayston, Rutlandshire, may be instanced as an illustration of an ordinary aisled thirteenth-century church (Fig. 68). Both of

THE PLAN

the nave arcades are Early English, but the north aisle is certainly the older of the two; its width is 5 feet 8 inches, but the width of the south one, probably widened at a later date, is 8 feet 6 inches. This widening of aisles after their first erection is not unknown, and there are examples in which an aisle has been widened for only a portion of its length at the east end, the development never being completed.

The addition of chapels to the chancel came about later, and certainly after a more gradual fashion than was the case with aisles to the nave. These additions were at first small chapels, usually of a chantry foundation, and not infrequently they still remain mere adjuncts with a single archway into the chancel, and another into the aisle. For instance, Freslingfield,

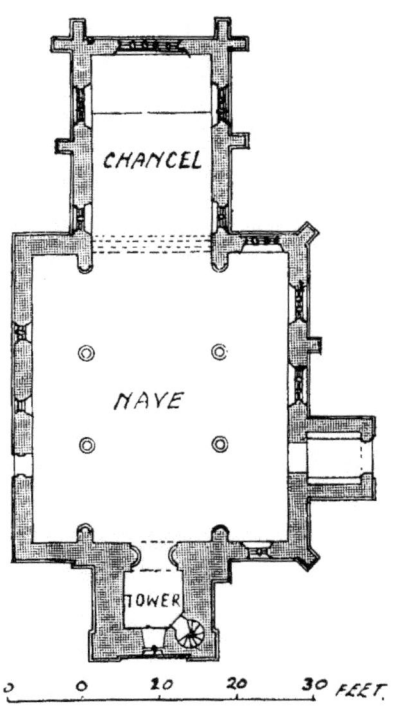

68. AYSTON, RUTLAND

Suffolk, has a Decorated chapel on the north side of the chancel. Even in important churches such as Raunds, Northants, there was but one chancel chapel, which in this case opened into the chancel by an arcade of three bays on the south side (Fig. 69). There is an almost endless variety of these chapels, which eventually develop into chancel aisles. At Weekley, Northants, there is a chapel on each side of the chancel, opening into it and to the aisle by single arches. On

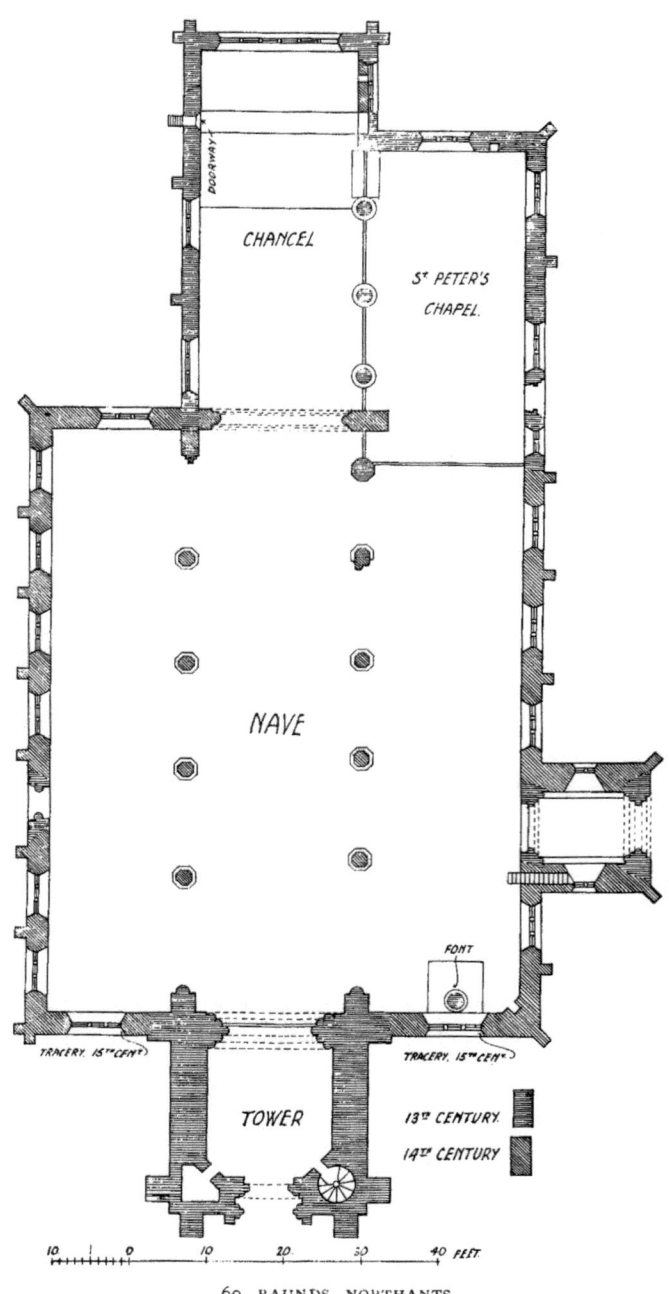

69. RAUNDS, NORTHANTS

the north the arches are of Early English date, whilst on the south they are Decorated. Another instance may be taken

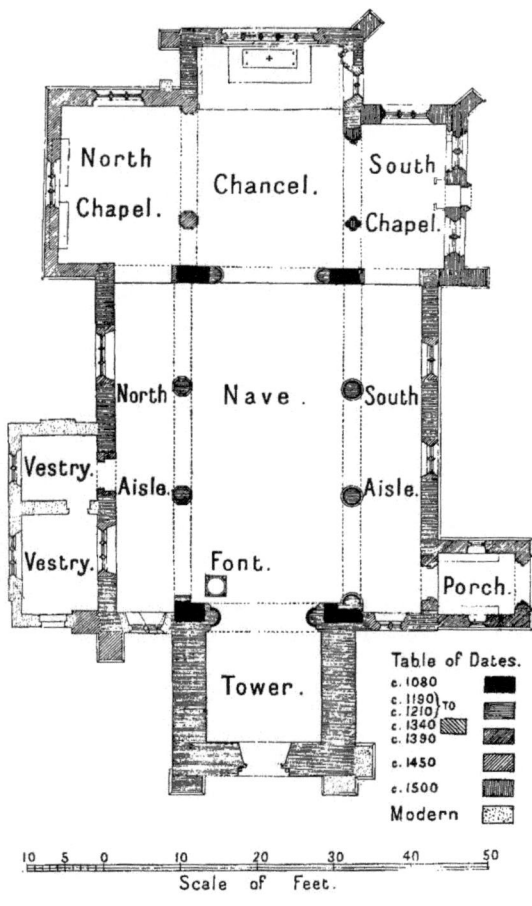

70. MERSTHAM, SURREY

from the interesting and varied church of Merstham, Surrey. In this case the chancel, originally Early English, has had its

71. LAUNCESTON

north side pierced for a Decorated chapel, and its south side for one of Perpendicular date (Fig. 70).

The next stage in chancel development was the production of chapels which ran for the full length of the chancel with an

72. NEW ROMNEY, KENT
[*Drawn by A. E. Newcombe*

arcade of two or three or more arches on each side. This later fashion often resulted in the "three-gable" termination at the east end which has already been mentioned (p. 81). This occurs in Cornwall, as at Launceston (Fig. 71), and Gwennap, and it is also to be found in Kent, as at Westerham; there is a fine lofty Decorated example at New Romney (Fig. 72). This arrangement can also be found in other parts, as at Little Easton, Essex.

In cases where aisles and chapels have been added to transeptal churches, the end wall of the transepts formed a convenient point for fixing the width of the aisle, and the projection of the transept is therefore merged into the general outline of the plan. The same is the case with the addition of

94   THE ENGLISH PARISH CHURCH

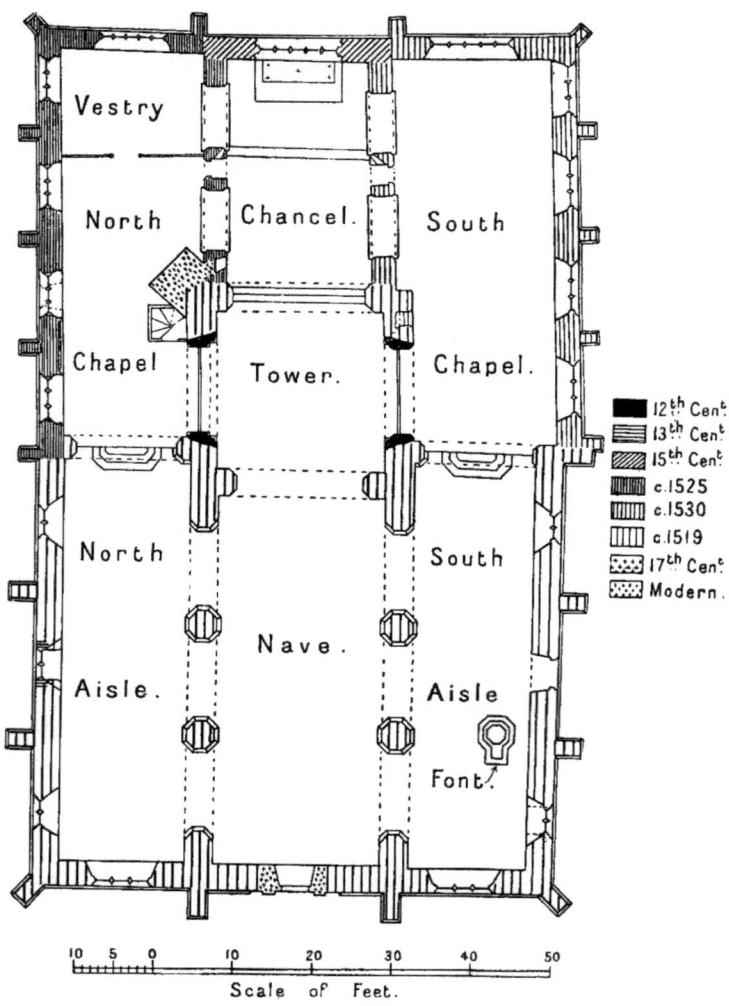

73. OLD BASING, HAMPSHIRE

aisles and of fully developed chantry or guild chapels to a
church of nave and chancel type. In both instances the plan

THE PLAN 95

is almost, if not entirely, reduced to a rectangular form, as at Tamworth; St. Mary's, Nottingham; and Basing (Fig. 73) and Odiham, in Hampshire.

The old constructive distinction between chancel and nave began to vanish in the average-sized churches, as well as in

74. CHULMLEIGH, DEVON

the larger ones of towns. Early chancel arches were rebuilt on an enlarged scale, and finally the chancel arch often disappeared entirely in some districts, as in the whole of Cornwall and the later East Anglian examples, during the rebuildings in the fifteenth century.

In some cases the rood screen was brought westward a considerable distance from the original entrance to the chancel, thus enlarging the quire space. Usually, in cases of rebuilding, the chancel division was maintained by a screen; Middleton, Lancashire, may suffice as an example. The abolition of a chancel arch division and of arches between aisles and chapels was usual not only in the West of England, where rood screens

96 THE ENGLISH PARISH CHURCH

assumed so fine a form, but also in the stoneless parts of East Anglia, where beautifully carved and finely painted screens abound. Here, as in the West, the screen frequently runs right across the church, including the eastern ends of the

75. SCREEN OF THE COPPLESTONE CHAPEL, COLEBROOKE, N. DEVON

aisles, as shown in the view of the chancel and north aisle of the beautiful Devonshire church of Chulmleigh (Fig. 74).

It need not, however, be supposed that no one save the priests, clerks, or singing men and boys were allowed on the further side of such an extended screen. The chapels on either side of the chancel were frequently shut off from it by parclose screens, and within such enclosed areas the family of the founder of a chantry or the members of a guild or fraternity were admitted, and the chapels practically became gigantic pews. As an example of such parclose work, an illustration is given of the south and west screens, with delicate lace-like tracery, of the Copplestone chapel on the north side of the chancel of Colebrooke, Devon (Fig. 75). During the last 200 years preceding the Reformation, chantry chapels

THE PLAN

founded by individuals or by guilds increased to such an extent as to add to the complexity of the plans of the larger parish churches. These chapels often took the form of screened enclosures within the churches, rather than of structural additions. Some of the most noteworthy of such additions are to be found at Coventry, in the two great churches of St. Michael and Holy Trinity. At St. Michael's two chapels were built on the north side aisle, and two small ones of peculiar shape attached to either side of the south porch; these served respectively for the trade guilds of the Dyers and the Cappers, whilst on the north side of the chancel was the chapel of the guild of the Drapers, flanked on the opposite side by the chapel of the Mercers. The yet more elaborately planned church of Holy Trinity, in addition to a variety of other chapels, made special provisions for the guilds of the Mercers, Butchers, and Tanners.*

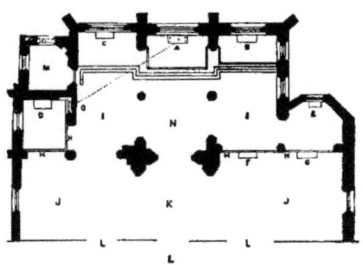

76. CHESTERFIELD, EAST END

The accompanying outline plan of the eastern limbs of the large church of All Saints, Chesterfield, originally cruciform, shows the sites of its various chapels (Fig. 76). This plan was originally prepared to illustrate the meaning of a large "squint" window of five lights, about 5 feet square, and 4 feet from the ground, in the south wall of the chapel to the east of the north transept, which was discovered and opened out in 1885. The mullions have no glass groove, and the opening was obviously designed to serve as a squint or hagioscope of a most unusually large size. Through this opening the majority of the worshippers in the chapel would

---

* See small plans, and excellent brief accounts of these two churches in Mr. Hamilton Thompson's Manual on "The Historical Growth of the English Parish Church," pp. 45–48.

be able to get a clear view of the high altar across the north quire aisle. In this chapel stood the Altar of the Holy Cross, a guild founded by the vicar of Chesterfield and various laymen of note in 1393, and here were the official seats of the "Brethren of the Gild of Our Lord Jesus Christ and of the Holy Cross in the north of the church of all Saints, Chesterfield," as they are described in the patent.

A squint window of these large dimensions is most unusual. It should be compared with a somewhat similar squint at Burford, Oxon, which takes the form of a long window in the east wall of the south transept, where the Mayor and Corporation have for a considerable period sat. It gives a full view of the high altar through a chapel which forms the south aisle of the chancel. The corporation at Burford is the lineal descendant of an old guild (as is not infrequently the case), and this transept was formerly its chapel, used as a pew for public services, and having its own altar for the guild services.

THE CROSS PLAN.—Turning now to the consideration of the cruciform type of plan, we find that the pre-Conquest central tower appeared with the advent of the Continental Benedictines in the tenth century. Romsey Abbey, Hants, was begun in 967, and Ramsey Abbey, Hunts, in 969. Both had central towers, while Ramsey had also a western tower; the like was the case with Ethelwold's cathedral church of Winchester. Significant instances of these Saxon central towers are to be noted at Breamore, Hants ; Norton, Durham; and at St. Mary's, Guildford, the last having transepts which open from the tower space by narrow archways.

The common notion that the Cross of Christ was deliberately selected for the plan of a cross church is nothing more or less than a popular delusion, and a study of early plans at once proves the idea to be baseless. Symbolism in this and in other matters was never the object aimed at, and was entirely secondary to utility. In the Eastern church the types of plan employed were on a circular and rectangular basis, whilst a comparison of plans, as development proceeded, makes it obvious that ritual growth and desire for special accommodation gradually brought about a fairly frequent adoption of the cruciform plan.

Here it may be well to point out that another popular notion that the builders deliberately planned a deviation of the chancel to one side, in order to denote the bend of Our Lord's head upon the Cross, is also a mistaken notion, for where such deviations occur they were the work of men building a century or so apart from each other, and arise from the methods used in the reconstruction of churches.

The average Saxon builder, as pointed out by Mr. Hamilton Thompson, did not possess the skill of constructing a central tower upon piers connected by arches. It was not until the close of the period, when Norman masonry had gained a footing prior to the Conquest, that two transepts, with a central tower supported only at its angles, came into being, as in the large church of St. Mary-in-the-Castle, Dover.

No sooner had the Normans firmly established themselves on our shores than the true cruciform plan began to assert itself, and this not only in fine and important structures, but in the humbler parochial churches. The distribution of the cruciform central tower churches is a subject which awaits full investigation and a careful survey. Professor Prior points out that churches of this type are found in the Upper Thames valley. They appear in a district extending each side of the river in its higher reaches west from Oxford. Churches like Witney and Broadwell in Oxfordshire may be mentioned in this connexion, but the type extends south-west into Wiltshire, as at Great Bedwyn and Potterne, into Hampshire, as at Kingsclere, and north-eastwards through Thame into Buckinghamshire (*e.g.* Aylesbury and Ivinghoe), and Cambridgeshire (Foulmire and Thriplow).

Not only are extant cruciform churches fairly numerous, but if any given district of the south or west of England is systematically examined, traces of original planning of that

100   THE ENGLISH PARISH CHURCH

character will be found in many other examples. A careful survey of the district forming the corner of South-East

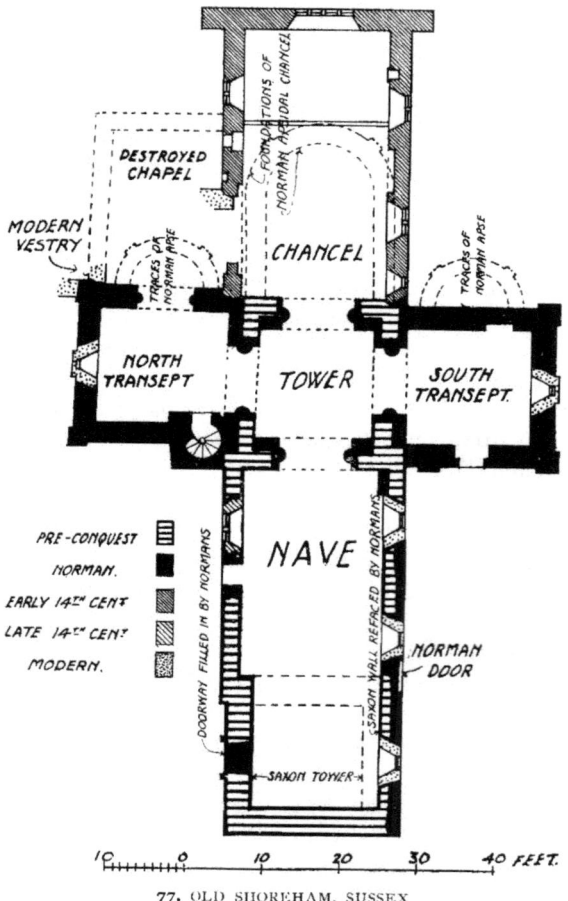

77. OLD SHOREHAM, SUSSEX

Devon showed that Buckwell, Axminster, Colyton, Honiton, Shute, Sidbury, Widworthy, and Clyst St. George are cruciform; whilst Awliscombe, Axmouth, Seaton, Feniton, and

THE PLAN

Woodbury yield evidence of early cruciform planning. In that interesting triangle of North Devon the angles of which are marked by Bideford, Hartland, and Torrington, fifteen of the twenty-two old parish churches show evidence of having once been constructed on a cross plan.

Abbotsham and the small churches of Welcombe and West

78. OLD SHOREHAM

Putford still consist of nave, chancel, and two small transepts. Bradworthy has a south transept, and a small embryo transept on the north side; the latter, which now forms a single pew, stands probably on the ground occupied by the north transept of the first church. The tiny church of Abbots Bickington, the internal measurements of which are only about 40 feet by 10 feet, has a small south transept. There are also south transepts to the churches of Clovelly and Woolfardisworthy, whilst Alwington, Littleham, and the chapel of Taddy Port have north transepts. The great church of Hartland, rebuilt in the latter part of the fourteenth century, has north and south transepts as well as aisles.

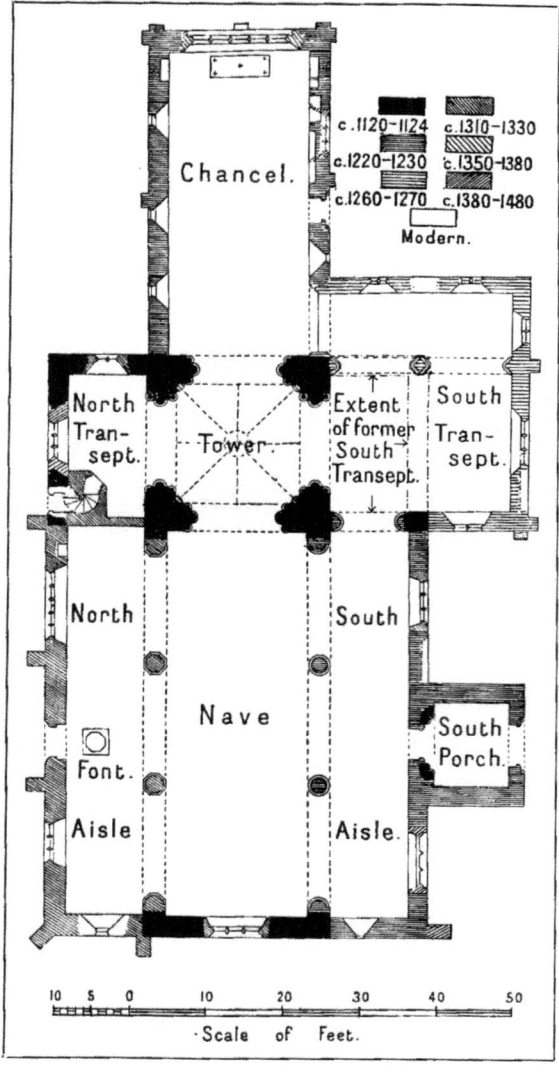

79. CASTOR CHURCH, NORTHAMPTONSHIRE

THE PLAN

In Cornwall, the typical church of Norman days was cruciform, and even when consisting originally of chancel and nave it not infrequently had transept chapels added to it in the thirteenth and occasionally in the fourteenth centuries, thus approximating to the cross form. The occurrence of a single

80. CASTOR

transept in many churches of this county must be mentioned, but a close study of the fabrics shows that one or other of the original transepts became absorbed in the aisle development of the fifteenth century. There are ninety-three Cornish churches which were undoubtedly either originally cruciform or were more or less on that plan; thirty-three of these are known to be of Norman origin.*

Sometimes the aisleless Norman plan is found with a western tower and transeptal chapels, but these are generally additions to

* See list in Dr. Cox's "Churches of Cornwall," 1912, pp. 14-16.

the building. As a rule the Norman central towers rest upon piers with arches to the nave, sanctuary, and transepts, and thus attain to the true cruciform plan. Of this Old Shoreham, Sussex, with its fine arcaded Norman tower, is a good example (Figs. 77, 78). North Newbald, in the East Riding, is another delightful instance of a Norman cruciform parish church, and happily it has suffered little subsequent alteration. The highly interesting Northamptonshire church of Castor, with an extant dedication inscription of 1124, had at that time an aisleless nave, transepts, and chancel; the central tower is a grand example of Norman work (Figs. 79, 80). Another fine and dignified instance of a central tower is that of St. John's, Devizes, and it is interesting to add that the chancel retains its Norman vaulting.

Following up the cruciform or transeptal plan in its later stages in the story of the English parish church, it may be noted that though, as already mentioned, transeptal chapels were occasionally added later, as at Branscombe, there are several instances of definitely designed Early English churches with transepts and without any central tower; of this the churches at Northwick, and Acton Burnell, Salop, are good instances. Many fine large central-towered cruciform plans were carried out at different periods during the thirteenth century. Such are the churches of Pottern, and Amesbury, Wilts (Fig. 81); Bampton, Oxon; Uffington, Berks (Fig. 41), and Hedon, E.R. Yorks. At Othery, a Somersetshire parish on the Sedgmoor plain, is one of the few instances of an aisleless cruciform Early English church on a small scale. The tall central tower has, however, been altered subsequently to its erection.

There are several good cruciform central tower plans in the Decorated style; special mention may be made of the two spire-crowned Derbyshire examples of Ashbourne (Fig. 28) and Chesterfield. Uffington, Berks (Fig. 41), and Doulting, Somerset (Fig. 187), have central towers carried up above the roof in octagonal form.

THE PLAN 105

By the fifteenth century most if not all parishes possessed their church, so that very few central-towered churches were freshly built in the Perpendicular period. Where they exist they generally replace an earlier cross church. Minster Lovell,

81. AMESBURY, WILTSHIRE

Oxfordshire, is a case of a late transeptal church. Crediton, Devon, is almost entirely Perpendicular, and has apparently a tower of that date, but the interior shows the Norman piers and arches on which it rests. The same is true of Wedmore, Somerset, but in this case the tower arches are Transitional (Fig. 82). The base courses of the Perpendicular central towers of Colyton and Axminster are probably of Early Norman, if not of Saxon masonry.

Up and down England are many instances of the tower having fallen or being taken down because of its dangerous condition, whereupon a new tower was built up at the west end

106   THE ENGLISH PARISH CHURCH

of the nave or elsewhere, and the centre of the church altered in design. Such new west towers chiefly, but not by any means always, date from the fifteenth century. It will suffice to quote

82. WEDMORE, SOMERSET

two examples out of some scores: Tintagel, Cornwall, and Kirkby Stephen, Westmorland.

Not infrequently we get a case in which a church has transepts, aisles, and western tower, as illustrated by Rushden. This plan usually occurs in churches of fourteenth-century date, as at Heckington and Frampton, Lincolnshire. The plan of transepts and western tower of late date has almost always descended from an original cross church with a central tower. Frampton, Lincolnshire, will serve to illustrate this type (Fig. 83).

In certain of our larger cruciform parish churches the transepts were developed to such an extent that, as in cathedral and great conventual churches, they had aisles. This is so

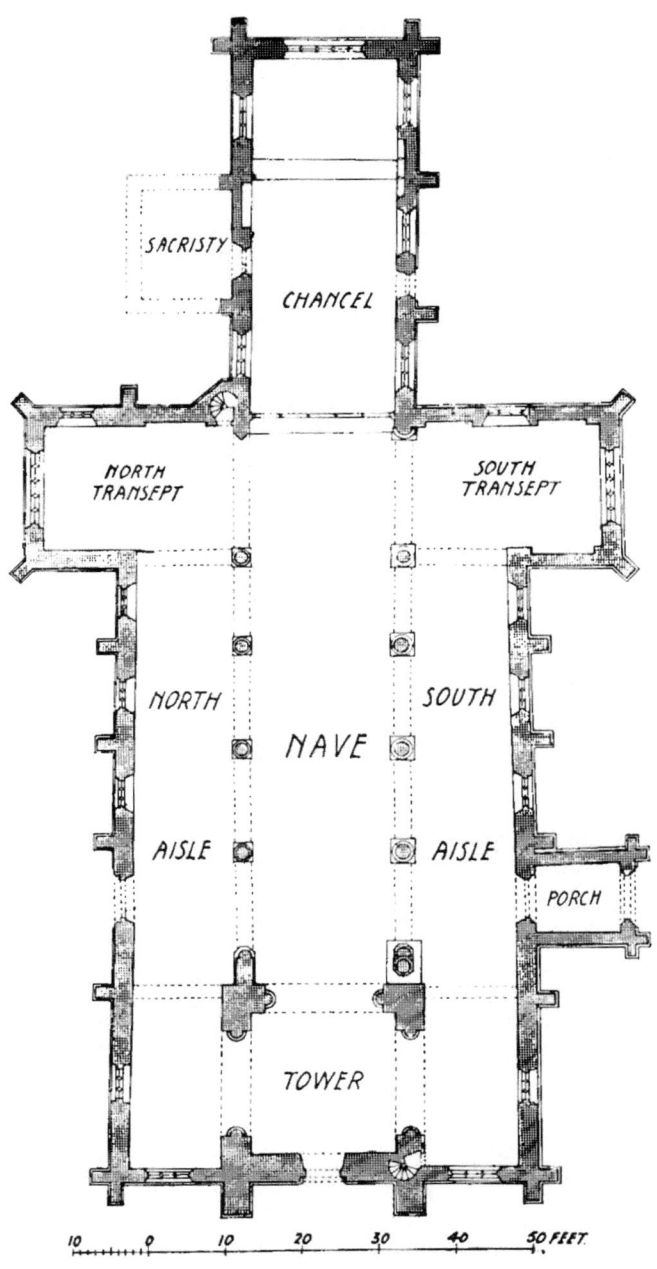

83. FRAMPTON, LINCOLNSHIRE
(Principally thirteenth and fourteenth centuries)

108　THE ENGLISH PARISH CHURCH

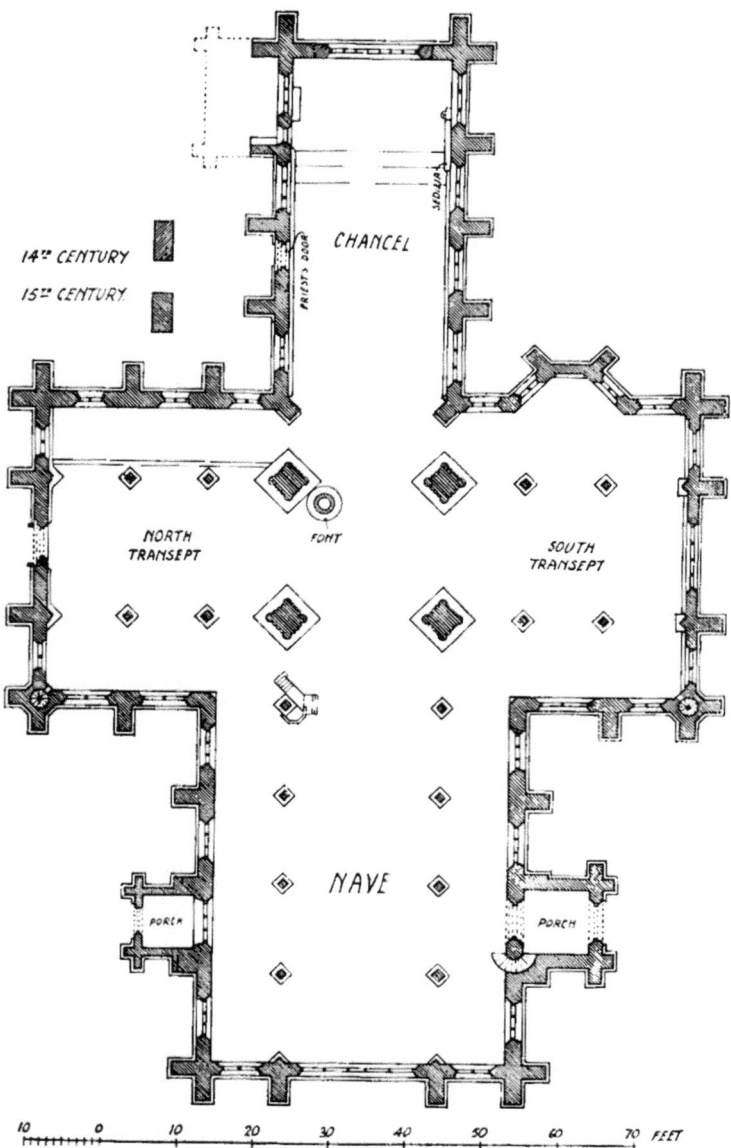

84. PATRINGTON, YORKSHIRE

with the transepts of the beautiful Leicestershire church of Melton Mowbray, Patrington in the East Riding (Figs. 84 and 141), St. Mary Redcliffe, Bristol, and Luton, Bedfordshire (Fig. 85). At Medbourne, Leicestershire, in which the transepts are of two dates, the north one Early English and the south Decorated, the latter has an eastern aisle. Both transepts of St. Michael, Penkivel, Cornwall, have three arched recesses of a remarkable character in the eastern walls. All such arrangements were made for extra altars, and this indeed was the cause of all transeptal chapels, for the body of the church but rarely supplied the necessary space for their increasing number. Such may be one cause for the existence of transepts, as in great measure it is for aisles to naves or chancel chapels, the former having also the advantage of affording more space for congregational use. The awkwardness of transepts for the latter purpose led to the use of squints, sometimes, as in Cornwall, of considerable size, so that those present in the transept could see to a certain extent what was taking place at the high altar. These were at best but meagre expedients, and the dropping of the transept form in favour of aisles and chapels may be due to their inconvenience for general use. The interesting cruciform church of Newchurch, Isle of Wight, of early thirteenth-century date, with widely projecting transepts, underwent a change of plan in the following century, when although the transepts remained, part of their west walls were cut away to afford openings to the aisles added to the nave at that time.

St. Mary's, Beverley, had an eastern aisle added to the south transept in the thirteenth century. Oakham and Langham in Rutland have large transeptal chapels with western aisles.

THE TOWER.—No tower, whether western or central, originally accompanied either of the two forms of early churches in the British Isles; but after a time a tower occurs in both. A tall square western tower became usual in the Saxon church of the ninth or tenth centuries. Its primary use was to carry bells,

THE PLAN

and the form it took was closely reminiscent of the ordinary Italian bell tower. A defensive refuge in time of danger was also another purpose to which many were put, as is plainly manifest in their construction. As at a later date various church towers in the further North of England show that they were built after a special fashion to resist the Scotch borderland raids, so did certain of the Saxon bell-towers assume defensive features, especially along the estuaries of the East of England, which were exposed to Danish incursions. Towers of this time are frequently without staircases, and therefore difficult of access, while the openings in the lower stages were insignificant.

86. INTERIOR OF DEERHURST TOWER

The late Mr. J. T. Micklethwaite was the first to establish conclusively that the carrying up of early west porches into tower form was nearly as much to provide safe and suitable dwelling-places as to serve for the accommodation of bells. The churches of Brixworth (Fig. 101) and Deerhurst (Fig. 86) had each an elaborate window looking into the church from a chamber at some height in the tower. An illustration of this window is given in chap. iii. (Fig. 108). One of smaller dimensions occurs in a similar position at Bosham. They could not have been contrived to provide light for either the church or the tower

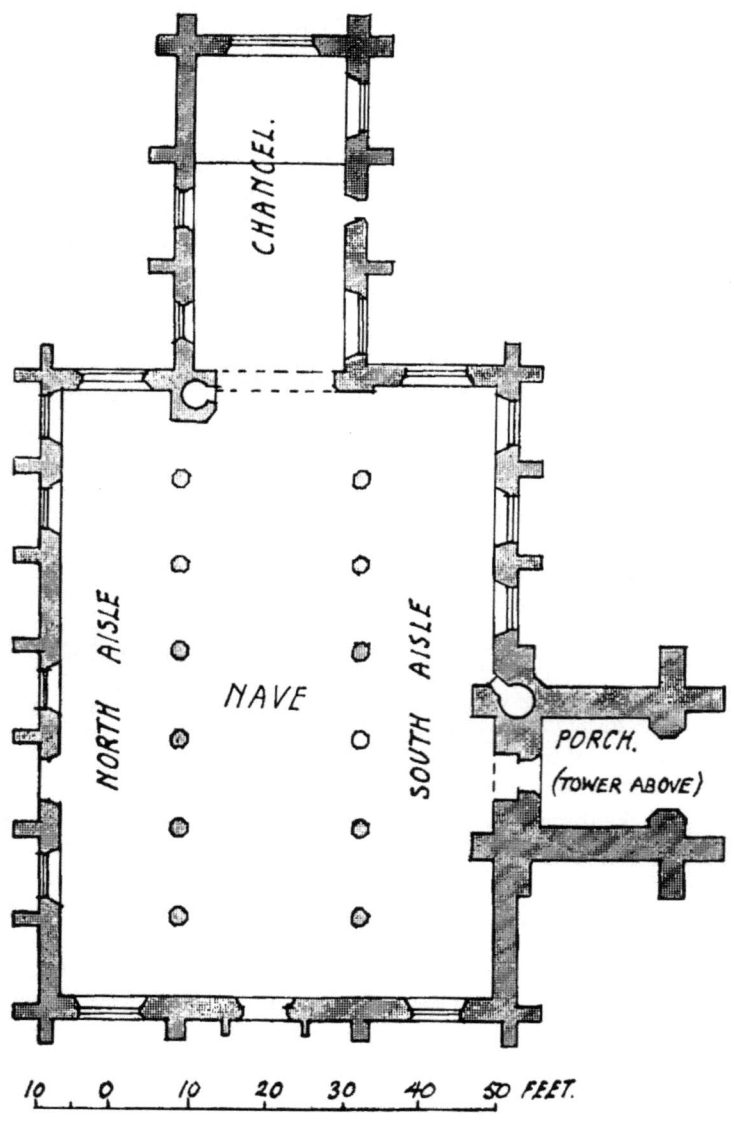

87. DONINGTON CHURCH, LINCOLNSHIRE

88. DONINGTON, LINCOLNSHIRE

114 THE ENGLISH PARISH CHURCH

chamber, and it has been conjectured with much probability that such windows were constructed to enable the inmates to say the night offices without descending into the church.

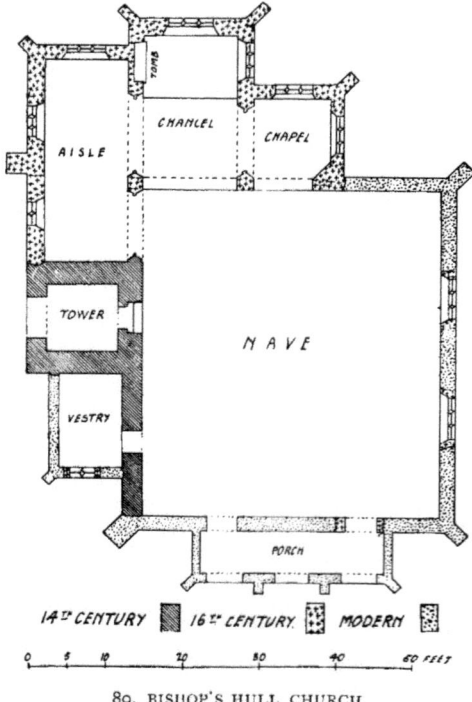

89. BISHOP'S HULL CHURCH

Evidence as to early tower dwellings is strong not only at these churches, but also at Wearmouth, Brigstock, and Broughton (Lincolnshire), and used to be especially interesting in the now destroyed tower of a much later date, at Irthlingborough, Northants.

The flues and fireplaces in the Norfolk towers of Billockby, Bradeston, Thornage, Thorpe Abbots, Thrigby, and Wicklewood, which are generally considered to be for the baking of

THE PLAN 115

wafers, may be tokens of habitation. The large chamber of the Norman central tower of Branscombe, Devon (Fig. 15), used undoubtedly to be occupied. In the chamber under the bells of the tower of St. Michael's, Penkivel, Cornwall, is a priest's

90. BISHOP'S HULL, SOMERSET
[*From a drawing by Roland W. Paul, F.S.A.*

room with an altar. In at least a score of other churches of Norman and Early Gothic days there are more or less conclusive proofs of tower chambers being used as dwelling-rooms; several, indeed, were thus occupied as late as the seventeenth century, as can be shown from churchwardens' accounts.

The west end of the nave is the most frequent position for towers in England, and has become a distinct charac-

116   THE ENGLISH PARISH CHURCH

teristic of English churches; nevertheless diversity of position is not uncommon, and is found in every part of the land, as is readily proved if any single county is selected for study.

For instance, Norfolk has flanking towers on the south

91. MELBURY BUBB, DORSET

side, the basement serving as a porch entrance, as at Little Ellingham, Hardingham and Hockwold. The fine church of Donington, Lincolnshire, is of this type (Figs. 87, 88). In Cornwall, the towers of Dulse, Lawhitton, and Veryan are on the south side, whilst that of St. Stephen-by-Saltash is at the west end of the north aisle, and that of Saltash on the north side. Bishop's Hull, Somerset, is on the north, over the porch (Figs. 89, 90). The towers of Bodmin St. Enoch and Blisland are attached to the north transept. Transeptal towers are occasionally found in other counties, and St. Mary Ottery, Devon, has a tower over each transept. The tower of Melbury Bubb, Dorset (Fig. 91), is above a south porch, projecting from an aisleless nave. St. Mary-in-the-Castle, Dover, on the other hand, which was also an aisleless nave, has the tower over an early north transept. Whaplode, Lincoln, and Clymping, Sussex, are other examples of south transeptal towers.

Mr. P. M. Johnston, in his summaries of the ecclesiastical architecture of the counties of Surrey and Sussex, in the Victoria Counties Histories, names seven cases of flanking towers in the former county, and twenty-three in the latter, several of which are of a transeptal character. Such towers were usually additions to the original plan. The reasons for their positions can often be traced to a falling away of the ground or other impediment in the site. Thus at Fordingbridge, Hants, a tower was built in the fifteenth century at the east end of the north aisle, the nearness of the highway preventing any extension westward. The tower and spire at the north-west angle of Lapworth church, Warwickshire, which is connected with the north aisle by a covered vestibule, could not, when a good bell-tower was desired, be placed at the west end, because of the presence of a raised chapel over an open west portico dating from the fourteenth century.

Occasionally, owing to some change in plan or loss of part of the structure, the tower is now in an abnormal position; thus they terminate the church eastwards at Chedgrave and Flitcham, where the chancel has evidently vanished, whilst Guestwick has the tower at the east end of the north aisle, this aisle having originally been the nave of the church.

There are various instances in which belfry towers in various positions stand detached from the body of the building, an arrangement which is usually due to the exigencies of the site, or through some defect in the ground. There are six such detached bell-towers in Cornwall, among them being Telland, St. Mylor, and Gwennac. They also occur, among other instances, at East Dereham and West Walton, Norfolk; Sutton St. Mary, Lincoln; Marston Moretaine, Beds (Figs. 92, 93); Ledbury and Pembridge, Herefordshire (Fig. 225);

THE ENGLISH PARISH CHURCH

Berkeley, Gloucestershire; Chittlehampton, Devon; and Brookland, Kent.

Towers were added to churches in various ways, and the edifice often presents interesting peculiarities of construction at the junction of the tower with the building, for which the

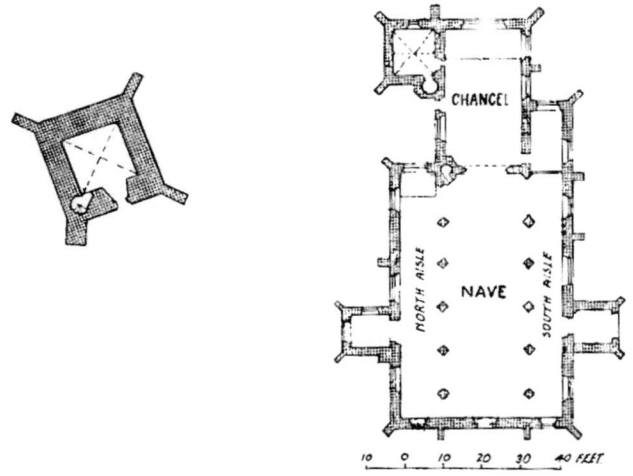

92. MARSTON MORETAINE, BEDFORDSHIRE
(Chiefly fifteenth century)

method adopted by the builders can be gleaned. Cases are not unknown in which towers were built entirely free of the west end of the church, the nave and aisles of which have subsequently been lengthened to join up to the tower, as at Gretton, Northants.

Occasionally, the west tower is engaged within the fabric, the nave aisles having been extended westwards. The tower in such cases stands on three arches, those on the north and south opening into the aisles. This plan may be observed at the churches of Newark, Grantham (Fig. 135), Ewerby, Lincolnshire (Figs. 94, 95), and in some Cornish churches. At Keyworth,

Notts, Milford, Hants, and other instances, the aisles were extended at a later date than the tower, forming mere lean-to additions against the tower walls, which are pierced by low

93. MARSTON MORETAINE, BEDFORDSHIRE
[*Drawn by F. L. Griggs*]

arches. In some cases the space thus gained was enclosed by screens, and formed chapels.

Sometimes the western tower stands out externally upon piers with archways north and south to admit of a passage-way beneath. Of this arrangement there are examples at Lostwithiel (now blocked up), Cornwall; Dedham, Essex; Wrotham, Kent; All Saints, Cambridge; and elsewhere. In most of these cases, and possibly in all, the explanation of this curious feature is that it enables the processions, as already stated, which might not leave consecrated ground, to make a complete outdoor circuit of the church. This plan of piercing the tower was adopted when, by reason of extension, it closely abutted on the highway or other unconsecrated ground, as at the church of St. John, Warwick. The same was the cause of external vaulted passages under the east ends of chancels

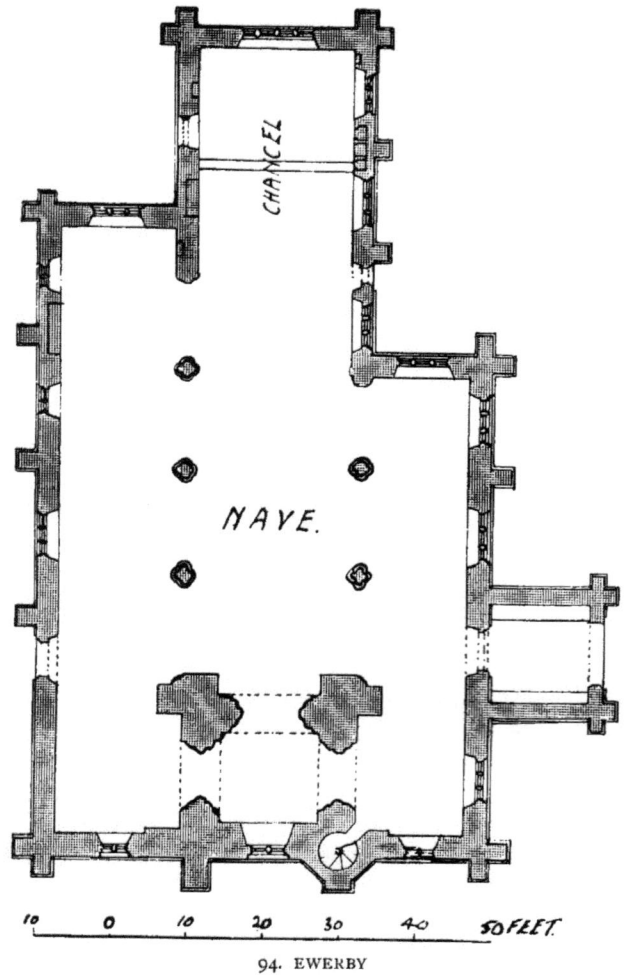

94. EWERBY

which occur at Hythe, Kent, and Walpole St. Peter, Norfolk.

One or two unusual tower forms may be very briefly noted. Many of the towers in small village churches in the Eastern

95. EWERBY, LINCOLNSHIRE

counties are of circular plan, and built of flint; this form is thought to be used so as to avoid square angles necessitating expensive quoin stones brought from a distance. This is dealt with at length under "Materials." At Maldon is a tower of triangular plan arising from the nature of the site. Occasionally the square was changed for the octagonal plan from the ground level and not only for the upper portion, as at Cotswold, N.R. Yorks; Stanwick, Northants; and Standlake, Oxon; but more often an octagonal upper stage rests on the square base, as at Coggs, Oxon, and Lowick, Northants (Fig. 161). The same form is used in the upper portion of the central tower resting on the square base, as at Uffington, Berks (Fig. 41); Tong, Salop; and Sutton, Cambs. Octagonal lanterns at the base of the spire also occur with some frequency, as at Wilby, Northants.

THE PORCH.—The use of porches was threefold—the utilitarian one of breaking the violence of the winds, and preserving the door from the weather; for the performance of the earlier parts of the services of Baptism, Matrimony and Churchings; and for secular uses, allusion to which has already been made in chap. i.

A late Saxon feature, possibly of monastic origin, but rarely met with in later times, was the rectangular western porch, usually with an opening on each face, the eastern one leading into the church. Wherever this remains it now forms the lower story of a tower, as at Monkwearmouth, Brixworth, Barton-on-Humber. The western porch of the ruined church of St. Pancras, Canterbury, has a much earlier form. At Bishopstowe there is a south porch, and transept porches occurred originally on both sides at Bradford-on-Avon.

In early times there was usually one porch, and in the great majority of cases this was on the south side; but where the manor house or the greater part of the village was on the north, no hesitation was shown in placing the chief entrance on that side and assigning to it a porch. In later times, and

THE PLAN

frequently in the fifteenth century, there were two porches, both south and north.

West porches are exceptional, though not nearly so rare as has been sometimes stated. Instances still occur among many

96. YAPTON, SUSSEX

others, at Cley, Norfolk; Woodstock, Oxfordshire; King's Sutton, Northants; Broadwater and Yapton, Sussex (Fig. 96); a large example at Boxley, and another at Otford, Kent.*

An inclination has sprung up to assign the word "Galilee" to every west porch. The name Galilee arises from the fact that the west porch was the last stage in the Sunday procession, and the celebrant on entering was supposed to symbolize Our Lord preceding His disciples into Galilee after His Resurrection. It is, however, improbable that there was anything of the nature of a regular Sunday procession at

* This list can be greatly extended. See correspondence originated by the writer towards the close of 1911 in the *Church Times*. There are seven old west porches in Surrey and ten in Sussex.

smaller village churches, and in some cases the western porch, quite apart from ritual signification, was the customary congregational entrance. This is put beyond dispute by a considerable number of holy-water stoups within such porches, and occasionally even on the outer wall.

97. WOOLPIT SOUTH PORCH, SUFFOLK

In a few churches, chiefly in Somersetshire, as at Weston-in-Gordano, Clapton-in-Gordano, Portishead, and Kingston Seymour, as well as at Caldicot, Monmouthshire, and Wroxall, Warwickshire, there are within the porch remains of a small gallery with special means of access. These galleries were doubtless used on Palm Sunday by the semichorus, who joined in the special refrains when the procession made a station before entering the church. They would also probably be used by singers or minstrels on other special occasions.

Upper chambers, commonly but erroneously called "parvises," were sometimes built over porches in Norman and Early English days. In the fourteenth century the custom of erect-

THE PLAN

ing these rooms increased, and they were still more frequently constructed during the Perpendicular period. Sometimes these chambers were built over existing porches, as at Boston, Lincs. The East Anglian porches of the fourteenth and fifteenth centuries are specially noteworthy for their elaboration and beauty. The strikingly individual "flushwork" treatment of patterned flint-work is described and illustrated under "Materials," pp. 234 to 300. Most of these late porches are two-storied. Woolpit (Fig. 97) and St. Nicholas, King's Lynn (Fig. 98), show excellently the variety in materials and treatment.

98. THE SOUTH PORCH, ST. NICHOLAS, KING'S LYNN

The various uses of these porch-chambers has often been discussed, but that they were occupied by anchorites or recluses may be at once dismissed. In a few cases they are furnished with a piscina, as at Sall, Norfolk, and this demonstrates that they once contained an altar and served as an occasional chapel. They are still oftener found with fireplaces, especially in later examples, as at Northwich, Cheshire; Westham, Kent; and notably in the noble, beautiful porch of Northleach, Gloucestershire, where the smoke escapes through a cunningly devised chimney in one of the bracketed pinnacles. Numerous instances also occur where there are squints in the inner wall, which command a fair view of the church, and not only of the high altar. Of this a good example occurs at Mackworth, Derbyshire.

There are various references in episcopal registers and churchwardens' accounts to church ornaments and valuables being kept within chests in chambers of this description. In 1324 the Rural Dean of Marton, Warwickshire, was ordered to provide for the safe keeping within the church of the books and ornaments at Grandborough. The Episcopal Register states that these church goods were to be placed in charge of the deacon, whose duty it was to minister continuously within the church and to remain there throughout the night. The room over the south porch of Tideswell, Derbyshire, was known within memory as the "dormitory."

In post-Reformation days these chambers were occasionally used as libraries, and still oftener as the receptacles for the parish armour. Where they were of a fair size, they occasionally served as schoolrooms, as in the cases of St. Sepulchre, London; Colyton, Devonshire; and Berkeley, Gloucestershire. Sunday school was held in the porch-rooms of Tottenham, Middlesex, and Colby, Norfolk, as late as 1879, and at the same date a day school was held in that of Malmesbury.

The largest porch-chambers occur at Cirencester, where the magnificent south porch of three stages had its upper rooms used by the trade guilds of the town; they afterwards served for a time as the town hall (Fig. 99). The north porch at Grantham was extended northward in the fourteenth century, and the upper chamber became the chapel where the chief relics were preserved. The chamber over the south porch of the same church was clearly used by the church watcher, who slept there, and a small inner window projects slightly from

THE PLAN

the wall, whereby he could gain a general view of the interior. There are several examples of two stories of chambers above the porch, as at Bodmin, Cornwall; Ingham, Norfolk; Burford, Oxon; and St. Sepulchre, London.

In addition to the western porches mentioned previously, it may be remarked that there are some cases in which there is a small porch, or portal, attached to the west doorway of the tower. The most beautiful example of this occurs at Higham Ferrers; other instances of these shallow porches may be noted at Raunds, Rushden, and Oundle, Northants. Very rarely a small porch is built over the priest's door in the chancel. There is a case of this at Trunch, Norfolk.

99. CIRENCESTER PORCH

VESTRY. — On the north side of the chancel there is frequently a rectangular projection, usually of fourteenth-century date and differing from a chapel; this was the vestry or sacristy. In smaller parish churches, it is possible that the place set apart for the purpose was under the tower, or in some screened-off chamber; nevertheless, definite structural vestries were fairly common. They open into the church by a door in the wall of the chancel, not far from the high altar, but have no external means of entrance. The following may be cited as examples:

Worstead and Hingham, Norfolk; Whitwell, Derbyshire; Islip, Northants; Wheathampstead, Herts; Willingham, Cambridge; and Burford, Oxon. In several cases they had an altar with a piscina, as at Hawton, Notts; Ewerby, Lincolnshire; and Dunster, Somerset. Vestries are sometimes of two stories, as at Raunds, Northants; Writtle, Essex; Chipping Norton, Oxon; Aylesbury, Bucks; Luton, Beds; and Heckington and Long Sutton, Lincolnshire. The upper rooms are occasionally provided with a window looking into the chancel, as at Roos, E.R., Yorks, in which case they probably served for a church watcher. More frequently there is a small aperture, or squint, which commands a view of the high altar, either from the upper chamber or from the ground floor; now and again, as at Warrington, Warwickshire, the upper room is furnished with a latrine.

Occasionally the vestry is found on the south side of the chancel, as at Darlington, Durham; Brigstock and Rushton, Northants. In certain cases it projects from the east wall of the chancel below the east window, as at St. Peter Mancroft, Norwich; Lavenham, Suffolk; and Langport and Ilminster, Somerset. Some vestries of this kind have been destroyed, as at St. Stephen, Launceston, and Crewkerne, Somerset. There are also a few cases in which a stone screen wall or reredos, against which the altar stood, was built across the chancel, the space behind it forming the vestry. This occurs at the two Derbyshire churches of Sawley and Tideswell. A similar treatment at the east end of an aisle is at Rushden and Higham Ferrers, Northants. Occasionally there are diminutive sacristies for special chantry altars, as in the two transepts of the remarkable church of St. Michael, Penkivel, Cornwall.

If we add that there are numerous instances of chancels which retain the north doorway into a vanished vestry, as at Ruislip, Middlesex; Taversham and Whittlesford, Cambs; and Barton Mills, Suffolk, it is readily perceived that such structures were fairly numerous. These vestry doorways are often of considerable beauty, as at Kislingbury, Northamptonshire.

THE PLAN

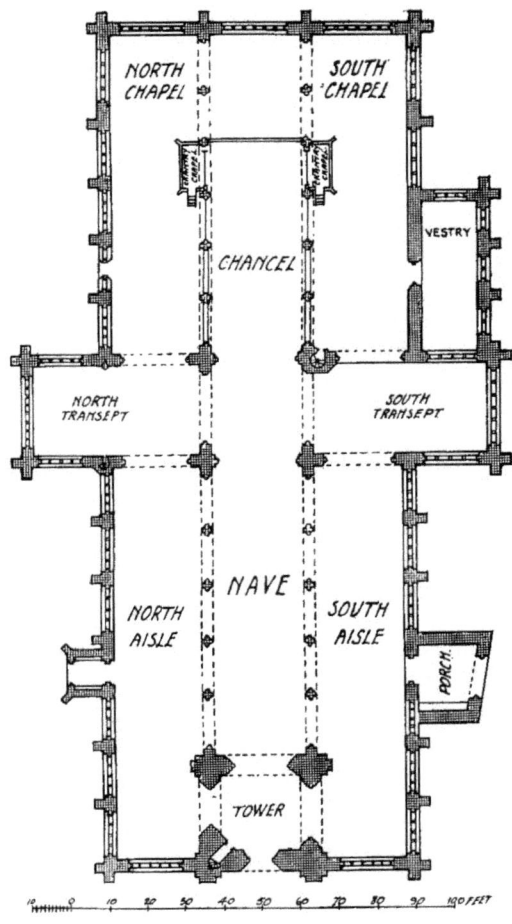

100. NEWARK, NOTTS
(Largely fourteenth and fifteenth centuries)

CRYPTS in parish churches are of somewhat rare occurrence. Among pre-Conquest examples are those at Brixworth and Wing. Norman instances of vaulted crypts may be seen at

St. Mary-le-Bow, London, at St. Peter's-in-the-East, Oxford, and under the chancel of the small Gloucestershire church of Duntisbourn Roos, where the ground falls away with abruptness. A thirteenth-century vaulted crypt, also occasioned by the sloping site, is under the east end of the chancel at Shillington, Beds. In the later mediæval period they are not usual, but in the fifteenth century, when great extensions of churches took place over graveyards, charnel or bone holes for the collecting of disturbed remains were sometimes formed under the new buildings; examples may be cited at Newark, Notts; Chipping Campden, Gloucestershire; Rothwell, Northants; and Hitchin, Herts; and, as illustrated earlier in the chapter, at Witney, Oxfordshire.

AMBULATORY.—A further development of the parish church, perhaps the finest of all, occurred at the end of the mediæval period. This was the extension eastwards of the chancel and chapels, forming an ambulatory from chapel to chapel behind the high altar reredos. This is the counterpart of the retro-choir of cathedral and abbey churches, and was only attained when the burghers of large mercantile towns realized their importance in the community. Examples of this rare device may be seen at Newark (Fig. 100) and St. Mary Redcliffe, Bristol, where chapels project beyond this aisle, and also at Hull, all three of these being cross churches. At Hitchin the arrangement existed as late as the eighteenth century, but has now disappeared.

With this extension, which added greatly to the dignity and mystery of the chancel, we may take leave of the parish-church plan, but not before casting one brief glance back at its sequence of evolution, noting that, infinite as is the variety in form and detail, its gradual growth is parallel with the national development, and its increasing beauty with the greater refinement of social life. The parish church, besides being the tutor, was also the companion, and even the playmate of mankind, and called all in their various capacities into its fellowship, in building, beautifying, or in service. Its immeasurable advance is realized in the contrast of the small, crude Norman church, so typically the offspring of its social order, built by the feudal usurper of some Saxon manor, with the fully developed structure, built, owned, and maintained by the people, its every part ablaze with colour, and pointing every one to its innermost sanctuary by the increasing enrichment of the fabric. Small wonder that it took five centuries to achieve this result, and deep regret that so much for which it stood should crumble away within a hundred years.

CHAPTER III

ARCHITECTURAL STYLES IN THE PARISH CHURCH

For the intelligent study and appreciation of English Gothic architecture it is essential to be able to recognize with some degree of accuracy the work of different styles and periods. At the same time it should be understood that mediæval architecture was for most of its history in a continual state of transition. The character of the work was always undergoing a process of change, one style passing unconsciously into another. The rate of advance was not uniform at one and the same time in every part of the country, whence it is obvious that we meet with contemporary work of very diverse character in different districts. It is not possible, therefore, to determine with nicety the precise date at which one period begins or another ceases. In the study of human life it is eminently useful to mark off such periods as infancy, childhood, youth, manhood, and old age, but the growth is continuous, and it is impossible to specify the exact month or year when the one ceases and the next begins. Moreover, the rate of development is not always the same, but depends upon organic and climatic conditions. Again, in the study of all branches of natural history it is essential to orderly methods to remember the round of the seasons, but it is idle to lay down precise calendar dates for their limits.

One of the essential differences between such early architecture as that of Egypt and Assyria on the one hand, and Mediæval Art on the other, consisted in the fact that the former was a fixed and stereotyped quantity, whereas the latter was energetically, even restlessly, progressive. No doubt Egyptian and

Assyrian architecture at an early period went through stages of development, most of which have not come down to us, but, having once attained maturity, they were dominated by a rigid and stereotyped conservatism. The mediæval artist, on the other hand, was never content to let his art stand still, but was continually experimenting to solve problems of construction and reaching forward to further developments in form and ornament.

The present chapter does not aim at giving more than bare outlines as to the successive periods. They can be amplified at will by the study of text-books which treat of the details of the subject.

Those authorities who are disinclined to use the names formerly assigned to the different periods have sought to supply the need of some terms by the employment of dates.

With regard to this latter plan, the use of "centuries," though on first thoughts sounding fair and simple, presents difficulties in application, for work of totally different character was carried out at the same time, and perhaps a somewhat better plan is to refer to reigns. Thus the transition from Norman in parish churches came about roughly under Richard I, though in some instances it occurs earlier, while the style known as Early English prevailed under Henry III, Decorated under the three first Edwards, and Perpendicular continued from Richard II to Henry VIII inclusive. But to this method there are again objections. The precise dates of the reigns, which few people bear in mind without a table of reference, do not by any means correspond with the changes of style, as in the days of John and Richard II. Moreover, overlapping is more extensive than is usually supposed, for wide divergences exist in different districts. For instance, the use of flowing or even rigid geometrical forms in window tracery and elsewhere continued far later in Norfolk than in most parts of England, whilst square-headed windows prevailed earlier in Nottinghamshire than in any of the other Midland counties. Such cases emphasize the value of adopting a classification by styles. At the same time the question of terminology in describing the successive phases of Gothic building is a controversial one, nor can it be said that the controversy is by any means finished. Though the matter cannot be discussed here at length, it must be mentioned that even the best experts of modern days differ as to the use of dates and terms. On the whole it is perhaps as well to continue the use, at all events at first, of descriptive names for successive styles. This is the plan still followed by such an eminent authority as Professor Lethaby. All are agreed as to the convenience of the terms "Saxon" and "Norman" for Romanesque work, and as to their approximate dates; the difficulty begins with the rise of Gothic architecture. The study of English mediæval architecture was first undertaken in a systematic manner about eighty years ago. Thomas Rickman, as the result of his analysis of styles, for which he will always be held in honour, suggested the terms "Early English," "Decorated," and "Perpendicular," terms which have become accepted as part and parcel of our English language, and which have so far resisted every effort at dislodgment. Thoughtful architectural students cannot fail to appreciate the happy inspiration which gave us the term "Early English"; and though it may be pointed out that much of Decorated is exceedingly plain, and that Rectilinear might be an improvement on the word Perpendicular, there is yet more in favour of their appropriateness, and it is advisable for students to acquiesce in their adoption, failing any effective substitutes, which their objectors have so far been unable to provide.

To these three terms two others may be added. It is best that the name Transitional be given to the latter half of the twelfth century, when the overlap occurred between Norman and Early English, and that its use be strictly confined to that period.

Then, again, a distinctive name might be found helpful for the intervening period between Early English and Decorated. There can be little or no doubt that the best term for this highly important overlap, which plainly calls for distinctive definition, is Geometrical.

It follows then that we have seven divisional names for the classifying of English styles. They are: (1) Saxon, (2) Norman, (3) Transitional, (4) Early English, (5) Geometrical, (6) Decorated or Curvilinear, and (7) Perpendicular.

As to pre-Saxon work, it is enough to mention the foundations and scanty remains of a small Romano-British church uncovered at Silchester in 1892, and another possible small church discovered at Caerwent in 1909. Parts, moreover, of actual Roman walls are incorporated in the present Kent churches of St. Martin, Canterbury, and Lyminge, and of the ruined church of Reculver.

We pass then to a rapid survey of churches of more distinctly Saxon date.

The converted Saxons used the bricks of ruined Roman buildings very largely in their churches, and occasionally the squared stones, as at St. Peter-on-the-Walls, Essex, and Escomb, co. Durham. The most striking and considerable use of Roman bricks in a Saxon church is at Brixworth, Northants (Fig. 101). The following may also be named out of a score or two of like instances in church Saxon work: Dover Castle, and Swanscombe, Kent (Fig. 102); Langford and Prittlewell, Essex; St. Michael, St. Albans; Ovingdean, Sussex; and in the early Surrey churches of Ashtead, Feltham, and Stoke D'Abernon. In stoneless Essex at least seventy-five parish churches, in addition to those already named, make a more or less liberal use of Roman tiles, occasionally for quoins, but more frequently for turning the heads of windows and doorways, for

101. BRIXWORTH INTERIOR

which purpose they were so well adapted. This common Essex use is usually pronounced to be Early Norman, but Dr. Laver has in several cases given good reasons for considering the use of these bricks to be of Saxon date. A drawing of a built-up early light in the church of Chipping Ongar (Fig. 103) may be taken as a good instance of this Essex use of Roman tiles. Note in this instance the thin strata of Roman bonding tiles introduced to strengthen the

102. SWANSCOMBE, KENT

flint-and rubble walling; this distinct copying of the Roman method is far more likely to be the work of the Saxon than of the Norman masons, for the former would have abundant examples all round them. The indents in the squared stones joining the window were for the purpose of retaining the outer plaster, as maintained in the "Materials" chapter.

103. CHIPPING ONGAR

It may also be remarked in passing that the ornamental stonework of the Romans has also been utilized in some of our parish churches. Their sculptured stones are built into the walls of Ilkley, Yorks, and Escomb, co. Durham, used in abundance in Hexham crypt, and of fairly frequent occurrence in the parish churches of both Cumberland and Westmorland. A Roman altar is utilized in a window at Daglingworth, Glos. Drums of

Roman piers form the bases of the fonts at Kenchester, Herefordshire, and West Mersea, Essex; whilst altars have been used for the like purpose at Stainton, Hereford, and at Haydon Bridge, Northumberland.

So far as the classification of pre-Norman architecture in England is concerned, the observations are not at present sufficiently comprehensive to warrant the same degree of assurance as to comparative dates which is generally felt with regard to buildings of the post-Conquest period. It should, however, be remembered that stone churches, occasionally of magnitude, existed in England for fully four centuries prior to the Conquest. During that long period there must have been certain changes and evolutions. As time went on the Saxon churches multiplied and gained in size throughout England, and their ground-plans developed. It seems probable that the earliest Saxon churchwork was the best, and that the tendency was downwards until the close of the tenth and the beginning of the eleventh centuries, when ornamental work, of which Earl's Barton tower (Fig. 104) is one of the most famous instances, was introduced.

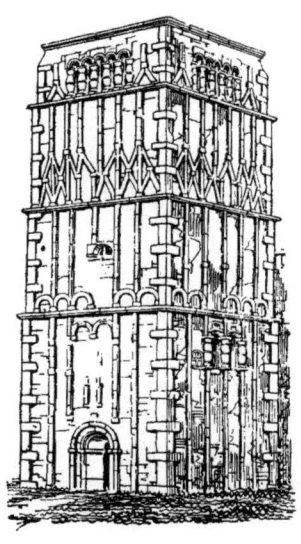

104. EARL'S BARTON

The reason for the better style of building at the beginning of the Saxon conversion, according to Benedict Biscop's well-known description of the churches of Wearmouth and Jarrow, is not far to seek. The method was traditional from the times of the Roman occupation, and there were ruined Romano British buildings here and there extant which naturally furnished ideas as to architectural structure as well as material for the fabrics. Of this, Brixworth is by far the most striking instance still remaining.

The fashion long prevailed of styling almost all mediæval architecture prior to the introduction of the pointed arch as Saxon. It was not until 1834 that Thomas Rickman pointed out the distinguishing characteristics between Saxon and Norman. Since that date ecclesiological research and minute investigation have grown apace, decade by decade. It is now well within bounds to state that pre-Conquest work can be traced with assurance in at least 225, and probably in 250 cases.*

105. ST. PETER, BRADWELL-ON-SEA

As to the distinguishing criteria for the recognition of Saxon

---

* On the question of Saxon church architecture see Mr. Micklethwaite's learned illustrated papers, "Something about Saxon Church Building," *Arch. Journal*, liii., 293-351; and "Some Further Notes on Saxon Churches," lv., 340-49. Also Professor Baldwin Brown's work, "The Arts in Early England," vol. ii., and Mr. Park Harrison's noteworthy paper on an examination of architectural details in Saxon illuminated MSS., *Arch. Journal*, xlvii., 143-53.

THE ENGLISH PARISH CHURCH 139

work, the following is a brief summary of the more noteworthy points :

(*a*) Saxon walls are, as a rule, thinner than Norman ; they generally vary from 2 feet to 3 feet 6 inches.

(*b*) Plastering originally obscured most of the outer and inner walling, but Saxon chevron tooling, as opposed to the diagonal strokes of the Norman axe, is often distinctive on the larger masonry ; it may be prominently noted on the inner work of the tower of St. Benet, Cambridge, and on the jambstones of windows, as at Wansford, Northants.

(*c*) The treatment of the outer angles of the buildings is twofold. In the one case large squares of stone are massed one over the other, after an irregular fashion, as at St. Mildred, Canterbury, and Stow, Lincolnshire, or at the seventh-century churches of Escomb and St. Peter-on-the-Walls (Fig. 105). In the other case the quoin stones are arranged after the

106. WOOLBEDING, SUSSEX

fashion so well known as " long-and-short "; the method is to alternate squared stone from 2 feet to 4 feet in height with flat slabs which project beyond the angles and grip into the walling. The examples of this last form of quoining are frequent, and are usually late in the style.

(*d*) The pilaster-strip is another easily recognized and significant feature, and frequently to be noted, as at Woolbeding, Sussex (Fig. 106); Repton chancel ; Braemore, Boarhunt, and Corhampton, Hants ; Barton-on-Humber, Lincolnshire, as well as on the well-known towers of Earl's Barton and Sompting. These pilaster-strips, or ribs, are usually late in the style; they are flat upright bands of stonework varying in width from 5 to 13 inches, and projecting but an inch or two from the wall. They are too slight to be regarded as anything but ornament, and are to be held as quite distinct from buttresses.

(*e*) The windows form a fairly safe criterion. The small narrow apertures for light may be sometimes confused with those of early Norman date, but the double-splayed form, the outer splay being frequently slight, is generally a Saxon mark. Good examples occur at Boarhunt, Barton-on-Humber, Diddlebury (Salop), and Wareham. A window of exceptionally deep outer splay occurs on the south side of the tower of Swanscombe, Kent (Fig. 102); the entire work is formed of Roman bonding tiles. Sometimes, especially high up in quasi-clerestory windows, the circular form occurs. Such windows, if Saxon, are always double-splayed, and rarely, if ever, exceed 9 inches in diameter. Openings of this description are conspicuous in the round tower of Forncett St. Peter, Norfolk (Fig. 106A). Yet more distinctive Saxon windows are the two-light openings of the belfry lights. Each half of the aperture is covered by a small round arch, both usually cut out of the same stone. In the midst is a stone prop, or shaft, usually of a baluster form, as though turned in a lathe. There

106A. FORNCETT ST. PETER, NORFOLK

is a triple opening of this kind out of the tower of Brixworth into the church (Fig. 101), and on belfry openings at Earl's Barton are fivefold, as shown in a previous picture (Fig. 104).

(*f*) The tower or chancel arches in Saxon work are usually of quite a distinctive character and not infrequently show long-and-short work in the jambs, as may be noticed at Brigstock, Northants, and Market Overton, Rutland.

(*g*) Triangular-headed archways, as at Brigstock

107. HOLY TRINITY, COLCHESTER. SAXON DOORWAY

108. DEERHURST CHURCH. SAXON WINDOWS

and Barnack, with two slabs forming the upper sides of the triangle, are a marked characteristic; at Holy Trinity, Colchester, such an archway is entirely formed in Roman bricks (Fig. 107). Triangular-headed windows occur at Bosham, Sussex; in the old towers of Weybourne, Norfolk, and Deerhurst, Gloucester (Fig. 108); in the round towers of Baslingham, Norfolk, and Herringfleet, Suffolk (Fig. 199); and over the Norman chancel arch of Sandiacre, Derbyshire.

The remarkably perfect

early church of Escomb, co. Durham, is the best example of a pure Saxon church of the square-ended chancel and nave type (Figs. 46 and 109). This small church, with a long lofty nave and diminutive chancel, is in all probability of seventh-century date. Many of the stones are of considerable size and show traces of Roman tooling. They doubtless came from Binchester. With the exception of the porch, it now stands very much as it was originally built. The walls are about 2 feet 3 inches thick. Blocks of a large size, as at St. Peter - on - the - Walls and Stow, are used for the quoins; they are laid alternately east and west, north and south; they show no trace of the technique of long-and-short work. On the south side of the nave is a pair of round-headed original lights or windows, with their heads cut out of single stones. A like pair on the north side have square headed lintels. The external apertures of all four measure 2 feet 8 inches by 1 foot 5 inches. These windows were not originally glazed; the groove for a shutter is visible in a south window. There are traces of plastering here and there on the inner walls. On the outer south wall of the nave is a mutilated circular sundial surrounded by a serpentine monster.

109. ESCOMB CHURCH, DURHAM

THE POST CONQUEST CHURCH ARCHITECTURE of England, so largely developed, followed the more advanced Romanesque lines usually denominated NORMAN. Rickman dated the Norman style from 1066 to 1189, ignoring Transitional; Parker considered that the Norman prevailed from 1066 to

1154; Sharpe's classification brought pure Norman to a close in 1145; but Professor Prior's well-marked and simple divisions assign the period from 1050 to 1160 to the Anglo-Norman style. The change at this period was not nearly so startling and overpowering in its results as when Norman gradually gave place to Gothic.

The characteristics of the Norman style are too well known to deserve here more than the briefest enumeration. In the earlier works the arches were simply moulded and the capitals of the plainest form of cushion type, while the windows in the smaller churches were little more than narrow slits in the walls. But as time went on ingenuity devised an infinite variety of mouldings, which are nowhere better illustrated than in the earlier issues of Parker's "Glossary." The earliest form is the well-known chevron, or zigzag, and this was followed, especially round doorways, by the characteristic beak head, of which Iffley west doorway affords a splendid example. Other of the more usual mouldings, all of them admitting of considerable variety, are known as the cable, the billet, the lozenge, the pellet, the studd, the chain, the cone, the scallop, and the star. The doorways, of which Kilpeck, Herefordshire (Fig. 110).

110. KILPECK SOUTH DOOR

is a noble example, increased in richness, especially on the south side of the nave, and in the number of orders in almost each successive decade of the period. The nook shafts of the sides of these portals number from one to five. The semicircular stone or tympanum, with which the head of the arch of the Norman doorway is often filled, is covered occasionally with geometrical patterns, but often with rude sculpture in low relief, as at Pipe Aston, Herefordshire (Fig. 111).*

111. TYMPANUM, PIPE ASTON

The windows, developed from those of small proportion, as illustrated at Nateley Scures, Hants (Fig. 112), grew in size, and became in the larger churches much more important features, having shafts with capitals and bases both in the interior and the exterior, as at Stow (Fig. 114). The arches of the arcades, and more especially the chancel arch, were treated with elaborate mouldings. It is almost idle to name special instances, for they are to be found in every county; but the chancel arch of Wakerley, Northants, is for its size one of the best in the country. Another delightful chancel arch is that of Winchfield, Hants, and there is one of some elaboration at Kilpeck, Herefordshire. The illustration of Kilpeck may well serve as a typical Norman interior on a small scale with chancel vaulting (Fig. 113).

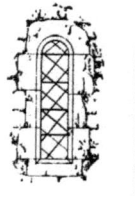 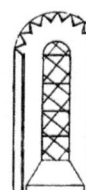

112. NORMAN WINDOWS, NATELEY SCURES

* See the whole treatment of this interesting subject in Mr. Romilly Allen's "Early Christian Symbolism" (1887), and more especially in Mr. Keyser's elaborate work on Norman tympana.

THE ENGLISH PARISH CHURCH 145

The capitals and bases of the piers supporting the arcades received equally elaborate treatment, and were often extraordinarily varied. A good Norman arcade is illustrated from

113. KILPECK CHANCEL AND APSE, HEREFORDSHIRE

Tilney All Saints in the previous chapter. Admirable and exceptional work is to be noted in the interior of the churches of Petersfield, Hants, and Stow, Lincolnshire (Fig. 114).

The Norman walls were usually of so great a thickness that no buttresses were required, even in the instances of certain larger churches, where the stone vaulted roofs of the aisles rested against them. The Norman buttress, when it was introduced later on in the style, is consequently only a slight development of the pilaster-strip of the Saxon churches. It was designed for ornamental purposes, or rather perhaps with the intention of defining the divisions or bays of an elevation, and not with the idea of giving any true support to the walling. The walls are occasionally enriched with moulded or carved string-courses, both within and without, and are generally crowned with a cornice, supported on corbels under the eaves of the roof.

114. STOW, LINCS. ARCADE IN CHANCEL

The roofs, mainly of timber, have naturally long since disappeared, and have been renewed after various fashions. Stone roofs, as time wore on, were more often erected. A succession of vaultings followed the same order here, as on the Continent. The plain barrel vault came first, and this was followed by the intersection of two such vaults at right angles; and finally the vault had well-defined arches between the bays, with mouldings or ribs under the intersecting angles.

Worked after Roman tradition, the Anglo-Norman walls were more or less a core of rubble, sometimes approximating to rubbish, faced with square stones. Hence under the stress of central towers, frequently not originally contemplated, the wall facings often became separated from the inner mass of rubble, with the result that disintegration ensued. But as the craftsmen advanced in skill they proceeded to remedy this defect, as Professor Prior points out, " by the device of arcades set on the

115. ADEL, YORKSHIRE

face of the wall, which with their covering strings made bonds, tying them to the interior core." This development, which began about 1130, may be considered as a step in scientific stone building, and hence the multiplication of arcadings became specially characteristic of later English styles for other than mere ornamental purposes.

Five parish churches may be just named as instances of those wherein the richest treatment of the late Norman period culminated: Iffley, Oxfordshire; Adel, Yorkshire (Fig. 115); St. Peter's, Northampton (Fig. 36); Barfreston, Kent; and the larger example of Castle Rising, Norfolk (Fig. 116). The illustration of this last example is from a drawing prior to Mr. Salvin's far too extensive restoration of 1844.

In these and other instances the trained craftsmen employed by the Church produced a marvellous wealth of mouldings

116. CASTLE RISING, NORFOLK, BEFORE RESTORATION

and sculptures. A scheme of decorative carving superseded the flat painting of surfaces, as practised by the earlier Norman school under Benedictine teaching; but it must not be imagined that colour ceased to be used in almost every direction, for not a little of the best late Norman sculpture bears, or used to bear, frequent traces of rich painting.

The Early Norman masonry had usually wide joints and a superfluity of mortar; but in the later work, after *c.* 1100, fine-jointed masonry became customary. A word or two must be added as to the *herringbone masonry* occasionally found in the earlier Norman church walling, and about which there has been much misconception. At one time it was generally considered that herringbone masonry (the method of laying rubble-stones in courses inclining alternately to the right and to the left) betokened pre-Conquest work.

117. HERRINGBONE, SOUTHROP, GLOS.

When, however, it was shown that several buildings wherein this method prevailed were undoubtedly post-Conquest, as in the chancel of Binstead, Isle of Wight, and the nave of Kippax, Yorks; and, further, that the method prevails in several Norman buildings on the other side of the Channel, a reaction set in, and nowadays it is too often customary to style all herringbone-work Norman. Probably much of such work is Norman, as at Southrop, Gloucestershire (Fig. 117), but it cannot by itself be taken as a test of date. The Romans used herringbone construction, and so undoubtedly did the Anglo-Saxons. Work of this nature, which is certainly pre-Conquest, occurs at Brixworth, and in the interior of Diddlebury, Salop, and at Deerhurst, Gloucestershire; also in the Sussex churches of Burton and Elsted, as well as in several examples in Nottinghamshire and elsewhere.

Derbyshire not only possesses an architectural gem in the delightful little apse-ended Norman church of Steetley, in the north-east of the county (Fig. 118), but also possesses one of

118. PART OF THE APSE, STEETLEY, DERBYSHIRE

the finest and most interesting parish churches of this period in the whole kingdom. The church of Melbourn, on its southern confines, is of cruciform plan, with central tower, chancel, transepts, nave with aisles, and western portico or narthex with two small flanking towers (Fig. 119). The full length is 100 feet, and the width across the transepts is 77 feet 6 inches. It was begun in 1190. The narthex has a groined stone roof, and over it is a chamber or gallery opening into the church, access to which used to be gained by spiral staircases in the tower. The circular piers between the nave and aisles are 4 feet in diameter and 15 feet high. Above the arcades are clerestory openings, but the two sides are of different dates, that on the south having been rebuilt in the thirteenth century after fire. The nave had originally a stone groined roof, or was, at all events, planned with that intention. The inner walls of the central tower are divided into three tiers of arcading, and it was planned to be open up to the groining; the bells would at that time hang in the small western towers. The chancel, as well as the two transepts, used to terminate eastwards in apses—their traces are obvious; they were removed in 1300. The chancel was originally in two stages; the upper one either served, as at Compton, for another chapel, or else as a priest's chamber.

If specific terms, rather than reigns of the kings or parts of centuries, are to be applied to our architectural periods, each of which cannot fail to some extent to overlap, the word TRANSITION is well deserving of persistent retention. About the middle of the twelfth century the pointed arch in its incipient stage appeared in certain of our parish churches. It was of earlier appearance in some of the great churches of religious houses: in the nave arcade of Buildwas Abbey as early as 1132, and but little later in

119. MELBOURN, DERBYSHIRE

several other houses of Cistercian foundation. For some time this pointed arch was only used occasionally, and blended with the rounded form, whilst the details and accessories remained much the same as before. This change very gradually led the way to the full adoption of First Pointed or Early English.

There will always be differences of opinion, as well as numerous conjectures, concerning the origin of the pointed arch. Among the guesses of an architectural nature are two: the first, popular but erroneous, is that it was suggested by the intersection of semicircular arches, a detail often found in

152   ARCHITECTURAL STYLES IN

ornamental arcades, as at Castle Rising, or St. John, Devizes. The more reasonable hypothesis is that it originated from the structural exigencies of vaulting. It was during the period of Transition that the science of stone vaulting received a great

120. NEW SHOREHAM, SUSSEX

impetus, and the whole architectural construction began to assume lighter and more graceful lines. So far as years go, it would be correct to say that the real Transition began in 1160, and did not die out till 1207.

The Transition style is met with in somewhat different phases all over England and in all parts of buildings, though, of course, it is in the main known by the occasional introduction of the pointed arch. At Castle Hedingham, Essex, there is a beautiful chancel arch with Norman mouldings but of pointed form, and the like occurs after a marked fashion at Walsoken, Norfolk, and Broadwater, Sussex. The chancel of Bloxham, Oxon, has some curious, large pointed windows, but the arches have zigzag, cable, and billet mouldings. The chancel arches of Clevedon, Somersetshire; Morbourne, Huntingdonshire; South Cerney, Gloucestershire; and Little Packington have the same Transitional characteristics; also the tower arch of Middleton, Lancashire.

In Northamptonshire the ball-like volutes of the capitals of the otherwise Norman arcades of Barnack, Polebrooke, Wittering, and Duddington seem to mark them as early Transition. Late Transition is to be noted at Addington, Hargrave, Northborough, and other churches of that county; but the most striking

121. SOHAM, CAMBS. CHANCEL ARCH

Northamptonshire instance is the tower (the spire is later) of Spratton, which is probably of the days of King John. One of the most important examples of Transition on a large and imposing scale is to be noted in the chancel aisles of the fine Sussex church of New Shoreham (Fig. 120).

There are a fair number of instances where circular Norman piers in the side arcades of village churches support pointed arches. In the majority of cases such arches are the undoubted result of rebuilding, but the practical eye will now and again detect, in certain instances, the simultaneous work of the Transition period. At Burton Agnes, in the East Riding, the north side of the parish church is thus divided from the nave by two plain pointed square-edged arches, which spring from a circular pier with scalloped capital of a usual Norman design. In this case the whole work is certainly of the second half of the twelfth century, and is a clear case of Transitional. The same may be said of the arcades on each side of the Worcestershire parish church of Tredington, and notably at Soham, Cambs (Fig. 121). Occasionally we find the reverse to be the case, namely, semicircular arches supported by Early English piers; of this there are several notable examples in Leicestershire, and a striking instance occurs at St. Mary's, Shrewsbury (Fig. 122).

As finally worked out, there was a broad difference between Romanesque and Gothic, but it is with the intermediate stages that we are now immediately concerned. Although good work of the Transition period is to be found all over England, it does not seem possible to point to any one church, large or small, where it entirely prevails or strongly predominates. Transition is well illustrated in the interior of Rothwell, Northants; and the four arches for the former central tower of Soham, Cambs, are delightful examples. The style is notable at Blewbury and Lambourne, Berks, whilst in Sussex it is more frequent than pure Norman.

By the time of the dawn of the thirteenth century the happily named EARLY ENGLISH STYLE, the first pointed period of the Gothic art, was firmly established. But all art was in a state of suspension, and church building was dormant in the latter part of John's reign, when the Interdict was in full force. It is therefore best, on the whole, to regard this beautiful Early English period, at all events so far as our parish churches are concerned, as extending from 1216 to about 1250 or a little later, for about this latter date it developed into the Geometrical, so well worthy of a distinct name.

The leading features of Early English are too well known to require any elaborate description. The windows are of long and narrow proportions, and are used either singly or in combinations of two, three, five, as in the Five Sisters of Bosham,

THE ENGLISH PARISH CHURCH 155

122. ST. MARY'S, SHREWSBURY

Sussex (Fig. 123), or even seven, as in the east window of Ockham, Surrey (Fig. 124). Occasionally they are surmounted by an arch embracing the whole group, as at Etton, Northants (Fig. 125). The space between this arch and the tops of the

123. BOSHAM, SUSSEX   124. OCKHAM, SURREY

main lights is sometimes pierced with circles, trefoils, or other openings, as in the celebrated case at Wimborne, thus gradually approximating to the dawn of real tracery in the Geometrical period.

Groined vaultings came into common use; generally they have only what are termed cross springs and diagonal ribs, but sometimes with longitudinal and transverse ribs at the apex of the vaults. The piers frequently consist of small shafts arranged round a circular or other shaped central pillar, of which Eaton Bray, Bedfordshire, offers a charming example. But it must be remembered that plain octagonal or circular piers, occasionally used alternately, are fairly common in the simpler country churches. The capitals in the ordinary examples consist of plain mouldings, or

125. ETTON, NORTHANTS, EAST WINDOW

encircled with a line of nail-head mouldings, as at Barrington, Cambs, but they are more usually enriched with a great variety of conventional foliage treated with consummate skill and beauty of design. A simple fact, which it is well to remember with regard to Early English capitals, is that the foliage thereon is almost invariably one presented with stalks, whilst in the fourteenth century the foliage is far more closely imitative of nature, and is generally, as it were, twisted round the capital.

Both Bedfordshire and Hertfordshire offer a considerable variety of thirteenth-century foliage capitals. In the former county those of Studham and Eaton Bray are specially notable. The south arcade of Ivinghoe, Bucks, has some admirable capitals of this style, whilst Woodstock, Oxon, has human heads curiously intermingled with stiff stalked foliage. For a yet more beautiful development of the carving of capitals, West Walton, Norfolk (Figs. 126, 127), supplies about the most exquisite work in any English church, as may be gathered from the examples selected. The most prevalent bases of the piers of this style have a close resemblance to the Attic base of classic architecture; the turn of the mouldings leaves a hollow which in current language is usually styled the "water-holding" mould.

126. WEST WALTON ARCADE

The most common ornament, used in this style with great frequency, on every kind of arch and on other details of the fabric, is the effective dog-tooth

127. WEST WALTON, NORFOLK

THE ENGLISH PARISH CHURCH 159

pattern. The south doorway of Mumby, Lincolnshire, and the west doorway (Fig. 128) and aisle window of the noble church of Warmington, Northamptonshire, may be mentioned as examples. The corbel-tables on towers and under the eaves of roofs are occasionally thus ornamented, as at Ketton, Rutland. One of the advantages of this pure English style was its elasticity or adaptability for almost every kind of church building, whether small or great, simple or stately. Good instances of this small, simple, and inexpensive kind of parish church, so well suited to country districts, occur at Chidham, Sussex, and Little Casterton, Rutland.

128. THE WEST DOOR, WARMINGTON, NORTHANTS
[*From a drawing by W. Twopeny*

This thirteenth-century style, though productive of many a noble tower or spire, such as those of St. Mary's Sutton, Whaplode, Lincolnshire, or Witney, Oxfordshire, or in the splendid example of Ketton, Rutland (Fig. 129), where, though the spire is later, the whole composition is entirely harmonious, was eminently suitable for comparatively inexpensive double bell cotes on the west gable. Rutland supplies two good instances of this in the churches of Manton and Little Casterton, the west fronts of which are both, in their respective ways, of real merit and quiet dignity.

129. THE TOWER AND SPIRE, KETTON, RUTLAND

Early English work dignifies and graces most parts of England. It is rare to find a county without some more or less effective specimens of the style in whole or in part. Even Cornwall, though the granite work of the fifteenth century thrust most which preceded it out of the way, has some beautiful and considerable remnants of the style. Essex, as might naturally be expected, is but little represented. Very little work of this period worth mentioning is to be found in the extensive West Riding. In the East Riding, on the contrary, there is work of great beauty and importance. Irrespective of the whole of Beverley Minster, east of the great crossing, most of the nave of Bridlington, and the grand transepts and quire of Hedon, Filey, and Sigglesthorne belong almost wholly to the period, whilst beautiful doorways or windows are to be found at Easlington, Elloughton, Hessle, Kirk Ella, and Middleton on-the-Wold. The North Riding possesses in the small church of Skelton—the dimensions are only 44 feet 2 inches by 32 feet 8 inches—a perfect gem of Early English craftsmanship.

130. AMBERLEY, SUSSEX

Amberley, Sussex, may be taken as a typical example of a good village church of this period (Fig. 130).

It is much to be wished that antiquaries, ecclesiologists, and church architects would agree to make a general use of such a term as GEOMETRICAL as applicable to the period when formal window tracery began to be used, when Early English had almost come to a close, and before Decorated had begun. As it is, writers and expounders of Gothic architecture are for ever confused and not infrequently contradictory in nomenclature about the close of the thirteenth century. It is comparatively simple to insist upon the definite use of the phrase Geometrical as applicable to the time between 1250 and 1290.

This is the line taken by Professor Prior in his two important works on "Gothic Art" and "Cathedral Builders." He also, to a great extent, carries us with him in considering this brief period the "summit of Gothic art." If, too, we follow his pithy adjectival nomenclature, it will be found useful to remember that the first Transition period was *Norman* and *monastic*, the second or Early English *insular* and *episcopal*, and the third or Geometrical, at the end of the century, *Continental* and *regal*. This last division earns its two epithets from Henry III, who had been brought up in France and remained in close touch with the French Court of St. Louis; he avowedly rebuilt Westminster Abbey on French lines, and adorned it with the aid of Continental craftsmen. But, though admiring Professor Prior's definition of this period as Geometrical, the epithets are scarcely appropriate, as they only apply in themselves to Westminster, with its apse and apsidal chapels.

The momentous change that produced such masterpieces as the "Angel Choir" of Lincoln, which in its soaring perfection differed *in toto cœlo* from the stiff sublimity of the best efforts of the first half of the century, was reflected after a dim but real fashion in the details of many a parish church. The change is to be chiefly detected in the windows. The lancet, when retained, began to lose the outline which gave it its name and to broaden out a little in width, whilst the dawn came of embryo tracery. At Brownsover, Warwickshire, the space over a double lancet comprised within a single dripstone was pierced with a lozenge-shaped opening. At Kibworth, Leicestershire, there are sets of like pairs of lancets with similar openings above them, whilst internally these windows have detached shafts at the jambs. At Etton, Northamptonshire, which Brandon mistakenly styles "a simple and pure specimen of an Early English church," the windows of the aisles are all similar, and consist of two lancets with a plain circle above, the whole being under one dripstone (Fig. 131). A little later the space in the head of a double window was occupied by a foliated circle, and in the head of a triple window by two such circles; this effective though simple

THE ENGLISH PARISH CHURCH 163

designing occurs in several parish churches, notably at St. Giles, Oxford. At Calbourne, Isle of Wight, the chancel was rebuilt and a south chapel added *c.* 1260; the east windows of both chancel and chapel consist of a pair of lancets separated by an interval of masonry; in the chancel

SOUTH AISLE WINDOWS   CHANCEL WINDOW
131. ETTON, NORTHAMPTONSHIRE

is a trefoil piercing above the lancets, and in the chapel a quatrefoil piercing (Fig. 132). At Arreton, Isle of Wight, the chancel was also remodelled and a south chapel added *c.* 1275; they are separated by an arcade of three arches of beautiful Purbeck marble; the chancel east window has three principal lights with three arches above them, whilst the chapel windows are of two lights with a single arch. There are also some excellent Geometrical windows at the east ends of the chancel and south chapel of Freshwater church.

Northamptonshire has abundant instances of the Geometrical style. The south porch of Woodford is a remarkably good example of the close of Henry III's reign. The inner doorway, with beautifully moulded cusped head, surmounted by a

132. CALBOURNE, ISLE OF WIGHT
[From a water-colour by J. C. Buckler

niche and foliated panels, is most effective; the groining ribs of the roof are simply chamfered. Northborough, Helpston, Irchester, and Rushden show much beautiful work, especially in the sedilia. Other memorable Geometrical work may be noted in Northants in the spire of Crick, in the tower of Harleston, in the north aisle and Lady Chapel of Higham Ferrers, as well as in certain portions of Little Addington, Tidmarsh, Watford, and Yardley Hastings.

Noble indeed were the works of the splendid though brief Geometrical period, as might be detailed through many a county did not space forbid. Thus in Oxfordshire, rich in architectural treasures, there are the fine north aisle of Dorchester, the charming east window of the chancel of Hampton Poyle, and the south aisle of Woodstock. Interesting later developments occur in the east window of North Crawley, Bucks (Fig. 133), and in a south aisle window of Rickinghall Inferior, Suffolk (Fig. 134).

THE ENGLISH PARISH CHURCH 165

If there is one church above all others which justifies the idea of this brief period attaining to the summit of Gothic art, it is the glorious church of St. Wulfram of Grantham (Fig. 135). Here can be studied all the styles, and it is an easy church to study, for the ground-plan, owing to the width of the aisles and

133. EAST WINDOW, NORTH CRAWLEY, BUCKS

134. A SOUTH-AISLE WINDOW, RICKINGHALL INFERIOR, SUFFOLK

their prolongation so as to include the tower, is one of much simplicity. It forms a parallelogram 196 feet by 69 feet, and is divided into three nearly equal parts, only broken by the porches and a single late chapel. The tower, with its wonderful spire, rising to a height of 231 feet, is one of the greatest works of the early fourteenth century, and there is other good later work of that century; but by far the most beautiful and grandest architecture in this great pile is that which was accomplished about

135. ST. WULFRAM, GRANTHAM, FROM THE SOUTH-WEST

1280, when the Angel Choir of Lincoln was in progress. At that time the nave was extended two bays to the west, the tower was begun, and the magnificent north aisle was built so far as

136, 137. WINDOWS AT GRANTHAM

the end of the first bay of the chancel. Admirable as is the effect of this splendid church with its blend of different periods, the later Decorated work pales before the purity of the Geometrical (Figs. 136 and 137), and it is impossible to resist the wish that the church had been finished ere the fourteenth century dawned.

With the close of the Geometrical period came the first ebb in the tide of architectural progress. "In the thirteenth century," says Professor Prior, "the flood of great Gothic art was as the majesty of a great tide; the national life was in its stately sweep, and though the turn had come, still broad and white lay the sheets of its foam, the limit marks of its achievement."

138. HIGHAM FERRERS CHANCEL, NORTHANTS

The term "DECORATED," as applied to a period of English Gothic architecture, was first used by Britton in 1807.

It was subsequently adopted and popularized by Rickman to such an extent that it has now become too crystallized to be discarded. The unsuitability of the term to much that was produced during the fourteenth century is obvious, especially with regard to country churches, for they are often remarkably plain, and show at once a distinct falling off from the stately beauties of the Geometrical division. Particularly is this the case with many of the village churches of Northamptonshire, where, notwithstanding the multiplicity of stone from the Rutland quarries and from the then unexhausted stone of Barnack, the masons of the first half of the fourteenth century seem in many instances to have been content to mark the advent of new conceptions by effecting changes

139. THE SOUTH PORCH, BYFIELD, NORTHANTS

in the simple mouldings of the capitals and the bases of the piers or jamb-shafts.

On the whole, however, it seems best to adhere to the term Decorated, but to confine its use to the period from 1290 up to 1348–49, when the Great Plague broke out.

In following up the best work of this half-century, amid the fascinating wealth of Northamptonshire church buildings Cotterstock claims particular attention; and more especially Finedon, where the nave, aisles, chancel, and transepts follow a simple design of late Edward II or early Edward III execution. Attention should be paid to the beautiful natural foliage of the capitals of the nave and south transept piers, and of the responds of the chancel arch. Another somewhat unusual feature in Northamptonshire is that the clerestory and several other windows have ogee-heads. This is a commoner feature of work of this date in Northamptonshire than elsewhere. It may be notably observed at Higham Ferrers (Fig. 138), and in the 1325

140. ST. CATHERINE'S CHAPEL, LEDBURY, HEREFORDSHIRE

windows of Harleston church, whilst several of the porches in the south of the county have a crocketed hood-mould of the same shape over the entrance.

The ball-flower ornament is as much a characteristic of fourteenth-century work as is the dog-tooth of that of the thirteenth century. Among the churches where it may be noted in Northamptonshire the following may be mentioned: The chancel arch of Raunds (a double row); the north porch of Ringstead; the capitals of the north arcade, Cransley; the west doorway and porch of Byfield (Fig. 139); the cornice of the south transept of Rushden; and the cornice of the chancel of East Haddon, where it is intermingled with grotesque figures.

141. PATRINGTON, YORKSHIRE

The windows of the north aisle of St. Catherine's Chapel, Ledbury (Fig. 140), afford a late example of an excessive and tasteless use of this ornament. It also abounds in Gloucestershire.

There is hardly a county which does not contain fine specimens of parish churches of this period, notably Cambridge and Buckingham; it is almost invidious to make distinctions, but two wonderful examples of the wealth of ornament and breadth of conception are chosen for a few comments. For

THE ENGLISH PARISH CHURCH 171

those who love the Decorated style there can scarcely be a greater pleasure than a visit to Heckington, Lincolnshire; it is a fine cruciform building, 150 feet long and 85 feet broad, with noble west tower and spire. It was begun in 1345; whether it was finished or not in its main conceptions before the out-

142. CHANCEL FROM NORTH, GRANTCHESTER, CAMBS

break of the Black Death is a matter of some doubt. An exceptional feature of the plan is that the nave extends without aisles, one bay east of the transepts. The chancel is regarded as "one of the special glories of Decorated architecture," and the east window of seven lights as "one of the finest in all England."

Patrington, E.R. Yorkshire, is another splendid cruciform church happily known as the "Queen of Holderness." "Beyond all cavil," as Mr. Joseph Morris writes, "it is one of the most beautiful and perfect parish churches in the kingdom." The prolongation of the nave beyond the transept is a feature shared with Heckington, but it is superior to that church inasmuch as the central tower, designed but abandoned for the western position in the Lincolnshire church, is well carried out (Fig. 141). The north and south aisle windows of flowing tracery follow a single pattern. There is a rose window in the gable of the south transept, a highly unusual feature in a parish church. Both of these churches have remarkable Easter Sepulchres with sculptured figures.

143. GRANTHAM, LINCS

The exuberant fancies of the first half of the fourteenth century, as the Decorated style came into being, were nowhere so strikingly manifested as in the windows. The size of the windows, as a rule, materially expanded, the mullions varying from two or three and onwards, in some extreme cases to even seven. These varieties as the style advanced were endless. The mullions were not carried out vertically through the head, but continued for a time to form in the head a more or less elaborate development of the dignity of the Geometrical style, as at Grantchester, Cambs (Fig. 142), and Westhall, Suffolk. More usually, however, the mullions at the spring of the arch turned aside and branched out into easily flowing lines, which are occasionally styled with much truth Curvilinear, as in a Grantham window (Fig. 143). Of this form of tracery the six-light west window of Snettisham, Norfolk, is a noble example, and an excellent one of five lights is seen in the south transept at Heckington. In some instances the branching out of the tracery produced flame-like compartments to which the term "flamboyant" is justly assigned, of which there are good instances at Salford, Warwick, Great Harwood and Preston Bissett, Bucks, and Chipping Norton and Ducklington, Oxon (Fig. 144). Now and again the main lights are left unfoliated, while the subordinate lights of the tracery are foliated and enriched; sometimes this treatment is reversed. Again, in one window the tracery is without a single cusp; in another every turn is cusped.

One of the commonest forms of Decorated windows is usually termed "net tracery," consisting of a series of quatrefoils in the head (Fig. 145). One other form must just be mentioned, namely, the reticulated, wherein the stonework runs in wavy lines diagonally across the window-head in each direction, subdividing the tracery into a series of quatrefoils and trefoils. A late development of some beauty is found now and again wherein the cusps terminate in circular and flower-shape forms. An instance is here given from Ledbury (Fig. 140). It is to be noticed in at least four Cornish churches.*

144. DUCKLINGTON

After recovering to some extent from the staggering shock of the Black Death, there came a breathing space between the real end of Decorated extravagant variety and the more sober and stately Perpendicular. During this interval square-headed windows, varied here and there by ogee-headed designs, were largely used. At Tideswell, Derbyshire, there are excellent examples of various forms of true Decorated windows

* See the author's "Churches of Cornwall" (1912), pp. 19-20.

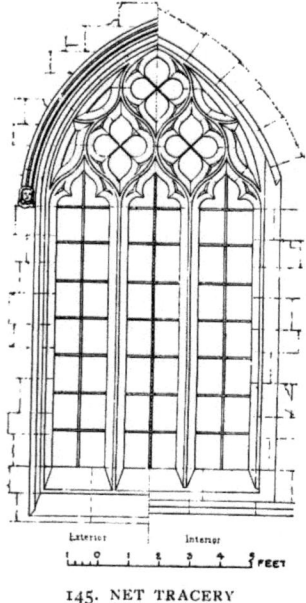

145. NET TRACERY

in the nave and transepts, but the side windows of the chancel are fine instances of the square-headed quatrefoil plan (Fig. 146). Such windows on a smaller scale are quite common in some districts, especially in Nottinghamshire, and are for the most part poor and ineffective.

A favourite adornment of the churches of the Decorated period was the introduction of a profusion of crockets and crocketed niches, especially on the open hoodmoulds over doorways, buttresses, and sepulchral recesses. This profusion is illustrated in the picture already given of Byfield porch, also in Fig. 148. Delicately designed imitations of foliage and flowers are found on capitals and corbels, on the mouldings of doorways, and in other less appropriate vantage-grounds, in all the more important

146. TIDESWELL, DERBYSHIRE

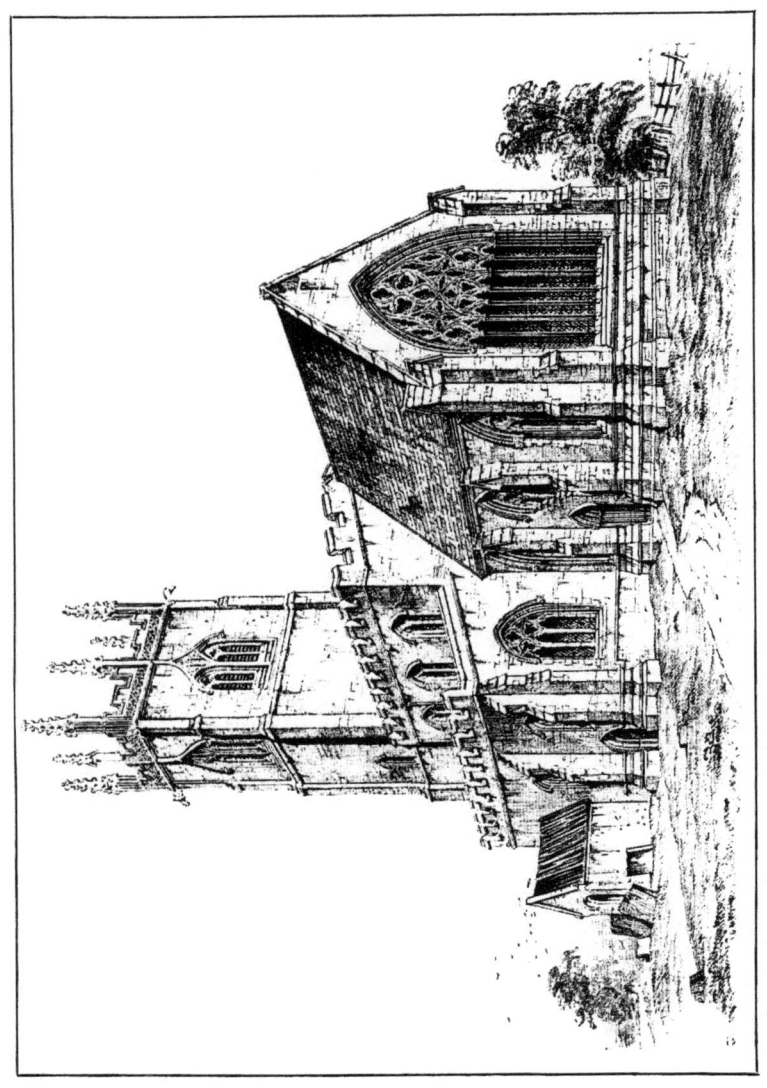

147. HAWTON, NOTTS, FROM THE SOUTH-EAST

176 ARCHITECTURAL STYLES IN

148. A CANOPY OF THE EASTER SEPULCHRE, HAWTON

churches. These illustrations from Patrington, and Bloxham, Oxfordshire, will suffice as examples.

Perhaps the most noteworthy achievement of the church sculptors in the heyday of Decorated elaboration occurs in the noble chancel of Hawton, Nottinghamshire (Figs. 147, 148), c. 1315-25. The arrangement of the tracery of the seven-light great east window is masterly and effective, while the elaborately enriched treatment of the sedilia on the south side and of the Easter Sepulchre tableau on the north, in the interior, are unsurpassed of their kind.

Many ecclesiologists and architectural antiquaries have been in the habit, from the days of Rickman's and Parker's earlier manuals, of regarding the period now under consideration as the acme of English Gothic art, and such an opinion is still largely held. But, from a religious and dignified point of view, there are now a large number of diligent students of England's church architecture of the past who agree with Professor Prior's contention that the summit was reached in the Geometrical period, and that it terminated about 1290. Notwithstanding all the brilliant exuberance of its sculptured ornaments, or the decorative blaze of the colour scheme of the interior, the great parish church of the fourteenth century can scarcely be regarded as devotional in its expression. The pride of human life, rather than the mysterious hopes of a purer life beyond the grave, was reflected both without and within the Houses of God. Even the very fonts of the initial Sacrament and the surroundings of the altar were stamped with heraldic achievements in the place of the symbols of the Faith.

Those days in England were times of emotional ostentation, of lavish extravagance, of gorgeous display, of wantoning in wealth, and of all the pomp and pride of the romantic sunset of true chivalry. Professor Prior, with his keen observation and ready power of phrasing, has framed many a paragraph expressive of these views, insisting that the fourteenth-century craftsmen were pressed into its service when dealing with the chancels or chantry chapels of our parish churches.

The canopy from the Hawton Easter sepulchre (Fig. 148) may serve as an example of exuberant ornamental treatment. The naves of this period, destitute as a rule of aristocratic

178 ARCHITECTURAL STYLES IN

149. A XIV-CENTURY INTERIOR, HEDON, YORKSHIRE

monuments, were generally treated after a more sober fashion, as we find in the nave of Hedon, E.R. Yorks (Fig. 149).

Just when this blaze of rampant architectural glory was at its height—at the moment, too, when England was delirious with triumphant joy over the capture of Calais, following close upon the momentous victory of Crécy—a sable mantle of the deepest dye descended on the land, producing for a time a total eclipse of all its splendour.* The awful, overwhelming shock of the Black Death of 1348-49 paralysed for some years all architectural effort. Its interruption to work in progress can be noticed all over England, from Durham to Sussex, or from the shores of East Anglia to the extreme limits of Cornwall. The nave and west front of York Minster were in process of building at the very date when the ravages of the pestilence broke out; and the survivors left the nave vault unfinished, and a mere makeshift vaulting of wood was all that could be furnished as the plague subsided. It was not until 1361 that the new quire was begun and carried through in quite a different spirit. Interrupted work, followed by a change in plan or style, may be specially noted in the large churches at Newark, Tadcaster, Patrington, Tideswell, and at Yarmouth, Rollesby, Cley-on-Sea, and Brumstead, Norfolk; whilst scores of others might be named as instances of the sudden check to plans in the smaller parish churches.

With regard to the inner embellishment of churches of the Decorated era, it ought to be remembered that the wealth of niches filled with imagery, and the richness in detail of the monumental effigies and of the tables on which they stood, demanded a more easily worked stone than could be procured from Doulting or Barnack, or from the quarries of Yorkshire grit. Hence it came about that there were "traders in monuments of Caen and Reigate stone in London, of Bathstone at Exeter, of clunch at Norwich, of Ancaster at Lincoln, of Huddlestone at York, of Dundry stone at Bristol, and of Cheltenham stone at Gloucester."† And as the demand for

---

* By a strange perversity, such an authority as Parker's "Glossary," followed by a multiplicity of handbooks, good, bad, and indifferent, insists on labelling plates of Decorated work either 1350 or *c.* 1350. And yet that was above all the very year when the mason's tools were silent from one end of England to the other.

† Prior's "Cathedral Builders," 80-81.

180 ARCHITECTURAL STYLES IN

150. RUSHDEN, NORTHAMPTONSHIRE

florid and canopied work grew greater, one and all of these stones were not only used for the delicacies of chantry chapel ornament and inner enrichment, but in the actual outer fabrics, with results which were often beautiful in themselves, but sadly lacking in permanence.

Though the Decorated ended with the Black Death, it was followed by a period, especially in East Anglia, wherein Decorated forms are found side by side with the newer Perpendicular. In short, throughout the latter part of Edward III's reign and during the whole of that of Richard II a time of transition can frequently be noted.

As England recovered from the shock and temporary stagnation that followed the scourge of the Great Pestilence, the Decorated work reasserted itself in several parts of the North and Midlands. Particularly was this the case in Northants. Irchester spire, for instance, is full of elegance and grace, but the best of all the spires of the second half of the fourteenth century is that of Rushden (Fig. 150). It is of this last named spire that Freeman says: "There cannot be a more perfectly beautiful example, whether for outline or detail."*

Nevertheless, after 1360 genuine Perpendicular began to establish itself with firmness in many parts of the South. It is held by some that the skeleton system of this Perpendicular

151. SOHAM, CAMBS. EAST WINDOW

* Freeman's "History of Architecture," p. 385.

building had its dawn about 1335 in the south transept of Gloucester Cathedral, and this was assuredly the case with the great

152. SUTTON, CAMBS. EAST WINDOW

quire, begun in 1351, when the English Perpendicular was definitely created in the development of panel and skeleton arch. Between 1370 and 1390 it was a struggle in different parts of the kingdom whether the entrance of the Decorated or the scientific marshalling of the draughtsman's school, as exemplified in the Perpendicular, should prevail. By the latter date Perpendicular had almost everywhere gained the day. The fine east windows of Soham and Sutton show the dawn of Perpendicular tracery (Figs. 151, 152).

"Perpendicular" was the term invented by Rickman to cover the period which extended from Richard II to Henry VIII; it is perhaps more rightly styled "Rectilinear" by Mr. Sharpe, but it seems that the former term will never be dislodged. Rickman took the name chiefly from the arrangement of the tracery, which is so often characterized by perpendicular lines, and forms one of its conspicuous features, of which the aisle windows of Northleach, Gloucestershire (Figs. 153, 154), are characteristic instances. This perpendicular arrangement is also to be noted in the panelling, which is often a particular feature of this period, not only in the jambs of arches and doorways, but also within the arches, and especially on buttresses. Panelling is also used abundantly on wall spaces both internally and externally, and it is an almost invariable feature of fan-vaulting. The window tracery, particularly in the larger examples, might often be as well termed horizontal as perpendicular, for transoms cross the mullions at right angles, and in the same way in the panelling vertical lines frequently produce a somewhat stiff rectilinear arrangement. The arches as the style advanced spread out, and for the last half of the fifteenth and the first half of the sixteenth centuries are almost invariably four-centred. A

153. NORTHLEACH, GLOS.   NORTH AISLE

plain octagonal pillar continues in use throughout the style, but with considerable variations of shallow hollow mouldings and fillets. A common arrangement is a clustered form of four three quarter circular shafts with intervening hollows. The plinths of the bases are almost invariably octagonal, and are frequently double; they may generally be distinguished from Decorated by their greater height. The capitals are usually plain, but are enriched occasionally with graceful foliage after a compact fashion, as at Tickhill, Yorkshire (Fig. 155), and now and again with simple flowers or patterns in relief after a coarse fashion.

154. NORTHLEACH, GLOS. SOUTH AISLE

The impressive and fine character of Perpendicular arcades can be better judged from views of the interiors of good parish churches of this period than by any amount of detailed writing. May not England well be proud of such interiors, from different parts of the country, as those of the large parish churches of Lowestoft (Fig. 156), Ludlow (Fig. 157), Hull (Fig. 8), Southwold, and Bideford? And the same thing is repeated in hundreds of other parishes on a smaller scale.

St. Petrock, Exeter (Fig. 158), may be taken as an example of the occasional sculptured figure additions to the capitals of Perpendicular piers. In this case the usual mouldings are crowned by a series of dignified shield-bearing angels.

Occasionally an exactly opposite treatment is to be noted in Perpendicular arcades, wherein the mouldings of the arches are continued down to the ground without capitals to mark the springing. This ineffective arrangement is far more common in the North of France than on this side of the Channel. It is to be found in the Cornish churches of Fowey and its neigh-

155. TICKHILL. NORTH ARCADE CAPITAL

bour Lostwithiel. There was a considerable Continental trade in the fifteenth century between France and the port of Fowey. A good example of lack of capitals is to be seen in the arcades of the church of Ormskirk (Fig. 159).

Another leading characteristic, usually to be found well treated in the west front of the tower, is the square arrange-

156. ST. MARGARET'S, LOWESTOFT

ment of the mouldings over the heads of doorways, creating a triangular space termed a spandrel on each side above the arch. The spandrels are generally filled with tracery, foliage, or a shield. Copdock, Suffolk, may serve as an example in the latter part of the style. The Tudor rose and the vine-leaf and grape design are often introduced with happy effect in various mouldings in stone as well as wood.

But it was in the windows, *par excellence*, that the startling change came about, a change so great that it would be recognized at a glance. The infinite and almost wearisome vagaries of English church window designs became exhausted by their very wantonness. Architectural extravagances died away with the expiring flames of a decadent chivalry. The nation became

157. ST. LAURENCE, LUDLOW

158. ST. PETROCK, EXETER

possibly more prosaic, but certainly more staid and generally devout, and this was speedily and almost universally reflected in the architecture of the churches. The reaction from the mere wantonness of diverse methods led to the formation and adoption of Rectilinear tracery. The enthusiasm for coloured glass and memorial windows, which at this time laid such a strong hold on the national development, had doubtless something to do with the greater width and the multiplicity of windows; but it is quite unreasonable to argue, as certain able men persist in doing, that the wider adoption of glass imagery affected to any large extent the lines of window tracery. This is in reality an obvious fact, and can be at once settled by resort to the measuring-tape or the foot-rule. The main portion—in fact, fully nine-tenths—of the glass effects or

159. ORMSKIRK

the fifteenth century could have been just as well produced in the larger and better windows of the fourteenth century—that is to say, within the straight mullions of the main lights. The size and shape of the subordinate lights of the upper tracery were comparatively immaterial.

160. STRATFORD-ON-AVON

The great change in the tracery of the Perpendicular days was brought about in the simplest of ways. The mullions or vertical members dividing the main lights were in the dawn of the style carried right through vertically to the top of the window, instead of diverging diagonally so soon as the spring of the arch was reached. When once this idea of the substitution of vertical for diagonal lines had gained ground the rest was an easy development, for it was obvious that other vertical portions of stonework could be introduced into the upper parts of the windows, starting from the heads of the principal lights. This method resulted in the dividing of the upper portion of the window into a series of panel-like compartments, of which abundant examples occur in every county. The fine east window of St. Margaret, Lowestoft (Fig. 156), may be taken as a good instance, though not very early in the style. The next step was the introduction of a horizontal transom or band, tying together, as it were, the vertical mullions, and thus producing a large panel effect in the main lights. Instances of

161. LOWICK, NORTHANTS

the use of transoms are fairly numerous, but it is not possible to judge with any precision as to the precise date of a Perpendicular window because of this attribute. The interior view of the noble chancel of Stratford-on-Avon (*c.* 1490) is a striking instance of glass predominating over stonework in the walls (Fig. 160). The Northamptonshire church of Lowick affords an excellent series of late Perpendicular windows in the chancel, and a still later south window in the south transept with double transoms (Fig. 161). A remarkable example of a vast east window of this style occurs at Colyton, Devon, where there are nine lights and double transoms; the window is carried down to the very floor, and has a doorway enclosed in it. The west window of St. Nicholas, King's Lynn, is another very large window of this type (Fig. 162).

162. ST. NICHOLAS, KING'S LYNN

In the tower of Lowick and Colyton the unusual feature of a lantern surrounding a tower proper linked to the pinnacles by diminutive flying buttresses may be noticed. The execution of fine west towers was usual throughout the period, and came to its greatest perfection in Somersetshire, with its superb triumph at St. Mary Magdalene's, Taunton (Fig. 3). Occasionally the nobility of the Somerset towers is almost paralleled by those of other counties, as at St. Neots, Huntingdonshire, or Fowey, Cornwall. Viewed from a general standpoint, the majesty of the tower has often the drawback of detracting from the dignity of the body of the church; this is particularly the case where a clerestory is lacking, as at Yate, Gloucestershire (Fig. 163); Huish Episcopi, Somerset; and Chittlehampton and Widdicombe, Devon. In the finest of the Somersetshire towers, and in those of like character elsewhere, as well as in all those of flint in East Anglia, the stairway is contained within an angle of the inner fabric. But in the Somersetshire towers of the second class, throughout Devonshire, and generally in the South of England wherever there are good towers, as

163. YATE, GLOUCESTERSHIRE

in the Tenterden district of Kent, an excellent effect is produced by enclosing the vice or newel stair in a projecting turret—most commonly of a semi octagonal form—at one of the angles, the stair turret rising several feet higher than the rest of the battlements. In South Devonshire there are two or three cases, as at Harberton (Fig. 164), where fine towers are by no means improved by placing the projecting turret in the centre of one of its faces.

Occasionally the towers were crowned with beautiful spires, as at St. Michael's, Coventry (Fig. 30), or in the wondrous aspiring effort at Louth, Lincolnshire, and emphatically in that district more grand with town and village spires than any other

164. HARBERTON, DEVON

area of Christendom, the county of Northampton, wherein the fifteenth century strove its best not to be outrivalled by the splendid efforts of its predecessor. In this Midland shrine

165. LAVENHAM, SUFFOLK

[*Drawn by A. E. Newcombe*

Perpendicular is of such supreme interest, both in fine and in comparatively simple churches, that it is a difficult task to name the most interesting examples. The whole church of Brampton Ash, save the chancel, is a notable instance of the beginning of the period, with a remarkably good, though not enriched, tower and lofty broach spire. King's Sutton possesses a singularly effective tower crowned with a most graceful spire. The noble spire of Kettering, fairly late in the style, taken in conjunction with the tower that it supports, is as good and impressive work of the date as can be found anywhere in the kingdom.

As to Perpendicular work throughout a church in this county, Ashby St. Legers, is a good instance. In this case the tower is somewhat earlier than the rest; its completion was, however, speedily followed by the rebuilding of the body of the church; this was accomplished by John de Catesby, who died in 1437.

The church of Islip in the same county may be regarded as a complete and almost model fabric of a good village church of moderate size, c. 1475.

The clerestory over the nave arcades was as a rule multiplied all over England, save in Cornwall and other parts of the West, and roofs lowered in pitch. The splendid high-pitched roofs, gloriously carved and painted, occasionally met with in Norfolk and Suffolk are an exception. Elaboration of treatment of the occasional fine ranges of clerestory windows is well illustrated in the grand Suffolk church of Lavenham (Fig. 165). The battlements of this church, with the pierced panels partly filled with a Tudor flower, are richly treated. The porch also of Lavenham is an admirable example of the elaborate treatment of porches of this period, especially in East Anglia; the heraldry is illustrative of the alliances of the De Vere family, and the bears in the spandrels of the entrance are the supporters of the De Vere shield. This church, one of the very finest of the Perpendicular period throughout the kingdom, was built between 1480 and 1530 by John De Vere, Earl of Oxford, and a local family of clothiers named Spring, whose arms appear both inside and outside the fabric.

The parapets of this style, though usually embattled after a plain or panelled fashion, are occasionally pierced with tracery after an attractive manner, especially in Somersetshire. The beauty of the church and tower at Winscombe (Fig. 166) and at Wrington (Fig. 167) is much enhanced by the light nature of the parapet; Oxbridge affords another good example, but

194   ARCHITECTURAL STYLES IN

the same cannot be said of the coarser pierced quatrefoil work of the tower of Fairford, Gloucestershire (Fig. 168).

The continued sameness in much Perpendicular work is an occasional drawback. Early in the style this was due in no

166. WINSCOMBE, SOMERSET   167. WRINGTON, SOMERSET

small degree to the battalions of pressed masons and builders' labourers marshalled for the King's work in consequence of the scarcity of workmen after the Black Death. They were supplied in batches by sheriffs of various counties, and learnt the then current rules of their trade under King's clerks, of whom William of Wykeham, the future renowned bishop, was

THE ENGLISH PARISH CHURCH 195

one of the most distinguished. Although this and other causes tended to the stereotyping of patterns and designs,

168. FAIRFORD, GLOUCESTERSHIRE
[*From a drawing by J. C. Wickes*

there were nevertheless essential differences up and down the country, shortly to be noticed, which were well maintained throughout the whole period.

196 ARCHITECTURAL STYLES IN

169. THE SOUTH NAVE ARCADE, LAVENHAM, SUFFOLK

The old Cambridge Camden Society, the "Glossaries" of Parker, and many a later writer on English Gothic have united in depreciating Perpendicular work as a distinct form of decadence from the previous pointed styles. Happily a certain reaction is now setting in amongst wider-minded and more reflective students, towards a due appreciation of the often stately and dignified outcome of the last stage of our homeland Gothic. Cleaving closely to the estimate already expressed as to the attainment of the summit of English Gothic architecture in the Geometrical period of the last part of the thirteenth century, we still hold strongly that there is more, at all events for the Churchman, to admire in Perpendicular work—for religion should above all be orderly and disciplined in its expression—than in the sensuous exuberance of the Decorated period.

It is sometimes vaguely imagined that Perpendicular, or the last expression of English Gothic, came to an end with the close of the fifteenth century. But this is by no means the case, for there are many dated church fabrics, of distinct value, which were erected in whole or in part in the later years of Henry VII or in the earlier years of Henry VIII, and this, too, was the very period when many of the finest of the later rood-screens were erected. The steeple of Louth, the superb tower of All Saints, Derby, the village church of Piddletown, Dorset, the tower of St. Neots, Hunts, and the best part of the grand church of Lavenham, Suffolk (Fig. 169), are all of Henry VIII's time or subsequent to 1500. Among church work of Henry VIII's reign may be mentioned the steeples of Mayfield, Staffordshire, and Oughton, in the East Riding, the chancel of Darton, in the West Riding, the south chapel of Collumpton, Devon, and the whole churches of Barton-under-Nadwood, Staffordshire, Great Panton, Lincolnshire, and Whiston, Northamptonshire. The last of these was built in 1534 by Antony Catesby, lord of the manor; it is a fabric of distinct interest and value. Nor should the last church of the reign be omitted, namely, that of St. Michael-le-Belfry, York, which was rebuilt between 1535 and 1545, and is excellent of its kind; but the present chancel and western bell-cote were added last century.

It is a complete though popular mistake to suppose that interest and zeal for parish churches were waning shortly before the repression and pillage of Henry VIII and Edward VI. To this idea both churchwardens' accounts and wills offer flat contradiction. For instance, a study of Henry VIII wills in the Northampton Probate Office has brought much information on this point to light. Rebuilding or considerable repairs were in progress at Whiston in 1526, at Rothwell in 1528, and at Hazelbeach in 1527; the building or substantial repairing of the steeple of Wold church was in progress from 1512 to 1519; the aisle of St. John Baptist at Kettering was building in 1512; a new porch was being built at Moreton Pinkney in 1520; and the middle window of the south aisle of All Saints, Wellingborough, was in process of reglazing in 1530.* The same story is repeated on a still larger scale wherever the old records have been consulted, as in Somerset, Yorks, Kent, &c.

170. WOODHAM WALTER, ESSEX

There was far less church building and less maintenance of church fabrics during the time that Elizabeth was on the throne than in any other half-century since the reconversion of England in early Saxon days. The Essex church of Woodham Walter was built by Thomas Earl of Essex in 1562-63; it consists of chancel, nave, north aisle, north porch, and western

* "Parish Churches of Northants as illustrated by Wills," by Rev. Dr. Cox, *Arch. Jour.*, lviii. 113-32.

wooden belfry with shingled spire (Fig. 170). The building is of brick with freestone facings, and closely follows the Late Gothic lines of the earlier part of the sixteenth century, with-

171. HANLEY, WORCESTERSHIRE
(*After the Rev. J. L. Petit*)

out any classical or Renaissance feature save that the gables of both the body of the church and the aisle have corbie or crow steps. It presents quite a comely appearance. Considerable Elizabethan repairs were done to the tower and chancel of Hanley, Worcestershire, after a rather debased fashion (Fig. 171). Boughton church, Northamptonshire, is sometimes cited as an example of late Elizabethan building; but this is a blunder, for the tower was considerably repaired in 1589, whilst the body of the church was rebuilt and enlarged in 1806, and again at a later date. There was much costly Renaissance building in England during Elizabethan days, but this was chiefly confined to the great houses for the more wealthy and the nobility and statesmen. When Sir Christopher Hatton erected the vast pile of Holdenby House, about 1582-84, with John Thorpe as his architect, much beautifying was done to the adjacent parish church. This included an imposing classical chancel screen, a manorial pew, and a fine Renaissance south doorway;

172. HOLDENBY, NORTHANTS

but a thoughtless restoration in the seventies of last century ejected screen and pew, and destroyed the doorway. The screen was eventually replaced, but in a mutilated condition (Fig. 172).

The rebuilding of our parish churches during the first half of the seventeenth century, after the upset of the Reformation period had in a considerable measure subsided, was frequently undertaken, and is well worth closer attention than has hitherto been given to it. A few of the more interesting instances may be just named: Arthwest, Cumberland, 1604; Fulmer,

THE ENGLISH PARISH CHURCH 201

Bucks, 1610; Stane, 1620, and Passenham, 1626, Northants; Baddesley Clinton, Warwickshire, 1634; Bletchley, Bucks, 1637; and Carrington, Derbyshire, 1648. A highly remarkable example of an effective instance to maintain Perpendicular traditions occurs at Staunton Harold, Leicestershire (1653).

Hampshire possesses some excellent classical brickwork of this century, notably in the towers of Odiham, 1647 (Fig. 173), and of Crondall, 1658; strange to say, in neither case do these towers, good of their kind, clash in any marked degree with the earlier work of their respective fabrics.

173. ODIHAM

Kent is perhaps the premier county for good church work, mainly classical, of the seventeenth century.* The following are its chief manifestations up to 1650: St. Nicholas, Rochester, 1620; Groombridge church and Ashurst porch, 1621; St. Nicholas, Plumstead, c. 1622; St. Botolph, Northfleet, 1628; Culpeper chapel, Hollingbourne, 1638; Charlton, 1640, a

* See a good article by Mr. Tavenor Perry in "Memorials of Old Kent," 1907.

fine, good example in red brick; and Plaxtole, 1649, an excellent reproduction of Late Gothic.

Middlesex used to be possessed of a really good example of seventeenth-century church brickwork, and it is still stately in a ruined and ivy-wrapped condition. The lofty embattled tower of the church of Stanmore was consecrated by Laud when Bishop of London. He says in his diary: "1632, July 17th, Tuesday, I consecrated the church at Stanmore Magna in Middlesex, built by Sir Jo. Wolstenham." At the trial preceding the Archbishop's martyrdom egregious charges were made that he outdid Popery itself in the consecration of chapels. One of the three instances alleged was that of "a chapel of Sir John Wolstenham's building." To this particular charge Laud replied that Stanmore was no chapel, but a parish church. Neither historical interest nor architectural value availed to preserve the church, and though in good preservation, it was ruthlessly destroyed, in 1849, for a pretentious successor of imitative fourteenth-century design.*

After the Restoration, a certain degree of vigour was shown in the repair or rebuilding of damaged parish churches, as at Compton Wynyates, Warwickshire, where there is a curious jumble of semi-Gothic and semi-Palladian styles. But the most interesting structure of this period is the church of Foremark, Derbyshire. Foremark and Ingleby were two adjacent ancient chapelries of Repton. At the Restoration both these chapels-of-ease were in too ruinous and decayed a condition to serve for any kind of worship. In 1662 Bishop Hacket consecrated a new church at Foremark to serve for both chapelries. He suffered the whole of the old chapel of Ingleby to be demolished on the condition that the whole of the stonework and timber were to be utilized in the building of the bell-tower and churchyard wall of Foremark. This demolition is justified in the official instrument inasmuch as the ruins would only serve if suffered to remain as *trophæum*

* See Dr. Cox's article on "The Ancient Churches of Middlesex" in "Old Middlesex," 1909.

temporis et approbrium negligentis incuriosi avi. This small church of St. Saviour consists of chancel, nave, and low west tower, and is of a debased Gothic style; there is no structural chancel division, but there is a remarkable high oak screen with large glazed openings. The altar is a large slab of grey marble resting on a wooden table.*

Other somewhat notable parish churches of Charles II's reign are those of Ingestre, Staffordshire, 1676; Mornington, Herefordshire, 1679; and St. Mary Aldermary, City. The last of these was rebuilt by Sir Christopher Wren, in imitation of its late Perpendicular predecessor. Wren, in his forty-nine City parish churches rebuilt after the Great Fire, paid special attention, in the majority of cases, to the interiors. Of later country parish churches of this century, two Warwickshire examples may be named, Billesley and Birmingham, both of the year 1692.

From the beginning of the eighteenth century the Italian mode prevailed in the building or rebuilding of parish churches to the exclusion of all that pertained to the latest form of Gothic or Tudor. Mr. Bloxam, in his section on the "Debased English Styles," gives a fairly long list of such churches. Here very brief mention may be made of four of the most remarkable examples of this century, none of which are named in that list.

When the Canon estate of the Middlesex parish of Whitchurch or Stanmore Parva came into the hands of James Brydges, Duke of Chandos, in 1710, he immediately began to build a vast and vulgarly ostentatious mansion, on which he squandered money without stint. In 1715 he took in hand the church, pulling down the whole of the body of the fabric and rebuilding it on classic lines. It now consists of chancel, nave, south porch, and northern mausoleum.

"No expense was spared in the beautifying of the new church. The best of materials and the best of artists were employed, with the result that the whole is still striking and

* In Dr. Cox's "Churches of Derbyshire" (1877), vol. iii. 443-45.

pleasing of its kind, though marred by recent tasteless interference. The ceilings and walls of the church are entirely covered with paintings." *

The mischief done by would-be improvers in 1897 and 1905 is most lamentable.

In a few other exceptional cases, when parish churches were for the most part in a sad state of neglect, and not infrequently

174. THE CHANCEL PANELLING, NORTH MOLTON, DEVON

of squalor, special repair was done to the sanctuary, the best work of the period being used in the interior. A striking instance of this is the Devonshire upland church of North Molton. The panelling of the east end of the church, with its elaborate seventeenth-century ornamentation, is well set forth in the illustration (Fig. 174).

The best example of admirable Georgian work of the eighteenth century is to be found in the chancel of St. Paul's Walden, Hertfordshire. The wooden screen at the entrance of the chancel has a central and two side openings divided by

* See full account by the present writer in "Memorials of Old Middlesex."

fluted Corinthian pillars, with richly carved entablatures, from which spring three circular arches (Fig. 175). Over the central arch is a pediment with elaborate finials. The walls of the chancel are panelled in delicately carved work, painted white, and at the east end is a lofty reredos with a central round-headed recess—the east window blocked at a modern restoration—flanked by Corinthian pilasters, whilst over the recess is a pediment enclosing the Book of the New Testament surmounted by a burning heart (Fig. 176).

The retired country church of Wolverton, in the north-east of Hampshire, was rebuilt on a cruciform plan, but with substantial western tower, in 1717,

175. THE CHANCEL SCREEN, ST. PAUL'S WALDEN, HERTFORDSHIRE

after a classic style, in red brick with stone facings (Fig. 177). The whole treatment of this village church is most effective, and the warm tones of the building are well set off by the surrounding growth of varied timber. The harmony of its proportions is somewhat marred by the obtrusion of a high-pitched gable between nave and chancel, but this was caused by the raising of the sound timbers of the old fifteenth-century roof, in their entirety, over the nave. This church is, so far as we know, the sole instance of its kind in an

English village, and was originally a masterpiece of good classic treatment on a small scale, both in fabric and fittings. But the restoring mischief-makers could not leave it alone,

176. THE CHANCEL, ST. PAUL'S WALDEN

and in 1872 did grievous injury both inside and out. The circular-headed windows were actually divided up, after a vulgar fashion, with brick mullions to procure a quasi-tracery effect. In the interior the fine projecting west gallery was thrown down; the good wrought-iron chancel gates were turned out into the churchyard; and the well-executed vase-font of right proportions was utilized as a flower-pot,

THE ENGLISH PARISH CHURCH 207

giving way to a feeble Gothic successor absolutely unsuited to the building. In 1905 it was much damaged by fire. In 1725 a classic body was united to the grand tower of All Saints, Derby. However incongruous, the new work was excellent of its kind. It was designed by Gibbs, the architect

177. WOLVERTON, BASINGSTOKE

of the Radcliffe Library and of St. Martin-in-the-Fields, Westminster. The great feature of the interior was the iron screen-work from the master-hand of Bakewell, but this and much of the rest of the fittings were grossly maltreated in an ignorant restoration of 1873.

The beautifully situated and well-timbered estate of Ossington, Nottinghamshire, was purchased from the Cartwright family in 1780 by William Denison, a wealthy wool merchant of Leeds and a man of considerable taste. The parish church, under the shelter of the Hall, was in bad repair, and Mr. Denison at once caused it to be rebuilt throughout after an effective classical design. The estate remains in the same hands, and the church is happily not only in excellent order, but has been preserved from any material interference.

The celebrated Horace Walpole in the latter half of the eighteenth century considered the idea of bringing about a Gothic revival. He set an example on his Strawberry Hill property in domestic Gothic between 1760 and 1770; Walpole succeeded in creating a furore for so-called mediævalism, but his own imitations of Gothic were poor and trivial, and for the most part retained those characteristics when introduced into church building. Amongst efforts of this character may be mentioned Combe d'Arbitot, Worcestershire, 1763; Tetbury, Gloucestershire, 1781; East Norton, Leicestershire,

178. ST. CHAD'S, SHREWSBURY

1783; Carlton, Northamptonshire, 1758; and Leek Wootton, Warwickshire, 1792. An interesting late example of a less trivial character was the rebuilding, with the exception of the fourteenth-century tower, of the little country church of Popplewick, Nottinghamshire. Throsby, in 1795, found this church in process of rebuilding, "in a very elegant Gothic style." The somewhat imposing church of St. Chad, Shrewsbury, was built after a severely classical design in 1792 (Fig. 178).

After this brief general survey of the successive styles that can be studied in English parish churches during the lapse of thirteen centuries, it remains to remark, before proceeding to the discussion of plans and main types, that the particular charm of most of our parish churches is that they consist of a patchwork of different periods. The very worst kind of restoring church architect—happily they are now rarely to be met with, and where found are rendered comparatively innocuous by a saner public opinion—is the able man who is absorbed in the beauties and perfections of a particular style—let us say, for example, the Early English. A fine old parish church in such hands may be thus treated, though originally a delightful medley in stone of local church history through half a score of sovereigns' reigns. The south transept, let us say, has a particularly fine five-light late Perpendicular window, with fragments of coeval glass in the upper tracery beneath its obtusely pointed Tudor head. There are some stately large Early English lancets in the chancel. The architect, enamoured of these designs, sets out a clever triplet of lancets and—if the funds are abundant—suggests that "the painfully debased transept window" should be removed in favour of his pretty sketch, and the roof pitch raised. The rector and his committee, overawed by the big man's name and impressed by the prettiness of the sketch, consent. One parishioner, of more knowledge than his fellows, offers a vain protest. The church-breakers are set vigorously to work. In pulling down the end of the transept several hidden fragments of undoubted mouldings of thirteenth-century Early English window-jambs come to light. The architect produces these in triumph, the objector is crushed, and the least intelligent of the committee regard the great man in hushed awe, as akin to a magician. Had the objector known a little more, he would have gone to the heap of dislodged masonry, turned up a stone or two closely marked with Norman axeing and another perchance bearing Saxon tooling, and told the architect that there was just as much justification in giving transept windows of the days of Athelstan or Stephen as those of Henry III. And this is exactly the kind of thing that went on in a score or two of highly interesting parish churches in the mid-Victorian epidemic of rash restoration, when many a period was obliterated to satisfy the ideal fancies of some would-be purist.

It is useless, however, to cry over spilt milk. Let us rather triumph in the fact that so many ancient churches have, after all, come comparatively scathless through the stormy times of senseless obliteration. Let us rather rejoice that in every county of England there is an abundance of old parish churches which, when carefully studied, yield memories of the art and the devotion of many a generation of our forefathers. Notable examples occur at Burford, Oxfordshire, and Bredon, Worcestershire, but you may select them almost at haphazard. But let us take Bredon as an example of a diversified church of a fair size, and Chaldon, Surrey, of one of small dimensions, and see what they have to tell us in the fewest possible words.

The parish church of St. Giles, Bredon (Fig. 179), consists of a large chancel, central tower, nave with short aisles of two bays, and north porch. Originally erected about the middle of the twelfth century, it retains a west front flanked by two square stone-capped turrets, a north porch with room over it, three doorways, and the west of the nave, all of good Norman work. The porch is groined; the room above can only be gained by a ladder. In the Early English period a short aisle or chapel was added on the south side of the nave, with trefoil-headed lancet lights, having slender detached marble shafts within. The chancel is a fine example of Decorated work of three bays, with excellent tracery in the seven windows. The chancel arch is Decorated, but the western or belfry arch of the tower is Norman. The south aisle of the nave is of like date and style with the chancel. The central tower, with a light and graceful octagonal spire, rising to a height of 160 feet, is also Decorated. In the Perpendicular period a good five-light large window was inserted at the west end of the nave over the Norman doorway. In the chancel, on the south side, are a triple sedilia and a piscina, with a low side window behind the piscina, and a curious slab with a crucifix and the busts of a man and wife under canopies. On the north side is an un-

THE ENGLISH PARISH CHURCH 211

179. BREDON, WORCESTERSHIRE

inscribed tomb with a richly ornamented and crocketed arch
and an almonry to the east of it. The tower is separated from
the nave by a low wooden screen. In the south aisle is a
sumptuous monument, with recumbent effigies, to Giles and
Katherine Reed, both of whom died in 1611. On the chancel

floor is a black marble slab, with brass inscription, mitre, and shield, to Dr. John Prideaux, Bishop of Worcester, who died here in 1650.

The small church of Chaldon, on the Surrey Downs, is best known for its wonderful west-end wall-painting of early thirteenth - century date, known as the "Ladder of Salvation"; but there is much more of interest. The church was originally Early Norman, consisting of chancel and nave, and of this period the west wall and a single small light remain (Fig. 180). Towards the end of the Transition period, c. 1200, an aisle was added on the south side of the nave, and a chapel on the same side of the chancel. About 1225 an Early English aisle was added on the north side, and a chapel (now no more) to the north of the chancel. In the Decorated days, about a century later, the two-light windows of this aisle were inserted and other changes made. The east window of the chancel and the chancel arch are Perpendicular, c. 1460. The south porch, with half-timbered gable, is early sixteenth century. There are many traces of subsequent repairs. The present tower and spire are comparatively modern. Note also (1) plain piscina in east wall and traces of two others; (2) Easter sepulchre, north side of chancel; (3) fragments of old thirteenth and fourteenth century glass in south chapel; (4) font of local firestone, thirteenth century, but altered; (5) handsome pulpit, inscribed "Patience Lambart, 1655"; (6) a

180. CHALDON

THE ENGLISH PARISH CHURCH

remarkable Renaissance tablet, 1562, with striking inscription, beginning: "Good redar warne all men and women whil they be here to be ever goode to the poore and needy," and (7) in the steeple the oldest bell in the county, certainly not later than 1250, inscribed *Campana Beati Pauli*.

Surely England should be proud of the possession of such composite historical buildings as these two churches of Bredon and Chaldon, representative of hundreds of others of equal interest. The latter is not of special beauty or of any magnificence within and without to attract the ordinary wayfarer, but to the man of intelligence it displays striking links between the past and the present.

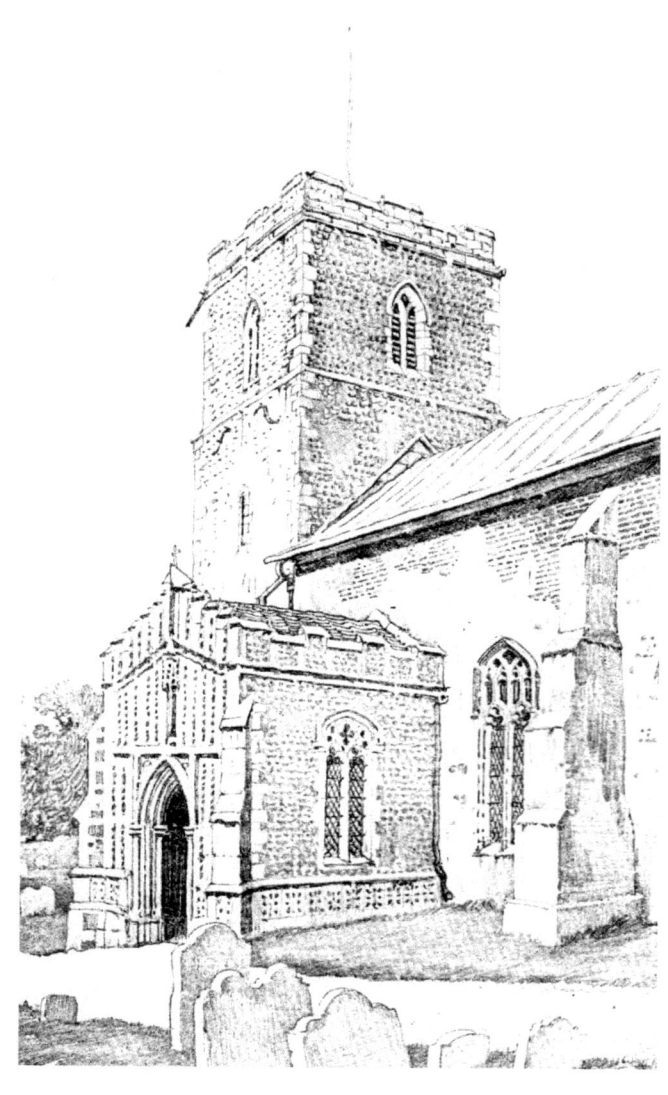

181. VARIETY IN MATERIAL: BADINGHAM, SUFFOLK
[*Drawn by A. E. Newcombe*

CHAPTER IV
MATERIALS
STONE

ALTHOUGH, as we shall presently see, churches were constructed of timber both in early and late pre-Conquest times, the general rule for Saxon churches was that they should be constructed of stone. In Bede's account of the illustrious Cedd at Lastingham, it is stated that he was first buried in the open air, but that in process of time a church was built of stone and his body interred in the same to the right hand of the altar. In the same writer's account of the construction of the oratory or small chapel at Lindisfarne, it is mentioned that it was made of rough stones. In the elaborate accounts of the building in the seventh century of the churches of Wearmouth and Jarrow (Fig. 182) by Benedict Biscop, it is expressly stated that they were built of stone after the Roman manner. When Wilfrid was made Bishop of York in 669 he found the stone walls of his church half ruined. After restoring it, he built the stone churches, fine for their time, of Hexham and Ripon. This must suffice to establish the existence of stone buildings soon after the reconversion of England to the Faith; but numerous other instances, some of even earlier date than those cited, could be readily supplied.

Saxon churches of stone, of a superior character both in design and craftsmanship, abounded towards the close of that period, after the brutalities of the Danish invaders had for the most part subsided.

For the reason that it furnished so large an amount of the stone that was used in the best-known examples of pre-Norman

216 THE ENGLISH PARISH CHURCH

ecclesiastical architecture, the place that demands primary mention is Barnack.

182. JARROW

The most important subdivision of building limestones is the Oolitic, so called because a broken surface resembles when magnified a conglomerate of small globular eggs. The best example of oolite was the stone from these prolific Barnack quarries in the north of Northamptonshire; they were in constant use in mediæval England, but have been long since exhausted. These once famous quarries furnished material for the masons of the great monastic houses and churches of Peterborough, Crowland, Thorney, Ramsay, and Norwich, and also afforded stone for the best parochial churches in the adjoining counties. This very durable stone was used in the Holland Division of Lincolnshire, in such noble churches as those of Boston (Fig. 183), Donnington, Gedney, Gosburton, Holbeach, Kirton, Moulton, Pinchbeck, Spalding, and Whaplode. It was also used, with striking effect, among the stately marshland churches of Norfolk between Wisbeach and Lynn, and in the fine Cambridgeshire churches of Over, Leverington, and Fen Ditton. In fact, Barnack stone penetrated wherever water-carriage rendered its transit feasible.

Second only to Barnack in merit and appreciation among

MATERIALS

Midland mediæval builders were the Rutland quarries of Ketton, an inferior oolite. This stone was used in most of the Cambridge colleges, at Bury St. Edmunds, and largely in the churches of Stamford (Fig. 184), and in those of its own immediate district; it is also occasionally found at greater distances, as in Essex and on the coast of Suffolk.

The Normans brought with them not only their Romanesque art of church building and masons to carry it out, but also, to no small extent, the stone which they were so accustomed to work from the great quarries round Caen. They were, however, sufficiently clever to adapt themselves to circumstances, and soon found that such an importation on any large scale was unnecessary, for the land of their conquest was in many parts well supplied

183. ST. BOTOLPH'S, BOSTON

184. STAMFORD ST. MARY

with workable freestones. Thus the Norman masons in remote Cornwall at an early date began to ply their hand-axes in dressing stones from the quarries in the parishes of Worbstow and Landrake, or from those of surviving local celebrity known as Polyphant and Pentewan. Their work in these stones can readily be followed in surviving remnants in the churches from one end to the other of this most western shire. The importation of Caen stone in reasonable quantities long continued to the stoneless counties of Norfolk and Suffolk, or in such coast counties as Kent and Sussex, when rubble or rag-stone required facings and quoins of a better and more workable material.

MATERIALS

Several of the best of the notable series of East Anglian fonts of the fifteenth century were formed of Caen stone. One of the finest of these stands in the church of East Dereham, Norfolk. The Churchwardens' Accounts of that parish for the year 1466 show that the stones for this font, and for the steps or risers on which it stands, were carried in seven loads from the quay at Lynn at a cost of 19 shillings.

The Churchwardens' Accounts of St. Mary, Sandwich, for this same year have many interesting entries relative to the rebuilding of the steeple. The facings were chiefly of stone from Caen, but partly also from the still-used quarries of Beer, on the coast of South Devon, whilst the ordinary walling was of Kentish rag.

Spendit on the mason of Crystchirche for to have an ynsyght yn the Cane [Caen] stone for the stepill	v d.
For v ton of Cane stone	xxv s.
For iiij of bere [Beer] stone for the stepill	xx s.
For vj ton and j pip of Folston [Folkestone] rag	vij s.

Sussex supplies instances of the use of Caen stone even in pre-Conquest days, as at Sompting and Ford, and also in the bas-reliefs from Selsey, now in Chichester Cathedral. After the Conquest its use in Sussex churches, especially near the coast, is frequent, as at Broadwater, Climping, Old and New Shoreham, Steyning, and West Wittering. Its use in this county died out after the middle of the fourteenth century, save for tombs, in favour of stone from the Brinstead quarries, in the Isle of Wight. It can be readily distinguished from Caen by its coarser texture and greenish colour.

The poet Lydgate tells us, when writing of the building of the great abbey of Bury St. Edmunds in the eleventh century, that Abbot Baldwin, in addition to stone from Barnack, used:

> Ston brought from Kane out of Normandy,
> By the se and set upon the strande
> At Ratlysdene, and carried forth by lande.

Rattlesden, nine miles from Bury, is about twenty miles from Ipswich with its port on the Orwell estuary. There is now but a little brook at Rattlesden; but drainage has much altered the surface of this part of Suffolk since the days when stone-laden barges could penetrate so far inland.

But even in districts well equipped with their own stone Caen stone, if near the seaboard, was occasionally transhipped down to the close of the Gothic period. Thus in Cornwall the church of St. Mylor, on the actual verge of the sea, with a small quay abutting on the churchyard, has a fifteenth-century arcade of Caen stone, whilst up the river to Truro a block of Caen stone was transhipped to be sculptured into a handsome Late Perpendicular font, and other large blocks to form a pulpit. About the same time another supply of Caen stone reached Egloshayle, up the Padstow estuary, on the north coast of Cornwall, to make a pulpit. These are the only two old stone pulpits in Cornwall. Caen stone is more compact in texture than Bath stone, and therefore more fit for delicate carving; but it does not stand the climate so well as freestone of local origin.

185. UFFORD, SUFFOLK

The constant use of Caen stone in Norfolk and Suffolk, to produce what is known as flush-work (Fig. 185), throughout the fifteenth century, is explained in the subsequent remarks as to flint. In short, so long as mediæval church building continued to thrive in England there was a steady, though not

MATERIALS

considerable, commercial demand for the freestone of Normandy along our eastern and southern shores.

Meanwhile the Norman masons were adapting themselves to the magnesian limestones of Tadcaster, used in the minsters of York, Beverley, and Ripon, and in the groups of parish churches around them, or to those of the Anston and Bolsover Moor quarries, as used at Southwell. After a like fashion this process of stone selecting of the best local quality went on throughout the different parts of England.

186. BLACK MARBLE FONT AT ST. MARY BOURNE, HAMPSHIRE

In the twelfth century the blue and black marbles of Belgium began to reach our shores to serve for memorial slabs, and more especially for expensive and attractive fonts. Seven of this beautiful series of fonts survive, namely, in the cathedral churches of Winchester and Lincoln, and in the parish churches of East Meon; St. Michael's, Southampton; St. Mary Bourne (Fig. 186); St. Peter's, Ipswich; and Thornton Curtis—all places easily accessible by water. From this comparatively trifling circumstance great results followed in the use of English building materials, a change, as will afterwards be seen, which had no small share in shaping the dawn of Gothic architecture. Just as the importation of the fine Caen stone brought about the discovery and use of homeland freestones, such as those round Bath and in a score or two of other places, so the importation of a comparatively few slabs and blocks of costly dark marble from Tournay aroused a wholesome jealousy to find local substitutes. It must, too, have been known to travelled masons that a certain custom was beginning to spring up between France and the Rhine of using detached shafts of Belgian marble in the nooks of light stone piers. The result of this English anxiety and activity was the discovery and use of the beautiful dark marble of South Dorset, which soon gained so great a repute under the name of Purbeck. About 1170 activity began among the masons of the Isle of Purbeck, and by the end of the century shafts for beautifying the larger of our parish churches as well as the great cathedral and monastic churches, together with blocks to be carved into fonts and certain ornamental details, had made their way to many distant parts of England, and were generally dispersed before the thirteenth century had made much headway.

Purbeck, on the sea-coast, had exceptional facilities for water carriage; nevertheless distance added not a little to its price, and price, combined with local jealousy and ingenuity, brought about the discovery and use, as Mr. Prior points out, of various fairly successful substitutes in different parts of the kingdom. The marblers, in this respect, proved their ability in seeking out fresh materials after the fashion set them by the white-stone cutters.* Although Purbeck marble had reached Durham as early as 1160, the spotted black marble of Frosterly was soon in use throughout Durham and Northumberland; Forest marble was the substitute used at Lincoln and elsewhere; Somerset used the Langport lias; whilst Kent discovered her own marble at Bethersden, and Sussex a quarry at Petworth.

Among the more noteworthy building stones of the thirteenth century and later developments, special mention should be made of the Doulting oolite, still largely quarried near Shepton Mallet, the creamy tones of which produce so charming an effect on the west front of Wells Cathedral, and added so much to the beauty of many a Somerset church; of the other noted Somersetshire quarry of Ham Hill, from which stones

---

* *Marmorarii* and *alborum cissores* appear as distinct craftsmen in the thirteenth-century accounts of Westminster Abbey.

were carried great distances on pack-horses to supply the dressed work of the churchyard crosses of further West Somerset ; of the various developments of Bath stone at Box and Corsham, in Wiltshire ; of the ancient quarries on the Devon coast at

187. DOULTING, SOMERSET

Beer ; of the best of the oolite freestone at Chilmark, which supplied the stone for Salisbury Cathedral and for many of the fine churches of Wiltshire ; of the famed Ancaster stone of the Kesteven Division of Lincolnshire ; and of the quarries round the Abbey of St. Mary of Quarr, Isle of Wight, which supplied the building stone for Winchester Cathedral and for various churches on the mainland.

Mention, too, should be made of inferior stones, such as the soft form of limestone known as clunch or chalk used so effectively in the interior of Norwich Cathedral, and found in the window tracery as well as in minor details in churches of Cambridgeshire, Essex, and other counties, but unsuitable for

224   THE ENGLISH PARISH CHURCH

external use; of the harder chalk quarried from the Downs of both Sussex and Surrey; of varied sandstones which soon

188. KILKHAMPTON, CORNWALL

became honeycombed or perished, as witnessed in the Cathedral of Chester and many former churches of that county and

MATERIALS

Lancashire, and of the warm-toned but perishable nature of so much of Lichfield Cathedral; of the Kentish rag so useful as a second-class stone for church walling, as proved within its own limits, and exported for tower building in the south of stoneless Essex; and of the Totternhoe quarries of Bedfordshire, the stone of which was once in much repute and used largely in that county and Hertfordshire, but eventually proved to be unfitted to withstand the weather.

With regard to Cornish granite, the earlier mediæval builders avoided any general use of a material unsuitable for work requiring high finish or delicacy of treatment.

189. ST. MARY MAGDALENE, LAUNCESTON

But, when a wave of church rebuilding and extension swept over the county in the fifteenth century, there was a general resort to this abundant local material. The granite then widely used for arcading was "moor stone," or blocks found lying near the surface of the open moor. Great mechanical skill was used in the necessary hewing, polishing, and shaping of this hard grey granite. The monolith piers of the granite four-centred arcades of the fifteenth and early sixteenth centuries are marvellously alike wherever they occur, being in clusters of four shafts with plainly moulded capitals. They are to be seen in about 90 per cent. of the old Cornish churches; the illustration of the interior of Kilkhampton (Fig. 188) may serve as an example.* The church of St. Mary Magdalene, Launceston (Fig. 189), built entirely afresh of granite between 1511 and 1524, is most profusely and ingeniously covered throughout the exterior with coarse sculpture.†

When we talk of a plan in connexion with a building, as in this chapter, we really mean the ground-plot or ichnography, but it is also quite legitimate to use the word in its primary significance as a scheme, a form, or a model. Looked at from this point of view, the roofing of a church is a most essenial part of its plan.

The subject of roofs divides itself into two branches—stone and wood, of which the latter is dealt with in the section of this chapter on Timber. The former, owing to its permanency and the effect it had on the general structure, is the more important in any general discussion on Gothic architecture. In fact, the whole story of the evolution of Gothic architecture on a grand scale is bound up with vaulting schemes, for buttresses, flying buttresses, and weighty pinnacles all came into being to resist the outward thrusts of the vaulting at given points where the ribs of the groining intersect. But all this mainly pertains to the erection of great cathedral, monastic, or collegiate churches. In the vast majority of cases English parish churches know nothing of stone roofing, and where it is found, save in a handful of cases, it only affects the roofs of small portions of the building, such as porches and tower basements, occasionally chancels or chapels, and still more occasionally the narrower forms of aisles. The treatment, therefore, of vaulting in such a book as this need only be brief and cursory.

The simplest and oldest form of stone roofing is the semicircular or barrel vault, springing from two opposite walls, and

* The noble and richly sculptured tower of St. Austell is not granite, as usually stated; it is a hard vein of Pentewan stone throughout the exterior but lined with granite.

† As to the use of Cornish granite, see Dr. Cox's "Churches of Cornwall," pp. 6-10, 21-22.

presenting a uniform concave surface throughout its length. Vaults of this kind were much used by the Romans, and were by them introduced into this country. They also were the first to employ cross-vaulting, a term descriptive of the intersection which occurs at the crossing of two semicircular vaults, the intersecting edges forming the groin.

There are barrel vaults to the early Saxon crypts of Ripon and Hexham; the much later Saxon roofing of Repton crypt is partly groined and partly segmental. The porch of Monkwearmouth is the only instance of Saxon vaulting now extant above ground.

190. STOWE, LINCOLNSHIRE

Examples of vaulting with stone are fairly common in the Norman period. Quadripartite vaulting was the customary church form, at first with plain groins, and afterwards with ribbed groining. The ribs at the beginning were square, then chamfered, next they had rolled edges, and finally the diagonal ribs were embellished with the chevron or other characteristic mouldings. All the Norman crypts have quadripartite vaults. Among Norman vaulted chancels may be named those of Stowe, Lincolnshire (Fig. 190); Darenth, Kent; Compton, Surrey; St. Peter's, Oxford; Easton, Hants; Cassington, Oxon; Elkstone, Gloucestershire; Warkworth, Northumberland; and the fine square-ended chancel of Hemel Hempstead.

Semidomes or coved roofs occur in various of the Norman apses, as at Checkendon and Swincombe, Oxon, and Kilpeck,

191. ST. MARY'S, GUILDFORD

Herefordshire, illustrated in the chapter on "Styles," Fig. 113. The late Norman apse of the beautiful little Derbyshire church of Steetley has roof ribs ornamented with beak-heads, uniting in the centre in an Agnus Dei medallion. The groining ribs of Iffley chancel bear the chevron ornament. It was quite exceptional for the aisles of a parochial church of this period

MATERIALS

to be vaulted. Traces of their former occurrence have been noted in two or three churches; at St. Peter's, Canterbury, there is an actual fragment of the groined aisle vaulting yet extant.

The late Norman chancel of Tickencote, Rutland, is the only example of a parish church with sexpartite Norman vaulting. The only

192. NEW SHOREHAM

193. THE CHANCEL, MINSTER, ISLE OF THANET

other English instance of this sexpartite vaulting is in the choir of Canterbury. The tower of Icklesham, Sussex, has late Norman vaulting.

To the Transition period belong the vaulting of chancel and nave of Lastingham, York; of the quire and aisles of Shoreham (Fig. 192), of the chancel of Broadwater, of the chapels off the transepts of Sompting, and of a chapel at the end of the south aisle of St. Anne, Lewes, all in the county of Sussex. The apsidal chapels and the chancel vaulting of St. Mary, Guildford, are also of the same period (Fig. 191). There are still two bays of remarkably fine quadripartite vaulting, with dog-tooth moulding on the ribs, on the chancel of Crondall, Hants, c. 1190.

In the Early English style, when the pointed arch was firmly established, the like form was given to the vaulting. Simple groining ceased and ribs were invariably employed. Except, however, in the great churches, there was but little vaulting during the thirteenth century. The chancel of Stoke d'Abernon, Surrey, is a beautiful example of early thirteenth-century vaulting, and so, too, is the original Early English framing of the fine chancel of Minster, Isle of Thanet (Fig. 193). The low chancel of Havant, Hants, is well vaulted with chalk groining ribs, springing from Purbeck shafts, somewhat later in the century. Burpham chancel, Sussex, is another instance of Early English vaulting. The vaulting of the central towers of Chipstead, Surrey, and of Kingston-on-Sea, Sussex, are also Early English, and so, too, are the vaults of the crypts under the chancel of Bamborough, Northumberland, and under the south aisle of Bosham, Sussex. The stone groining of the

194. ST. MARY, REDCLIFFE

MATERIALS 231

chantry of the south transept of Rye is of the same period. The basement of the tower of Saltfleetby All Saints, Lincoln-

195. CHANCEL, NANTWICH

shire, has considerable remains of former thirteenth-century vaulting.

In the fourteenth century the vaulting, as a rule, followed

the simple quadripartite form, especially in the great cathedral and monastic churches of the North of England. But in the South and West of England additional connecting ribs, termed liernes, were introduced; this produced a more complicated effect, though it did not make much structural alteration. This system of net vaulting was further developed in the next century. Large churches such as St. Mary Redcliffe (Fig. 194), Ottery St. Mary, and Patrington (Fig. 271) and Nantwich (Fig. 195) were vaulted wholly or in part. The Decorated chantry chapel, separately gabled, on the north side of Willingham church, Cambs, has a high-pitched stone roof, the vaulting of which is supported on ribbed arches after an original design. The north transept of Limington church, Somerset, is another example of high-pitched ribbed vaulting. There is interesting advanced fourteenth-century vaulting to the "Flemish Chapel" of St. Mary's, Beverley.

The Perpendicular period of the fifteenth century produced vaulted roofs more complicated in detail, owing to the increase of the groining ribs; they frequently spring at various angles, forming a diversity of geometrical panels or compartments; but examples are almost entirely confined to great churches. The basements of various towers of this period are vaulted, especially in the South of England, as at St. Clement's and All Saints, Hastings, and Carisbrooke and Shorwell, Isle of Wight. Perpendicular porches, too, were often ceiled with good groining, especially if they carried an upper chamber. Good instances occur at Worstead, Norfolk; Southwold, Suffolk; Long Sutton, Lincolnshire; and Southminster, Essex. Even in Cornwall such groining is shown in the porches of St. Creed, St. Juliot, Landewednack, and North Hill.

It was in this century, too, that the most beautiful and most essentially English of all forms of stone groining for vaulting came into being. Towards the end of the fifteenth century and the beginning of the sixteenth century this form of curved and expanding ribs, termed fan-vaulting, came to marvellous

MATERIALS 233

development.* It can be equally applied to such a diminutive vault as that of a chantry chapel in Oxford Cathedral, or to the vast high vault of King's College Chapel, Cambridge; it had also the great advantage of exercising but little thrust, and that thrust could be entirely concentrated upon the points of support. The grandest displays of fan-vaulting occur in great cathedral or abbey churches with which we have no concern. But it is to be found in certain parish churches in much beauty and perfection: over the Lane aisle of Collumpton, Devon, and the Dorset aisle of Ottery St. Mary; over the south porch and over St. Catherine's Chapel, Cirencester; the Lichfield chapel at Ely; All Saints, Evesham; the Wilcote chapel, North Leigh, Oxon (Fig. 196); the porches of Burford, Oxon; Torbrian, Devon; Hillesdon and Maids Moreton, Bucks; Spalding, Lincoln; and Bodmin, Cornwall; and in several Somerset towers, of which Wrington and Axbridge may be taken as examples, and Highworth tower, Wilts.

196. NORTH LEIGH, OXFORDSHIRE

* The dawn of it is considered to have occurred in a small and ignoble form in the monument at Tewkesbury to a Sir Hugh Despencer and wife, *c.* 1350, but the earliest complete fan-vaulting dates from 1412. See a most admirable and profusely illustrated article on "Fan-Vaults," by Mr. F. G. Howard, in the *Archæological Journal* of March 1911.

FLINT

Flint, as distinct from building stone, plays a very important part in English church architecture; it is but rarely used in

197. THORPE-NEXT-HADDISCOE, NORFOLK

198. HADDISCOE, NORFOLK

any part of the Continent. Flint is one of the hardest and most enduring products of Nature; it is nearly pure silica, and consequently defies time, weather, or the hardest of usage. The drawbacks to its more general use are twofold, namely, the smallness of the size in which it is found, and the impossibility of carving its surface. Flints, when regularly quarried, are found in the chalk, and can be obtained in fairly large size and regular form; but the smaller ones more commonly used occur in other geological formations, particularly in gravel, and are found scattered over alluvial soils. In almost all parts of England where there are chalk downs the use of flint in

MATERIALS

church building is of common occurrence. But it is in East Anglia that its use is so continuous as to put stone or any other material completely in the background. The building flints of Norfolk and Suffolk were, in the first instance, mostly gathered from the seashore or from the surface of the fields. The small, simple churches of the days of St. Felix in the seventh century, and of his immediate successors, would probably be constructed of the surface flints or seashore pebbles. The earliest of these church fabrics disappeared before the fierce onslaughts of the bands of pagan Danes who so constantly harried East Anglia in the ninth century.

It is possible that some of the round towers of East Anglia were partly constructed as a defence or place of refuge if such onslaughts were continued.

199. HERRINGFLEET, SUFFOLK

A few of these towers, about which there has been so much discussion and conflict, are possibly even ninth century, whilst about thirty are certainly pre-Norman. These round towers are everywhere built of flints or sea pebbles, with an occasional use of general rubble, and bonded together with an abundance of mortar. They are without staircases, and were obviously built to serve as belfries. The circular form, once adopted, naturally commended itself to the intelligence of the builders, for in the stoneless regions of Norfolk, Suffolk, and parts of Essex the expense and labour of bringing and working stone quoins for the angles—essential in square towers — were avoided. Irrespective of ruined portions, the round towers of Norfolk number one hundred and thirty, and those of Suffolk forty.* There are also seven in Essex, three in Sussex, two each in Cambridgeshire and Berkshire, and solitary examples in Northamptonshire and Surrey. The round tower of St. Peter Forncett has already been given as an example of Saxon work. In the case of Thorpe-next-Haddiscoe (Fig. 197) the lower stages of the tower are indubitably Saxon, and the upper stage, with double belfry lights, Norman. Herringfleet, Suffolk, round tower, though much altered in Norman days, shows its Saxon origin in the east belfry window (Fig. 199).

200. BRADFIELD, NORFOLK

* For full lists, &c., see Dr. Cox's " County Churches of Norfolk," i. 4–9, and Mr. Bryant's " County Churches of Suffolk," i. 20.

MATERIALS 237

A fair amount of undressed flint walling, especially in Essex churches, when taken in combination with the use of Roman tiles, is of pre-Norman date; but the use of this material throughout East Anglia, and in other parts where chalk abounded, continued in rubble form until towards the end of the fourteenth century. The earliest use of what may be termed dressed or gauged flint can be traced back in a very few instances to the reign of Edward III; so also is Haddiscoe, Norfolk (Fig. 198). Thus at Bradfield, Norfolk (Fig. 200), the chancel shows regular faced flint-work, the date of which is supposed to be c. 1340. But in the great majority of cases wherein such flints are used with advantage on anything like a large scale, they occur subsequent to the middle of the fifteenth century. Thus the highly elaborate example of St. Peter Mancroft, Norwich, was finished in 1455; whilst in Suffolk, Long Melford was begun in 1450 and Southwold

201. THE TOWER, EYE, SUFFOLK

in 1460, and Walberswick was built between 1472 and 1493. The exceptionally fine tower of Eye (101 feet) was built by the parishioners in the days of Edward IV (Fig. 201). Saxmundham was finished in 1483, and the aisle and porch of Wetherden in the same year. To improve the look of flint walling, the first step taken was to gauge or select them in sizes, arranging them in rough courses. The next advance was to break the

202. WORLINGWORTH, SUFFOLK

flints and use them either in courses or otherwise. The third step was to split the stones with greater care to obtain a fairly even surface, removing in all cases the white or yellowish-white coating so as to present a dark or glossy black appearance.

Coeval with this third step came the introduction of that exceedingly graceful ornament of the East Anglian churches which is usually termed flush-work. It is not known how the idea of the flush-panel and diaper work of split-flint and stone first came to be used, but, having once started, it appears to have spread with great rapidity and multiplicity of design throughout the two East Anglian counties. It partly originated through

MATERIALS 239

the expense of carrying the Caen stone across the seas in any large quantities, and by the ingenious device of cutting these blocks of freestone into thin slabs its use was much economized. The flints formed the panel or centre work of the pattern, whilst the stone on the same face, without any moulded work, and not even raised from the surface, formed the margin, or division, between the panels. This style of work began in comparative simplicity, as in the case of the Suffolk porch of Ufford (Fig. 185) and Worlingworth (Fig. 202), but ere long the enrichment of the porches in flush-work was much elaborated, as at Framsden (Fig. 203). The towers also soon began to be invested with this special form of ornament, of which the west front of the tower of Southwold is a remarkable example (Fig. 204). The tower parapets were specially rich in detail of this kind, as in the Suffolk churches of Walberswick and Long Melford. Among the best examples of flush-work porches may be named those of Reddenhall, Bunwell, Halvergate, and East Dereham, the two Pulhams, in Norfolk; and those of Southwold, Halesworth, Blyth, Ford, and Mendelsham, in Suffolk.

The particular emblems characteristic of the dedication of

203. FRAMSDEN, SUFFOLK

the church were frequently introduced into the ornamental work of the plinths and battlements of the tower. Thus the church of Burlingham St. Andrew has crosses of that apostle; St. James's, South Repps, the cockleshells; St. Mary's, North Repps, and St. Mary's, Erpingham, crowned M's; St. John's, Coltishall, chalices; St. Michael's, Cressingham, crowned M's and erect swords with wreaths; St. George's, Saham Toney, G and M; SS. Peter and Paul, Fakenham, crowned P's; SS. Peter and Paul, Griston, crosskeys and swords; and St. Laurence's, Hunworth, L's and gridirons.

204. SOUTHWOLD, SUFFOLK

The pattern on the tower plinth is occasionally continued round the body of the church, as is the case at Martham, Norfolk. The parapets of the body of the church, and also the face of the clerestory between the windows, are occasionally subject to this beautiful treatment, as at Tunstead, Norfolk, and at Coddenham, Bacton, and Earl Stonham, Suffolk (Fig. 205). In a few cases the whole exterior of the church is richly treated after this fashion, as in the cases of St. Peter Mancroft and St. Michael Coslany (Fig. 206) Norwich.

The proportion of churches in Essex built of flints with stone dressings is very large, whilst flints are used for the

MATERIALS 241

walling in quite two-thirds of the old churches of Surrey, though sometimes mixed with stone rubble. There is but little use of dressed flint-work in the latter county, but at Esher, Leatherhead, and Mickleham there is a little chequer-work of flint and stone.

In Sussex the ordinary walling of most of the coast churches is formed from seashore flints or pebbles; also in some of the west and central parts of the county flints are commonly employed in the walls, either dug from chalk or gathered from the fields. The fine cruciform church of Poynings, 1360-70, has some excellent squared and coursed black flint-work, and the tower of Steyning, c. 1535, is in chequer-work of flint and stone.

205. EARL STONHAM, SUFFOLK

It may also be mentioned that a certain amount of this chequer-work exists in East Anglian churches, as on the west face of the tower of Southwold (Fig. 204). The nave walls of the small church of Wittlewood are of alternate courses of brick and flint, and at Cliffe, Kent, there are alternate bands of flint and stone.

Flints are largely used in the chalk districts of Wiltshire;

and in Berkshire, where good stone is scarce, there are many churches which are built chiefly of flint and chalk.

It is unnecessary to go through all the shires as to the proportion of flint walling in the churches, but Hertfordshire, destitute of any good building stone, ought not to be omitted. All the old churches are built of stone or flint rubble, in which the latter considerably predominates, whilst in some of the later instances the walls are faced externally with split flints. There is, however, an entire dearth of flush-work, though here and there are a few examples of flint and stone chequer-work. The Churchwardens' Accounts of Exning, Suffolk, yield evidence of the collecting of surface flints when repairs were necessary. The following entry occurs in 1590:

206. ST. MICHAEL COSLANY, NORWICH

> Paid to Sparrow of Moulton the furste day of Maye for gatheringe of ten lodes of flinte stones for the Church wall xxijd.

An earlier entry in the account of North Elmham, Norfolk, shows that child labour was employed when the chapel of St. James was being added to the parish church:

> To ye scolers for bred and drynk when they gathered stones ijd.

BRICK

In one of the earliest of Sir Gilbert Scott's lectures on the "Rise and Development of Mediæval Architecture" there is an eloquent passage descriptive of the extraordinary facility with which ordinary materials of varied character were converted, in the hands of Gothic builders, into structural beauty :

"No material was either too rich or too rustic to find an honoured place in the works of these truly Catholic builders. The varied marbles of the Apennines, the polished amethysts of Bohemia, the glass mosaics of the Byzantines, with gold and silver, enamel, brass and iron, were all brought under tribute to make their richer works glorious ; yet they were equally at home in the use of brick, or flint, or rubble, and did not despise even a homely coating of plaster, if only it were honestly and truthfully used."

With regard to the mediæval use of brick in church fabrics, although there is much more of this in England than is usually supposed, especially in the county of Essex, our own country was far behind many parts of the Continent in its beautiful adaptation to such purposes. Particularly was this the case in the Low Countries, North Germany, and all round the shores of the Baltic. For the most part it attained to its fullest use and finest development in districts that were destitute of useful building stone. But this was by no means always the case ; Mr. Tavenor Perry has pointed out that brickwork overran even such stone-producing countries as Sweden and Norway. In the Hansa town of Bergen the two churches were of brick ; Upsala Cathedral is mainly of brick ; and the later additions to the west fronts of the churches of Linkoping, Lund, and Orebro are wholly in red brick. The same writer has also pointed out that the influence of the Hanseatic League, during the fourteenth and fifteenth centuries, exercised a strong influence in the direction of the general employment of brick in civil and domestic work as well as in church fabrics. Hull was one of the important Hansa towns of England, and here we find that not only were the town walls of Kingston-on-Hull refaced with brick, but that the same material was also used in the construction of the vast church of Holy Trinity in that town. Another most important port of that part of our sea-

207. SANDON, ESSEX

board was King's Lynn. There the Franciscan church was of brick, and the interesting chapel of the Red Mount on the outskirts of the town is of the like material.

When Edward IV restored the forfeited privileges of the Hanseatic League in 1474, after they had been in abeyance for some thirty years, there came about a remarkable and almost complete displacement of stone in favour of brick throughout the London district, and more particularly on the Essex or northern side. Of this change, at a somewhat later date, the gateway of Lincoln's Inn, 1518, still bears witness in the heart of the city. The study of Continental brickwork as applied so extensively to churches in various parts of the Continent is one of great interest, but it is not possible to follow it up even in outline in these pages.*

* See "Brickwork in the Middle Ages," by G. E. Street, the *Church Builder*, 1863, 1864, 1866; "The Mediæval Brickwork of Pomerania," by

MATERIALS

More particular attention will be immediately drawn to the comparatively small amount of pre-Reformation church brickwork in different parts of England; but it may here be remarked that this material was laid very largely under contribution in much of the English work of the latter part of the seventeenth and eighteenth centuries. Red brick was also frequently used by Wren, mostly in the unseen parts, when rebuilding the churches of the City after the Great Fire; it was, for instance, exposed to view a few years ago in the quire vaulting of St. Paul's Cathedral, when Sir W. Richmond began his mosaic decorations.

Mention has already been made of the frequent use of Roman bricks in English church building.

208. FEERING, ESSEX

It has often been stated that the art of brick-making in this country died out with the Romans, and that it was not resumed until early in the fifteenth century, when it was supposed to be reintroduced by Flemish workmen. Such a notion, however, is quite erroneous. Late thirteenth and early fourteenth century brickwork, almost certainly of local make, exists in the East Riding of Yorkshire and in other parts. Essex, through its

J. Tavenor Perry, Trans. Roy. Inst. Brit. Arch., 1873; "The Influence of the Hanseatic League on Architecture," *ibid*. 1894; and "Mediæval Architecture of Sweden," *ibid*. 1891.

lack of stone, stands first among our counties for the use of church brickwork, as it also does for timber-work. At St. Nicholas' Chapel, Coggeshall, there are thirteenth-century arches of moulded brick, and it is at least possible that the

209. GREAT BADDOW, ESSEX

three-light brick lancet window at Ongar is also of that century, though somewhat renewed.

In domestic architecture the date of brickwork of Little Wenham Hall is 1266. Towards the close of the fifteenth century brickwork became common in the church fabrics of Essex. In fact, in the days of Henry VII and Henry VIII brick was the usual material in this county for either church building or repair. Fine effects of a massive character, involving a number of special mouldings, were produced in brick in both tower and porches. There are twenty-one old brick towers, the best of which are to be noted at Fryerning, Ingatestone, Rocheford, and Sandon (Fig. 207). At the last

MATERIALS 247

of these churches the massive tower has several St. Andrew's crosses in black brick, and on the west side two great Latin crosses. Other towers also show diapered work.

It may be here remarked that the colour of bricks is determined by the proportion of hydrated oxide of iron and other ingredients contained in or artificially mixed with the clay, and also by the degree of heat in burning. It was the latter expedient which was used in the production of the black or dark-coloured bricks of the later mediæval period in England. The introduction of lime to produce a creamy brown seems to have been then unknown.

There are a fair number of brick porches, the best of which are at Great Baddow, Feering (Fig. 208), and Sandon. The clerestories of Great Baddow (Fig. 209) and Castle Hedingham are effective instances of the use of this material. Occasionally there is cunningly devised window brick tracery and good hood-moulds, as at Little Bursted, Chignal St. James, Feering, Mount Bures, and Sandon (Fig. 210). In several cases the whole church is of brick, as at Chignal Smealey, East Thorpe, East Hornden, North Fambridge, Kelvedon Hatch, Layer Marney (1520), Topsfield (1519), and Woodham Walter

210. WINDOW, SANDON, ESSEX

248   THE ENGLISH PARISH CHURCH

(1564) (Fig. 170); or the nave is in this material, as at Feering (Fig. 211). The church of St. Osyth (Fig. 212) has some fine brick arcading of late fifteenth-century date.

211. FEERING, ESSEX
[*Drawn by J. L. Griggs*

There is also a great deal of church brickwork of both seventeenth and eighteenth centuries.

The next county to be considered in connexion with this material is Norfolk, though it is destitute of the really noble examples to be found in Essex. At Shelton there is a noteworthy church of brick throughout; it is a specially interesting example, as it is known to have been built between 1495 and 1500. At Potter Heigham there is an excellently designed fifteenth-century porch in moulded brickwork; this church also contains a font of moulded brick. The brick porch of Repps is *c.* 1500. A fair amount of pre-Reformation embattled brick parapets may be noticed up and down the county, and bricks are also used in turning the window arches

MATERIALS

of some of the later clerestory windows. Apart from surface work, the church use of bricks in Norfolk was considerable throughout the fifteenth century. The unhappy number of ruined, or partly ruined, churches show that bricks were freely used in the unseen parts of stone or flint tower archways and windows. Fully a fourth of the inner walling of the fine lofty tower of South Walsham St. Laurence, which is half ruined, is formed of brick.

Repairs in brickwork occasionally produce quite picturesque effects, as is the case with the steeple of Downham Market, Norfolk, or in the tower and clerestory of West Theddlethorpe, Lincolnshire.

212. ST. OSYTH, ESSEX

There are several of the later mediæval stone towers still standing which are lined throughout with brick, as in the case of Chelmsford, or Clare, Suffolk. Suffolk possesses a certain amount of interesting work in this material. At Shaddingfield there is some good moulded brickwork in the south porch, and the like is the case with the porch of the old church of Melton, now only used for mortuary purposes. The porch of Great Ashfield is an exceptional example, for the moulded brickwork is inlaid with flints. The north porch of Great Bealings is of brick, c. 1500, with a niche over the entrance, and octagonal turrets at the angles. The graded or corbie gables of Rushbrooke

250   THE ENGLISH PARISH CHURCH

church and the headings of the windows are brick, and usually considered to be of Elizabethan date. Waldringfield has an embattled brick tower, whilst in several cases, as at Badley, Kesgrave, Holton, and Yedding, the upper stage of the tower is of brick. Hargrave has a sixteenth-century tower of this material, whilst the porches of Bayham; Meesden, Herts; and Onehouse are of late brick.

The south chapel of Mapledurham, Oxon (Fig. 213), is a striking instance of excellent brickwork, *c.* 1600; it was constructed as a chapel for the Blount family, and contains a monument to Sir Richard Blount, 1619, and wife.

213. MAPLEDURHAM, OXON

Middlesex possesses a few good examples of pre-Reformation work in this material, such as the large porch of Tottenham, the clerestory of Littleton, and the north chapel of Isleham. In the last of these instances the moulded bricks of the windows still retain traces of the thin layer of plaster with which they were originally coated in imitation of stone. This thin plastering of brickwork is also to be noted in one or two Essex instances. The old church of Stanmore, Middlesex, erected in 1632, is a really splendid piece of effective massive brickwork, though now it is roofless, half ruined, and much buried in ivy. In the eighteenth century several Middlesex churches were rebuilt throughout in brick, the stone tower only being spared; the earliest instances of

MATERIALS

these are Isleworth (1705), Twickenham (1713), and Cranford (1716).

In Surrey bricks seem rarely to have been used till the middle of the sixteenth century. In the seventeenth century

214. OLD BASING, HAMPSHIRE

the church of Malden was rebuilt in brick in 1610, the church of Morden in 1636, and the tower of Wandsworth in 1630.

With regard to Sussex, Twineham, Thakeham, and Stonton have early sixteenth-century brick porches, and there is one of seventeenth century date at Ford.

Kent possesses a really grand tower of this material at Plumstead, with moulded brickwork for the cornices and window dressings. It is of early seventeenth-century date, with massive buttresses at the angles, and in both outline and proportion it is essentially Gothic. Charlton church, built between 1630 and 1640, is almost entirely executed in red brick. It has distinct merits, and, as Mr. Tavenor Perry writes, "taken as a whole, it is a not ungraceful composition or unworthy of so unique a position on the hill-top overlooking the river." Groombridge church was built of brick in 1621, whilst the church of Upper Deal has a massive tower of red brick with stone facings erected 1684.

Mention is subsequently made of the bricks inserted diagonally in the timber framework of the Hampshire church of Mattingley, of fifteenth-century date. This county has also much good seventeenth-century brickwork in the church fabrics, of which there are good examples in the towers of Basing (Fig. 214), Crondall and Odiham (Fig. 173), whilst Wolverton (Fig. 177) is a most noteworthy instance of a village church, erected in 1717. It has also been already noticed (pp. 205-7). The instances of early church brickwork of any particular interest are very few and far between in the Midlands or the North of England. Exception must be made in favour of the diapered brick tower of Edwalton, Nottinghamshire, which was built in the days of Queen Mary.

PLASTER

In considering materials, plaster demands brief mention. Though apparently an insignificant substance, made mainly of an admixture of lime, sand, and hair or straw, it played a really important part in English church building from the earliest days. Whatever church building there was in the times of the Romano-British Church, judging from the analogy of domestic and public buildings, it is quite safe to assume that they would be plastered in the interior. There were, indeed, traces of the use of a special kind of Roman plaster in the remains of the early church at Silchester; it was largely composed of pounded tiles, and was red throughout. Patches of smooth red plaster remain within the nave of St. Martin's, Canterbury. Plastering was a common and probably a normal finish to Saxon church walling. The wall face was set back on an average half an inch from the surface of the upright stones of the quoins, and the plaster of the small stones or rubble of the general walling was brought up flush with the edge of the corner-stones. The plaster has for the most disappeared from these churches, partly through weather and wear, but too often from ignorant removal. A certain amount remains at Escomb, Durham (Fig. 109), and Britford, near Salisbury. The tower of Sompting church, Sussex, is an excellent example by way of showing how the thin external plastering was applied. In this case the long-and-short quoins are regularly dressed so as to form a set-off to take the plaster. It must also be remembered that the Saxon churches invariably had an inner coating of plaster, which was sometimes a mere thin mortar dashing. It is to be noted in small patches in various churches, and was recently found at Corhampton, Hants, stamped with the pattern of a cross within a circle.

The early rubble walling of Norman days in different parts of the country was also for the most part plastered on the outside, after a fashion termed in later times rough casting. This, too, was the case with undressed flint-work, especially in Essex, but notably in Herts and Wilts, and, indeed, wherever flints were used. In the case of the interesting little early Norman church of Farly, Surrey, the intervention of Mr. P. M. Johnston was recently just in time to save the knocking off of the charming yellow-tinted twelfth-century exterior plastering, which was about to be done for the purpose, forsooth, of "showing the flints."

On the surface of the simplest and boldest of early Norman piers and other interior smoothed surfaces came a coat of thin plaster whereon were traced and coloured the fine distemper decorations and figure-pieces of the painters. This was the case not only in huge buildings such as Durham Cathedral, but in a great number of small parish churches. When Romanesque piers have been stripped for "restoration," whole series of twelfth-century paintings have been discovered, but they have usually been found only to be immediately destroyed. It is scarcely necessary to say that this system of plastering the interior walls of our churches, in all cases save the few which were dressed throughout in ashlar, prevailed to the very close of the Gothic period throughout the length and breadth of the land. The rough flint walling of the churches of many counties was covered with a thin layer of plaster, which produced an irregular undulating surface and gave a very charming effect. One of the most outrageous evils of the wholesale Victorian restorations has been the Philistine skinning of the inner walls so as to expose their intentionally hidden rubble anatomy. They were thus invariably plastered by their builders of the different styles, not only to conceal the jumble of broken stones and rubble, and to present a smooth surface for the work of the painter in distemper (not *Fresco*, as generally stated), but also for reasons of sweetness and cleanliness, the rough surfaces forming so inevitable a lodgment for dust and dirt. The destruction of this plaster skin has not only wrought immeasurable mischief to the story of church art and painting over a period of four and a half centuries, but has given a repulsive appearance to great surfaces of the walls of the Houses of God, such as would not be sanctioned for a moment in the dwellings of squire or parson, or even of the humblest cottager. One appalling instance of the hideousness of such a treatment may be here named, namely, that of the church of St. Just-in-Penwith, Cornwall, where the stripping has not only destroyed a highly remarkable series of wall-paintings, but has exposed surfaces of granite rubble, each atom of which has been emphasized by being outlined in black cement!

215. GRANTCHESTER, CAMBRIDGESHIRE

The tower of Grantchester, near Cambridge (Fig. 215), may be taken as a representative instance of the occasional

MATERIALS

plaster-coating of the exterior of fifteenth-century work. It is quite a mistake to assume, as is often the case, that external plastering of inferior masonry was unknown in the fourteenth and fifteenth centuries.

WHITEWASHING

The use of whitewash or colour-wash on the inner walls of churches is still popularly supposed to be a post-Reformation enormity. But the custom strongly commended itself to our ancestors throughout the whole period of church building. The whitewashing of large surfaces of inner walling, especially when too vast to admit of design or figure painting, was of general and continuous adoption. Eddius tells us how St. Wilfrid, when restoring York's ruined Minster, washed the walls whiter than snow. Five hundred years later Paul of Caen did the like at St. Albans.* Instances could readily be cited of each intervening century, from the white-liming of the Norman quire of Peterborough in the twelfth century down to the latest sacrists' rolls of the sixteenth century; but it will be best to give one or two specimen extracts from parish church accounts.

Notwithstanding the abundance of good mural figure and design painting, there were frequently large surfaces in our parish churches which, from their uneven surface or from lack of funds, were treated, from time to time, with the whitewasher's brush.

In the 1394 accounts of St. Michael, Bath, full record is made of the whitewashing of the church both within and without (*tam infra quam extra*); the lime cost 12.4d.

1482-3 (St. Edmund, Sarum). Et sol' circa dealbacione
pariet' capelle Sci Johis Baptist ex una parte Chori
ecclesie caipendo in toto   iiij s iiij d.

---

* When taking part in the excavation of Dale Abbey, Derbyshire, in 1876, I noted whitewash on many stones that had been buried three and a half centuries; and I also noted the same thing under like circumstances in 1893 at Walton Priory, E. R. Yorks.

1490 (St. Dunstan, Canterbury). Receyvid of the beqweth of Mother Bollyng to the whyte lymynge of the Churche — vj s viij d.
Payde to Wyllyam Ingram a bargain penny for the whyte lymyng of our Churche — j d.
Payde to the same Wyllyam for whyte lymyng of the churche — vj s viij d.

MORTAR

Just a word or two must be said about mortar, without a free use of which it would, of course, be impossible for stone or brick churches to stand. Not only the width of the mortar joints but the actual composition of the mortar are helps to the understanding of the dates of our earlier churches. The mortar of Roman wall work, instead of being a simple mixture of lime and sand, is often compounded with coarsely pulverized tiles. This colouring matter gives to the mortar a pink tinge, which is to be noted in parts of the masonry of St. Martin's, Canterbury, and in the Roman pharos adjoining the church of Dover Castle. The early mortar of the walls of St. Pancras, Canterbury, shows, however, in one place yellow colour, which was used in the beginning of the work, and in the later work white, with fragments of sea-shells. And yet in this most interesting historic building the material is re-used Roman brick, with the original Roman mortar still adhering in some cases to the surface.*

The mortar joints in Norman masonry offer some guide as to approximate dating. The early thick mortar joints begin to give way to thinner joints in the beginning of the twelfth century. The use of rough flint walling or of any form of outer rubble-work naturally involved a bountiful supply of mortar.

TIMBER

The earliest legendary account of a Christian church in the British Isles comes under the head of timber construction. The church of Glastonbury, so famed in after days for its progressive

* See Professor Baldwin Brown's "The Arts in Early England," vol. ii., and more especially his technical articles on mortar contributed to the *Builder*.

MATERIALS 257

splendour, originated in a small building of the humblest materials. William of Malmesbury relates how Joseph of Arimathea and his eleven companions came into Britain in the year 63, and obtained from the barbarous king a grant of land whereon the Abbey was afterwards raised. There, guided by the Archangel Gabriel, they built a chapel, the walls of which were made of twisted osiers.

The church of Greensted, near Chipping Ongar, Essex (Fig. 216), is the one building now standing in England which has the walls of the nave composed of the trunks of split oak trees of very ancient date. There is no reason to doubt that it is the actual building which sheltered the body of St. Edmund on its return to London from Bury St. Edmunds in 1013.

216. GREENSTED, ESSEX

This wooden chapel had probably been standing for a long period before it was used for this purpose. The special veneration attached to the memory of the great East Anglian Saint has secured its existence for nine centuries. The walls are formed of split trunks placed upright, with the curved side outwards. Though repaired in 1848–49, these walls may be said to be much the same at the present day as when they were used to protect the relics of St. Edmund in 1013.*

There is a remarkable and little-noticed passage in the Ramsey Pontifical of the end of the eleventh century denoting the possibility of a bishop being called upon to consecrate a church of timber. It is therein provided that if the church was of wood (*si vero lignea fuerat*), the antiphon *Vidit Jacob scalam* was to take the place of *Lapides preciosi*.

The record evidence of wooden churches during the Saxon era is fairly abundant, but there is little or nothing to show that timber was actually used for the walls of parish churches during the eleventh, twelfth, or thirteenth century. It is not until the close of the fourteenth century is reached that timber construction of this character is again met with, and in the first instance it was revived for the erection of towers or belfries.

Essex is the county wherein by far the most of church timber-work still survives; it is singularly destitute of any kind of building stone, and used also to be one of the best wooded of English shires. None of its now standing timber towers, spires, turrets, or porches appear to be earlier than the beginning of the fifteenth or the end of the fourteenth century. The main reason which brought about this somewhat sudden and general use of timber throughout Essex and in portions of several other shires at a given period was the almost feverish anxiety of the church-folk not to be outdone by their well-to-do neighbours in other parishes in the matter of rings of bells, which were then becoming so popular. Up to that period the majority of village churches had been content to be called to worship by a single bell, or perchance two, swinging in an open bell-cote on the west gable. The poorer parishes in the stoneless districts could not afford to build towers of masonry; hence this rage for belfries had to be satisfied after a cheaper

* For full details, descriptive and historical, as to this church, see article in the *Builder*, October 8, 1904, by the present writer. The logs are certainly oak, and not, as is sometimes alleged, chestnut.

MATERIALS

fashion. In the majority of such cases the parishioners were content to construct a fairly substantial oak belfry of squared timbers rising from the roof over the western bay of the nave, and of sufficient strength to carry four or more bells of average size. The question then arose as to how such a framework, with its swinging bells, could be safely supported. The simplest device, of which an example remains at Aythorpe Roothing, was to carry the belfry on horizontal beams resting on the wall plates of the nave. The far more usual plan, of which there are many Essex examples—as at Little Braxted, Doddinghurst, Laindon (Fig. 217), Mountnessing, Stondon Massey, and Thundersleigh—was to carry the supporting framework of the belfry and spire, often of considerable size, from the floor of the church inside the nave right up through the roof. The simpler examples of this treatment are where four great baulks of timber rise from the ground unconnected with each other; but the more general plan, to give greater strength, was to lock these baulks together by diagonal or straight cross-

217. LAINDON, ESSEX
Drawn by Ernest Godman

pieces ; or in the more elaborate examples to support them still further by buttresses extending to the nave walls, or even, as at Mountnessing, into the side aisles. In this last case the timber supports have a natural arch or elbow in them, to afford greater space for the unencumbered use of the aisles. In old days the timber-hewers in the forests set considerable store on oaks which had a natural bend or twist ; such elbowed timber was useful in roofing, and also for the ribs of ships.

218. BLACKMORE, ESSEX

The Essex churches of Laindon (Fig. 217), Doddinghurst, Horndon-on-the-Hill, Shenfield, and Stondon Massey are among the more remarkable examples of intricacy and elaboration of the timber framing within the nave. In the case of Laindon the framing within the nave is supplemented by a cunningly constructed two-storied timber priest's house at the west end. The belfry is strong enough to carry five bells.

In a few cases in Essex the more wealthy country parishes caused great timbered towers, surmounted by shingle covered spires, to be erected towards the west end of the naves, obscuring, as in the case of Blackmore (Fig. 218), a good west front of Norman date. Such towers are also to be found at Bobbingworth, Great Easton, West Hanningfield, Margaretting, Navestock, Ramsden Bellhouse, and Stock. To strengthen these lofty spire-crowned towers, the base or lower story was surrounded with arched or diagonal-framed beams, projecting outwards and covered with lean-to roofs, thus

MATERIALS

making on the plan the appearance of a narrow aisle or succession of small chambers all round the tower. At West Hanningfield these projecting supports assumed the form of a Greek cross.

Much skill was used in carving the tracery work of the windows of these towers, and in some cases of the mere belfry turret, following the fashion of the stonework of the period. Good instances of this occur at Blackmore, Stock, and Margaretting. The effective appearance of these timber towers has suffered materially during the cheap period of "Churchwarden" treatment. They are now usually covered with plain overlapping weather-boarding, applied horizontally and repainted from time to time, usually in white. The exterior of the lower story is, however, for the most part covered with wide oak boarding placed vertically. This latter arrangement is most likely original; but Mr. Godman considers, with much probability, that the structural timbers were intended to be shown on the outside, and that the intervening spaces were plastered, or filled with wattle-and-daub.

219. SHENFIELD NAVE, ESSEX

In addition to towers solely of timber, Essex has a number of cases in which old stone towers, for the better development of bell-ringing, were crowned in the fifteenth century with wooden belfries. Out of twenty-three instances, those of Little Baddow, Great Braxted, and Chrishall may be mentioned. In a still larger number of cases the complete tower of stone or brick is crowned with a spire or spirelet having a wooden frame, as at Chelmsford and Witham.

Essex also possesses some exceptionally good timber porches, chiefly of the latter half of the fifteenth century. The best examples are those of Margaretting (two), South Benfleet, Doddinghurst, Laindon, and Runwell (two). As to the interior use of timber in Essex, apart from roofs and doors, there is a fine arcade of timber, supported by piers of solid oak with well-carved capitals, between the north aisle and nave of the church of Shenfield (Fig. 219). At Masbury and Navestock the chancel arch is of timber, whilst at Rayleigh there is a like arch to the south chancel chapel.

220. SOUTH HAYLING, HAMPSHIRE

Wooden porches are by no means uncommon in the southern counties, and are occasionally found in the Midlands. There are notable examples at Horsmonden and Brookland, Kent ; at Warbledon and South Hayling, Hampshire (Fig. 220) ; and at Crowle (Fig. 221), Huddington, and Northfield, Worcestershire. There is also a fourteenth-century example of much beauty at Boxford, Suffolk.

Surrey is the county, next to Essex, in which there is a constant occurrence of timber porches. They are for the most part of fourteenth-century date, with well-cusped vergeboards. Among the best examples are those of Bisley, Elstead, Ewhurst, Merrow, Pyrford, Seale, and Wisley. Next in frequency are the wooden porches of Sussex, though in most

MATERIALS 263

cases they are of mixed timber and stone construction. The earliest examples are Barnham, West Chiltington, and Rustington, all thirteenth-century. Lurgashall has a peculiar early seventeenth-century narthex of timber, which extends along the south wall of the church, abutting against the tower at the east end.

In Surrey, which has always been one of the best-wooded counties, timber was used for church construction with a certain amount of frequency. It was by no means destitute, in parts, of decent building stone; but the roads were bad, and there was very limited opportunity for water-carriage, except along the northern bound-

221. CROWLE, WORCESTERSHIRE
NORTH PORCH

ary. A timber arcade has disappeared from the old church of Haslemere, and at Frimley a wooden plaster church was removed last century. In the south-east of the county are three old spire-crowned western towers of timber, all of fifteenth-century construction, at Burstow, Horne, and Newdigate; the inner framework of the last of these is most noteworthy (Fig. 222). About forty of the churches have wooden western turrets or belfries over the west end; in some cases they are of considerable dimensions, supported by huge beams resting on the floor of the church, as in Essex. The principal examples of this construction are at Alfold, Great Bookham,

Buckland, Byfleet, Crowhurst, Dunsfold, Elstead, Hawley, Tandridge, and Thursley. In the last case the timber tower, with well-moulded side supports, rises from the centre of the church.

222. INTERIOR OF BELFRY, NEWDIGATE, SURREY

In Sussex the instances of mediæval timber spires covered with oak shingles are numerous. They amount to about forty, and include the fine examples of Alfriston, Billinghurst, Bosham, Buxted, Cuckfield, Horsham, Lurgashall, Rotherfield, and Tarring. There are also many timber belfries surmounted by spirelets, as at Chalvington, Denton, Folkington, Wilmington, etc. Three towers with massive oak framework from the floor of the church, each crowned with a spire, remain at Itchingfield, Rogate, and Tangmere. The two former are of early fourteenth-century date, and Tangmere probably earlier. At Yapton (Fig. 96) and Lyminster are skeleton frameworks of oak, within the stone towers, to take the weight of the bells. At Selmeston is one of the rare instances of a timber arcade. It is of early fourteenth-century date.

There are a few curious instances of church timber in Kent, including several examples of shingle-covered spires supported by massive timbers within the tower. At Brookland is a remarkable detached octagonal belfry, 60 feet high, and constructed in three diminishing stages. At Wingham there is a timber arcade supported by tall octagonal oak piers. Kent

MATERIALS

has a variety of good timber porches, some of them of much beauty; that of Shoreham is a notable example (Fig. 258).

Middlesex, though stoneless for building purposes, was always well wooded. In the less populated rural parts of this small county, which were at some little distance from the convenience of water-carriage, timber was used for towers in the fifteenth century, concealing the older simple west front. Examples of this remain at Perivale and Greenford. In other cases of small towerless churches, they were content to erect substantial square wooden belfries, surmounted by small spires, as at Cowley, Ickenham, Kingsbury, and Northolt, supported in each case by great timbers springing from the floor.

In Hampshire the small late fifteenth-century church of Mattingley is entirely constructed of timber and brick. The body of the church is divided into *quasi* nave and aisles by four arches of well-moulded timbers, having side aisles which are but 6 feet wide; the walls are composed of squared beams of upright timbers with 7-inch intervals between them, filled up with diagonally placed thin bricks. In this county timber was

223. THE TIMBER FRAMING OF BELL-COTE, DIDCOT, BERKS

freely used in church construction of the fifteenth century in the north-east and other parts where wood abounded. There are examples of towers of wooden framework at Hurstbourne Tarrant, Michaelmarsh, and Rockbourne. The timber-work at Hartley Wespall is exceptional and noteworthy, particularly at the west end. There are a fair number of examples of square belfries of wood over the west bay of the nave, supported, as is usual, on four great baulks of timber formed from single trees.

224. WARNDON, WORCESTERSHIRE

There is not much church timber-work in the South-west, but it is occasionally met with in that beautiful district of West Somerset which includes the interesting small towns of Dunster, Minehead, and Porlock. In these parts stone lies near the surface, which is of a lasting character for all rougher forms of building; it is, however, quite unsuitable for use where mouldings or any kind of sculpture are required. When good stone was required for church doorways, window-frames, mullions, and tracery or battlements, the nearest available material had to be brought from the distant quarry of Ham Hill. Oak was fairly abundant in the beautiful combes and valleys; it was used in the well-known grand old rood-screens and carved bench-ends of this district, and occasionally in the actual structure of the churches. At Stoke Pero, in the wilds of Exmoor, the pointed south doorway is formed of two solid

MATERIALS

blocks of oak. At Minehead there is a rude arch of roughly hewn timber opening into the north-east chapel. The romantically situated diminutive church of Culbone (Fig. 21) has a two-light, square-headed window with cinquefoil heads made of oak; it is an almost exact facsimile of one on the south side made of Ham Hill stone.

Proceeding towards the centre of England, Berkshire may be noted as having several small churches with belfries supported on internal wooden framework. The shingled belfry tower, topped with a broach spire, at the west end of the south aisle of Didcot, Berkshire, is supported by a somewhat remarkable framework of strong timber, as illustrated by the charming old drawing about 1830 (Fig. 223). The church of Winkfield has a remarkable wooden arcade down the centre of the nave, dated 1587. The county of Worcester is noteworthy for a few cases of exceptional church timber-work. Warndon (Fig. 224) has a half-timbered black-and-white tower of three stages, which has a singularly domestic appearance. At Ribbesford the nave and chancel are divided from the south aisle by a wooden arcade supported by five octagonal oak piers. Besford is a small building of rubble and plaster with timber framing; the nave, apparently fourteenth-century, and the chancel probably earlier; at the west end is a square-headed two-light window with wooden tracery.

The most interesting use of timber in the churches of the well wooded county of Hereford is at Pembridge (Fig. 225), where there is a detached wooden belfry of late fourteenth-century date resting on an octagonal stone base. At Holmer there is another detached belfry tower, the upper part of which is of half-timber construction. The detached belfry at Yarpole consists of two square stages, the lower one of massive stonework, but the upper one of timber. There are also several shingled spires.

Shropshire, which abounds in beautiful instances of half-timbered domestic work, supplies an example of small churches or chapels of a like construction, at Melverley, of upright timbers with lath and plaster, dating from the fifteenth century. The church of Condover has a half-timbered gable to the south transept.

The county of Chester, as might be expected by those who know its wealth of half-timbered houses, supplies several

225. DETACHED BELFRY, PEMBRIDGE, HEREFORDSHIRE
[*Drawn by F. L. Griggs*

instances of churches of that style. Of these the church of Marton, a former chapel of Presbury, founded in 1343, is the most interesting (Fig. 226). It was of timber throughout, but considerably restored in 1850, and again in 1871. The framework chiefly consists of uprights, a short distance apart, banded

MATERIALS

226. MARTON, CHESHIRE

227. WARBURTON OLD CHURCH, CHESHIRE

270   THE ENGLISH PARISH CHURCH

together by a horizontal transom. The church of Siddington, which was also a former chapel of Presbury, was originally timber and plaster throughout. At present it is only the chancel which is of that construction, together with the south porch and belfry or square turret over the west end. At first

228. CHURCH AND PRIEST'S HOUSE, FLAUNDEN, HERTFORDSHIRE
[*Now demolished*]

sight the west front appears to be of an elaborate black-and white design, but this is merely a bit of modern painting. The old church of St. Werburgh at Warburton (Fig. 227) was at one time entirely of timber; the interior of both church and chancel affords remarkable examples of timber arcading. Nether Peover is the best-known example of an old timber church now extant, but it has to be remembered that it was so considerably rebuilt at the hands of Mr. Salvin in 1851-52 that it is practically a new building.*

In Staffordshire there are fine timber arcades in the church of Betley. At Rushton Spencer the church, built about 1360,

* For other remains of timber-framed churches of this county and for detailed descriptions of the ones above mentioned, see the article by Dr. Cox in " Memorials of Old Cheshire," 1910.

MATERIALS

is supposed to have been entirely of timber, and there are considerable remains in the interior. External half-timbered work also survives at Harlaston and Whitmore.

Flaunden, Herts, used to possess a most picturesque timber tower in the priest's house adjoining, as shown in a drawing

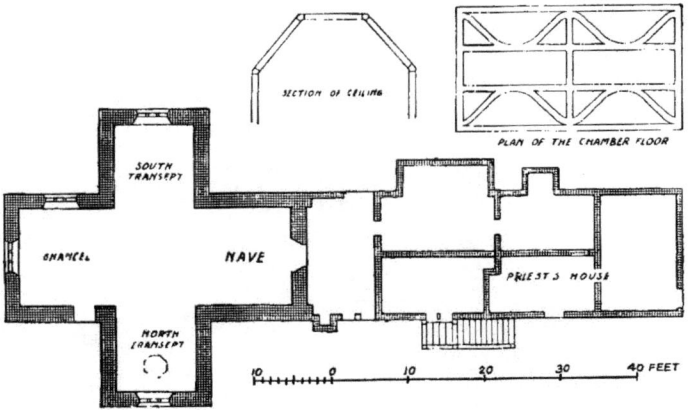

229. PLAN OF CHURCH AND PRIEST'S HOUSE, FLAUNDEN

of about 1825 (Fig. 228; the plan is shown in Fig. 229). It gave way, alas! to a modern church, which is claimed to be the earliest effort of Sir Gilbert Scott.

This brief summary of the more important remains of timber construction in the old churches of England must not be taken as exhaustive. Another instance should be just mentioned, namely, the large half-timbered church of Denton, a former chapelry of the once great parish of Manchester.

TIMBER ROOFS

As might naturally be supposed from their perishable nature, the very large majority of the timber roofs of our old parish churches are comparatively modern. Of Norman parish church roofing there is practically nothing left. It is, however, quite possible that some of the old woodwork in simple

272   THE ENGLISH PARISH CHURCH

early roofs, such as those of Burpham, West Chiltington, Ramsey, Lyminster, and Tortington, all in Sussex, may have certain Norman or Transition timbers incorporated in their present structure. The only undoubted Norman roof beam *in situ* which we have seen—and it is here noted in print for

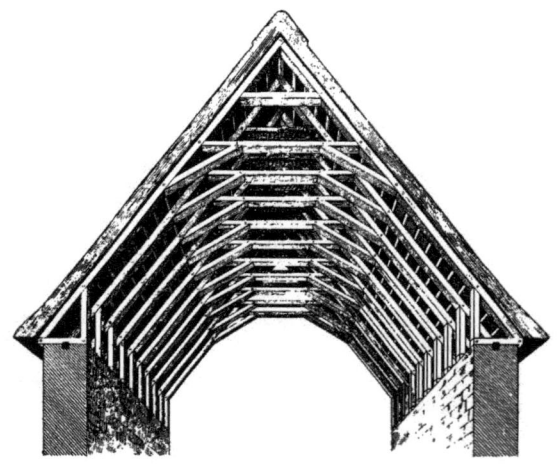

230. STOW BARDOLF, NORFOLK

the first time—is the beam over the east arch of the nave of Old Shoreham, which is ornamented with the alternate billet moulding. It has been stated, but it is doubtful, that the roof of Adel, Yorks, is Norman.*

It may safely be assumed that our Norman parish churches were tied together with great oak beams, resting on wall plates, and that from the plates rose simple trussed rafter roofs; in the better churches they would be ceiled beneath with boarding and painted, as in the cathedral churches of Peterborough and Ely. The main portions of the roof framing are termed trusses or principals; they are placed together at regular intervals, and in cases of early open roofs are sometimes rendered more or

* Assoc. Soc. Reports, xix. 110.

less ornamental. Various forms of trussed rafter roofs were erected as the outer covering of stone vaults.

With the Early English period came a change; the carpenter found it necessary to raise steeper roofs over the pointed vaultings of the greater churches, and the framings were of lighter scantling. By degrees the shapeliness and beauty of open ceilings grew upon their constructors' imagination as they came to roof in the unvaulted churches. The open thirteenth-century roofs were generally of high pitch and acutely pointed, and it was only occasionally that tie-beams were used.

A few fairly perfect examples of Early English roofs are extant, such as the roofs of chancel, nave, and aisles of Morborne, Hunts; the chancel of Overton, Hants; the nave of Hales Owen, Salop; parts of Binsted, Burpham, Lyminster, and Tortington, Sussex; and parts of Banstead, Chiddingfold, Fetcham, and Limpsfield, Surrey; and Stow Bardolf, Norfolk (Fig. 230). The nave roofs of Long Stanton, Cambs, and Filby, Norfolk, may be taken as good examples of the plain trussed rafter form. As to remains of thirteenth-century roofs, the following may be noted: nail-head ornament on timbers in the north aisles of Orston and Cromwell Bishop, Notts; on the wall plate of Up Marden, Sussex; and on the kingpost of Old Shoreham chancel.

Towards the close of the thirteenth century and the dawn of the fourteenth the custom came in of roofs of somewhat lower pitch, with arched braces below the moulded tie-beams. Excellent roofs of this construction, all about 1300, are to be noticed at Polebrook, Northants; Sparsholt, Bucks; St. Martin's, Leicester (Fig. 231); and Kiddington, Oxon. The geometrical designs that pierce the substantial braces at Sparsholt are especially effective.

Roofs of distinctly Decorated fourteenth-century character are not numerous. Dunsfold, Surrey, is a fine example early in the century. Another early one of exceptional interest is that of Starston, Norfolk (Fig. 232), with arched braces and moulded principals. Trotton, Sussex, has a very wide span, with

274   THE ENGLISH PARISH CHURCH

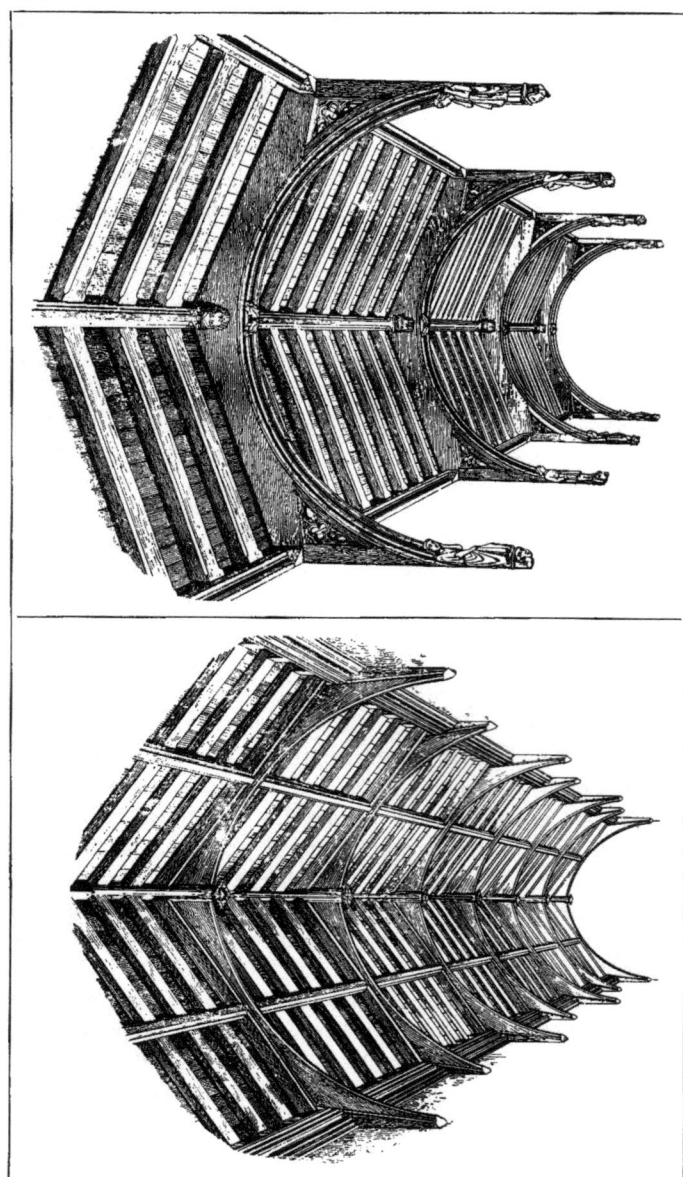

231. ST. MARTIN'S, LEICESTER

232. STARSTON, NORFOLK

MATERIALS 275

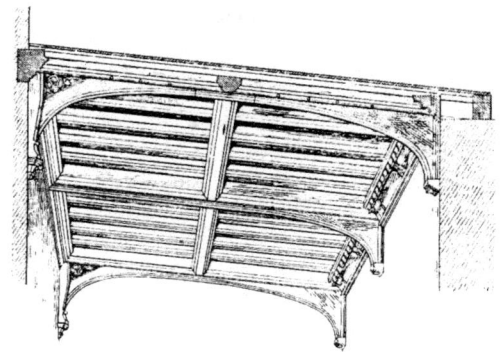

233. SOUTH AISLE, IXWORTH, SUFFOLK

arched principals, purlins and wind-braces. Bloxam adduces as good instances of Decorated roofs Byfield, Northants St. Mary's, Leicester; Adderbury, Oxon; nave of Higham Ferrers, Northants; north transept of Andover, Hants; and chancel of Wysall, Notts.

In the later years of the fourteenth century, and on to the close of the Gothic period, there came about a considerable change in the roofing of churches. In the large majority of cases the slope or pitch of the roof was considerably lowered, so that the form became more obtuse,

234. ST. NEOT'S, HUNTINGDONSHIRE

and sometimes approaches to actual flatness. The roofs of this style were supported by horizontal tie-beams resting directly on the wall plates, and supported below by comparatively small spandrels in place of the curved braces of earlier design; the actual roof is often divided into panel-work of intersecting timbers, as in the south aisle of Ixworth, Suffolk (Fig. 233).

Good examples of Perpendicular roofing can be found in almost every county. The whole system of diverse roofing of this date at St. Neots, Hunts (Fig. 234), has been justly described as of exquisite beauty; Buckden roofs, in the same county, are also notable. Bedfordshire has exceptionally fine fifteenth-century roofs at Marston Moretaine and at Dean. The tie-beam roof of Upwell, Norfolk, is relieved by finely carved angels, with wide expanding wings, rising from the wall plate. In Sussex, Billingshurst and East Dean have good panelled ceilings, whilst Friston, Suffolk, is a notably massive structure. The nave roof of Burwell, Cambridgeshire, is a fine example, with well-carved bosses and tracery pierced spandrels. One of the best roofs of Early Perpendicular in the South of England is the beautifully carved ceiling, *temp.* Richard II, of the north chancel chapel of Fordingbridge, Hants.*

There are two exceptionally fine late Perpendicular tie-beam roofs in Somersetshire, namely, at Martock (Fig. 235), and at St. Cuthbert's, Wells; in both cases angels with

* It is always insisted upon in that neighbourhood that the roof is of sweet or Spanish chestnut. This is a popular but baseless notion applied to a variety of good roofs. It may, however, be definitely stated that there is not a square inch of chestnut wood in all the old church roofs of England. The Spanish chestnut was not indigenous to England, and was a great rarity in mediæval days. Evelyn led many astray by giving a falsified annotation from Fitzstephen as to a great forest of chestnuts near London in the seventeenth century. The timber of the two indigenous varieties of English oak, *sessiflora* and *pedunculata*, is of different texture and grain. Whenever the so-called chestnut timber has been tested by experts, it proves to be the close-grained oak of the *sessiflora* variety. See "Royal Forests of England," pp. 70, 71; also *Arch. Journal*, 1858 and 1878, &c. There is a fond and oft-cited superstition that our ancestors chose chestnut wood because it is invariably shunned by spiders!

MATERIALS 277

expanded wings rest on the arches of the beams. There is another beautiful angel roof at Long Sutton, in the same county.

One of the simplest forms of Perpendicular roof was formed by the use of single kingposts from the centre of the tie-beams;

235. MARTOCK, SOMERSET

the Middlesex churches of Bedfont, Cowley, Harmondsworth, Northolt, and Perivale retain this plan.

At Cowley, where there is no chancel arch, the limits of nave and chancel are defined by bold open arcading of six timber arches between the tie-beam and the high-pitched kingpost-supported roof.

There are two considerable exceptions to the general prevalence of the obtuse roofs of the Perpendicular period. In the South-west of England—throughout the whole of

236. ST. ENDELLION, CORNWALL

Cornwall, in many parts of Devon and Somerset, and occasionally in Dorset and Hampshire—the roofs of the fifteenth century assume the coved wagon-head or cradle type, the intersecting timbers dividing the interior into square panels. The wall plates and bosses are generally well carved (particularly in the chancels), and often all the braces, ribs, or purlins. The mediæval plan usually adopted (St. Ives, Cornwall, is an exception) was to use laths, plaster, and whitewash to fill up the panels, thus considerably lightening these unclerestoried buildings, and showing up the beauties of the carving. St. Endellion retains the plastered roofs throughout

237. LANTEGLOS, CAMELFORD

(Fig. 236). Unfortunately, the restorers of not a few of these Cornish churches insisted on clearing out all the plaster, leaving either a foolish-looking open grille, or else superseding the original cool relief of the plaster by planed boards. At Lanteglos-by-Camelford the nave and south aisle retain the

238. BADINGHAM, SUFFOLK

plaster, but the chancel has been stripped by the restorer (Fig. 237). The carved work of these wagon-roofs of Cornwall is exceptionally good at St. Ives, Lansallos, Menheniot, and Fillaton, and over the south aisles of Egloshayle and Padstow. It was usual to roof the porches after the same fashion; over a score of examples remain; a notable one is that of St. Nighton. In the better churches, particularly in the chancels, it was customary to have small full-length figures of angels against the wall plates, placed at the springing of the braces. Some of these angels still remain at Bodmin, St. Ive, St. Ives, St. Kew, St. Mullion, St. Neot, Padstow, and St. Stephen-by-Saltash. There are beautiful Somerset examples of these wall-plate angels in the church of St. Decuman's, Watchet, and in the south aisle of Selworthy. The interior of the interesting church of Porlock shows a trussed rafter-roof over the nave, but a panelled wagon-roof over the chancel.

The second variation from the low-pitched tie-beamed roof was the form known as hammer-beam, essentially fifteenth-century, though one or two instances are possibly just at the close of the fourteenth century. The hammer-beam is a projection from the wall plate at right angles used to strengthen the roof framing, and to diminish the lateral pressure on the walls. They project sometimes as much as 5 or 6 feet opposite to each other, until they almost represent a tie-beam with the centre cut out.

239. BLAKENEY, NORFOLK

Badingham, Suffolk, has an exceptionally good hammer-beam roof, with richly carved wall plates, angel supporters, etc. (Fig. 238). Norfolk has a good instance over both nave and chancel at North Creake, which retains much of the original colouring. The chancel roof has figures of angels and apostles, the latter carrying scrolls with articles of the Apostles' Creed. The nave roof of Blakeney (Fig. 239), in the same county, also is a fine piece of hammer-beam construction.

The hammer-beam offers special facilities for ornamental

MATERIALS

treatment, and frequently terminates in angels with outspread wings. These beautiful roofs, most exquisite when fully coloured, seem almost ready to be lifted heavenward by the angelic host carved on every vantage-point, especially in those

240. NEEDHAM MARKET, SUFFOLK

of the double hammer beam form. Such roofs, as far as churches are concerned, are almost entirely confined to East Anglia. The three most glorious instances occur at Knapton, Norfolk; March, Cambs; and Woolpit, Suffolk; but there are other good Norfolk examples at Swaffham, Tilney All Saints, and Wymondham, and from Suffolk at Bacton, Grundisburgh, and Worlingsworth. Needham Market (Figs. 240, 241) is another handsome Suffolk example on an exceptional plan.

At South Harting, Sussex, is a rare example of a fine Elizabethan roof over the chancel, dated 1574; it is Gothic in its main features, but its details are Renaissance. There is a hammer-beam chancel roof at Haydon, Lancashire, of the year 1663. Early Victorian restorers played extraordinary pranks with old roofs; in two or three cases they had iron girders grained in oak to imitate tie-beams! An 1850 restoration of

241. DETAIL OF ROOF, NEEDHAM MARKET

Wigan church brought about the reproduction in terra-cotta of the corbelled angels!

Aisle roofs, save when they are exceptionally wide, are usually of sloping lean-to design, especially when there is a clerestory to the nave. Occasionally at a late date they are almost flat, as in the handsome panelled sixteenth-century roof of the north aisle of Tisbury, Wilts.

ROOFING

THATCHING. The earliest record of the roofing of an English church was the covering of it with thatch. Bede tells us that when Finan succeeded St. Aidan in the bishopric, about the middle of the seventh century, he built a church on the Isle of Lindisfarne, constructing it, after the manner of the Scots, of hewn oak, and covering it with reeds. He also mentions

MATERIALS 283

that, later in the same century, Bishop Eadbert took off the thatch, substituting lead.

The later use of thatch for the humbler churches doubtless continued because it served excellently to protect the walls

242. ACLE, NORFOLK

from the damage of rain-drip, saving the various devices of corbel-tables and parapets to attain a like end.

With regard to thatching, it is necessary, by way of caution, to remark that the old word "to *thack*" or "thatch" used to signify no more than to cover, and was sometimes employed with reference to roofs of tiles, slates, shingles, or lead, as well as for roofs of reed or straw. Old Churchwardens' Accounts have several times been misread through forgetfulness or ignorance on this point. Thatch was a very prevalent form of covering for the roofs of East Anglian churches. The various good qualities of such a material are shown by its long-continued use on the village churches, for it requires a fairly frequent renewal if it is to look well or be serviceable. Everywhere else in England a thatched church would nowadays be regarded

284   THE ENGLISH PARISH CHURCH

as an eccentricity, but in Norfolk and Suffolk, more especially the former, its survival is nothing unusual. The use of thatch

243. BRAMFIELD, SUFFOLK

in these counties and in a few cases in Cambridgeshire arises, to a great extent, from the resources of the Broads; it is generally formed from carefully cut water-reeds (*Phragmites communis*), which thrive on marshy ground, instead of from wheat or other straw. But the sedge (*Cladium mariscus*) of

244. FRITTON, SUFFOLK

MATERIALS 285

the fens was largely used in Cambridgeshire for thatching, and made better roofing than the reed, for its sharp serrated edges kept birds from building and rats from burrowing in its substance. Bishop Montague of Norwich, in his

245. BRAMFORD, SUFFOLK. NORTH AISLE

visitation articles of 1638, inquired whether the church was thatched with reed or straw. A large number of churches lost their thatch throughout the last century, particularly during the period of the earlier Victorian restorations, when it was fashionable to regard such roofing as mean.

In the first half of the nineteenth century upwards of 270 Norfolk churches had thatched roofs, as can be proved from the Dawson-Turner drawings and from the Ladbrook lithographs. The list, however, of Norfolk churches which still retain this seemly and pleasant-looking covering is by no means insignificant; they amount to upwards of fifty and are chiefly in the neighbourhood of the Broads.* Acle is a good example of this county (Fig. 242).

* See Dr. Cox's "Norfolk Churches," 2nd ed. i. 27-28.

In two instances, namely, at Irstead and Stokesby, the interwoven inner side of the reed-thatching shows through the rafters in the interior of the church after a primitive but not unseemly fashion. This used also to be the case at Little Melton, but the reed roofing unhappily disappeared in 1896.

The proportion of thatched church roofs which disappeared in Suffolk during the nineteenth century was nearly equal to those of Norfolk.* Eighteen still retain reed roofing, of which Bramfield, with its detached round tower, is a good instance (Fig. 243). Pakefield and Ringsfield have the continuing roofs of nave and chancel thus treated, whilst at Barsham only the nave is thatched. The charming little church of Fritton has thatch on both nave and apsed chancel (Fig. 244).

246. BARNSTAPLE, ST. PETER

Church thatching used to be common in the north part of Cambridgeshire. It has only been suffered to remain at Rampton and Long Stanton St. Michael. Among other churches which lost their thatch in comparatively recent years

* See Bryant's "Suffolk Churches," i. 9.

MATERIALS

were those of Coventry, Over, Thetford St. George, Wllingham, and Witcham.

Yorkshire had a few small straw-thatched churches in the East and North Ridings early in the nineteenth century; the last to survive was that of Beswick, near Driffield.

The roofs of Markby, Lincolnshire, were stripped of tiles in 1672, and thatch substituted. Another thatched church of this county is Somerby St. Margaret. One side of the nave of the Cheshire church of Restherne remained thatched until about 1870.

LEAD. The use of lead for church roofs is of very old standing. When St. Wilfrid repaired the church of St. Peter at York, in 669, he covered the roof with lead. Joceline's "Chronicle" records lead-roofing at Bury St. Edmunds in 1189. A much earlier instance is recorded by Bede in connexion with the church of Lindisfarne in 638. Lead came into greater use as a church roof-covering in the later Gothic days, partly owing to the increase in English lead-mining and its consequent comparative cheapness; it was, too, more suited for use in the times when the English roofs became so nearly flat. Bramford, Suffolk, may serve as an example (Fig. 245). It was also of important service in forming an admirable covering for timber spires.

247. GODALMING

Lead-covered spires are essentially English; the cathedral churches of Old St. Paul's, Durham, Canterbury, Norwich, Hereford, Rochester, and Ely, and the minsters of Ripon, Southwell, and Hexham, used to be thus crowned, and at least as many more parish churches as now retain lead spires were at one time similarly adorned. They were older than stone spires. The highest, oldest, and most perfect lead spire now extant is that of Long Sutton, Lincolnshire; it is in itself 85 feet high, and is of early thirteenth-century date. In addition to the celebrated crooked spire of Chesterfield, the best examples of lead spires, mostly of fourteenth-century date, are to be found at Hemel Hempstead, Herts; Minster, Kent; Hadleigh, Suffolk; Great Baddow, Essex; Godalming, Surrey; and Barnstaple, Devon. The Barnstaple example, which has stood for over five centuries, is a perfect broach, the lead sheeting overhanging the tower (Fig. 246); but at Godalming the cardinal faces of the spire stand a little within the wall of the tower (Fig. 247).

TILES. There is a third kind of church roof, which is also of considerable age, namely, tiling. The tile was a thin plate of baked clay used to cover roofs. Although the Romans were such masters of flat brick-making, often called tiles, their usual roof-covering was small stone slates. In the later Saxon and early Norman days roof tiles were constantly baked in kilns; churches were frequently covered with them in those days and during the three periods of Gothic architecture. More especially was this the case in districts where no fissile stone was to be had, as in Surrey and the eastern counties.

It may be mentioned that in the days of Richard II the houses of London were ordered to be covered with slates or "burnt tile" in the place of straw.

The section on the price of building materials in the first volume of Professor Thorold Rogers's "History of Agriculture and Prices in England," extending from 1259 to 1400, shows that there was a considerable and continuous manufacture of tiles, not only of the plain flat description, but of others that were needed for ridges and gutters. Cresting tiles, to cover the ridges of slated roofs, were much dearer than those bought for tiled buildings.

Pantiles, which occasionally occur in old parish churches, especially in Norfolk, are of a curved shape, so that each tile

248. DUNTISBOURNE ROUS, GLOUCESTERSHIRE

overlaps the edge of that next, and protects the joint from rain intrusion.

SLATES were also used for roofing from very early historic days. The term must not be understood as applying only to the thin blue or bluish-green slates chiefly to be found in Wales and Cornwall, but also to those fissile stones which are easily laminated into sections and which present a far more picturesque appearance than those of the thinner kind. The most celebrated quarries for the supply of stone-slates, as they may be termed, were those of Stonesfield in Oxfordshire, Colley Weston in Northamptonshire, and the Horsham slabs with which so many churches of Surrey and Sussex were picturesquely covered. They are characteristic of the Cotswolds, and Mr. Vallance's charming view of the church of Duntisbourne Rous (Fig. 248) shows the effect where nave, chancel, porch, and tower are all roofed with this appropriate local covering.

SHINGLES is the name given to thin pieces of oak forming as it were wooden tiles. These thin pieces of oak were usually from 8 inches to 12 inches in length by 4 inches in width. Shingles were, and still are, in fairly constant use for the covering of timber spires, especially in stoneless districts such as Essex. A good example of a shingled spire occurs at Bersted, Sussex (Fig. 249). In earlier times there were very many instances in which shingles were used as coverings for the roofs of the bodies or aisles of the smaller churches.

249. BERSTED, SUSSEX

> Item payd to the shyngler for shyngleng off the body off the church in serten places   xiij d.
> Item payd to Thomas Parris for iij c. being occupyed in the same work off shynglyng   xviij d.

Early in the reign of James I the roofs of this church were again shingled throughout, including the chancel.

In 1568, when the church of Eltham, Kent, was under repair, 6s. was paid for 200 shingles. In 1594 an elaborate document was drawn up by Dr. Bynge and twelve other Doctors of Civil Law, " assembled together in their Common dyninge Hall at Doctors Commons, London, touching a course to be observed by the assessors in their taxation for the reparacions of the Church of Wrotham, Kent, to be applied generally upon occasions of like reparacions to all places whatsoever." In a schedule of the details requisite to be repaired occurs : " The coverings of lead slabs, tiles, or shingle." *

The nave of the parish church of Tenterden, Kent, is still covered with shingles. A small portion of the church of Morwenstow, Cornwall, also retains some of the old shingles. These are, we believe, the only surviving instances of shingles on old churches, otherwise than on spires or belfries.

DOORS

Old wooden doors and their accompanying ironwork should certainly be included, after a brief fashion, under " Materials."

The woodwork of Norman doors, both early and late, appears to have been generally used as a vehicle for the display of good ironwork.† The doors are otherwise devoid of ornament, formed of narrow boards arranged perpendicularly, and nailed to wider horizontal boards on the inner side. In several cases Norman ironwork has been reapplied to later doors. Sometimes the hinges take the form of plain prolonged straps, as at Southchurch, Essex, but the ends are oftener turned into short scrolls, as at Navestock, Stafford, Castle Hedingham, Margaret

---

* A copy of this decree is given in the Churchwardens' Accounts of Spelsbury, Oxon.

† See Mr. J. Starkie Gardner's admirable and well-illustrated South Kensington manual on " Ironwork from the Earliest Times to the End of the Mediæval Period," 2nd ed. 1907.

292 THE ENGLISH PARISH CHURCH

Roothing, Warmington, and Wrabness. Frequently, too, there are large crescent scrolls on each side, which assume the form of a highly floriated letter C. Essex * has more extant Norman doors than any other three or four counties collectively, and these large C scrolls occur on the remarkable examples of Willingale Spain and Eastwood, and on the plainer instances of Waltham Abbey, Margaret Roothing, Castle Hedingham, Stifford, and Little Totham, all in Essex. At Buttsbury north door (Fig. 250), in the same county, the ends of the C's terminate in dragon-heads; the highly interesting ironwork of this door has evidently belonged to an older and larger door. The following are among instances of these Norman C scrolls on doors in other counties, the first three showing in addition ironwork of elaborate beauty: St. Margaret's, Leicester; Edstaston, Salop; Hartley and Erith, Kent; Westcott Barton, Oxon; Compton, Berks; and Merton, Surrey.

250. BUTTSBURY, ESSEX

At Haddiscoe, Norfolk, the C's are bent back into a squared form, and branch out into a profusion of scrolls. The centre of this door is also occupied by a large foliated Greek cross. Other modifications of the C hinge scrolls occur on doors of the Berkshire churches of Kingston Lisle and Sparsholt; at

* See the late Mr. Godman's "Norman Architecture in Essex," 1905, where there are various good plates of Norman doors.

MATERIALS

Sowerby, N.R. Yorks; and at Houghton-on-the-Hill, Lincolnshire.* Another remarkably fine example of smithcraft, embodying the C scrolls amongst a multiplicity of other ornamental ironwork, is to be seen at Leathley church, W.R. Yorks.†

There are two remarkably elaborate examples of door ironwork at Stillingfleet, E.R. Yorks, and Staplehurst, Kent, where the ends of the C scrolls form serpents, and a Viking's ship occurs as part of the independent iron ornaments. The arrangement of the latter is more confused because the ironwork has been transferred to a later door. Skipwith, near Stillingfleet (Fig. 251), and Hormead, Herts, have also remarkable and exceptional ironwork. These four notable Norman doors are all c. 1150. Skipwith has a unique arrangement in ironwork of a geometrical lining of intersecting circles, with crosses and swastika knots in the intervening spaces.

251. SKIPWITH, YORKS

Kenilworth west door is another elaborate rather late example, a good deal spoilt by restoration. The Transition doors of Arborfield and of Baulking, Berks, have also good ironwork.

* Beautiful drawings of these last two examples are given in Twopeny's "English Metal-work," 1904.

† Well illustrated in *Reliquary*, n.s., xi. (1905), 207.

The elaborate hinge-work and other ornamentation nearly covering the double doors of Sempringham, Lincolnshire, is fairly early in the style; it is well illustrated in Mr. Starkie Gardner's work. At Upleadon, Gloucestershire, the doorway is remarkable for being wrought with small iron crosses, in addition to scroll-work. Among other ironwork of a more or less elaborate character on Norman doors may be mentioned the instances of Hales, Raveningham, and Kirby Bedon, Norfolk; White Roothing and Colne Wakes, Essex; Woking, Surrey; Stanford Bishop, Herefordshire; Brightwell Salome, Oxon; St. Michael-at-Thorn, Norwich; and Terwick, Sussex.

With the advent of the Early English period a complete change came over the ornamental ironwork of church doors. A beautiful system of flowing foliated scroll-work, starting as a rule from the hinge, but offering a complete contrast to the stiffness of the Norman and Transition work, came into being. Probably the earliest example occurs on the double south doors of Market Deeping, Lincoln, where the slender foliations, branching out copiously from the four hinges into flattened leaves, are of exceptional grace. The door at Caister, in the same county, is nearly as beautiful.

A different early development occurs on the double doors of Worksop church, Notts, where the foliated scroll-work, unconnected with the hinges, sweeps round in boldly conceived circular designs terminating in conventional flowers, covering the whole woodwork in patterns of genuine beauty. Mr. Gardner considers that the hinge-work of Burford, Oxon, and of Abbeydore, Herefordshire, are taken from this Worksop design.

The Berkshire churches of Faringdon and Uffington have Early English doors, with an abundance of good scroll-work, proceeding from crescent hinges (strictly crescent, not of the Norman C form), and strengthening pieces, which have many terminations in stamped rosettes. The like stamps occur at Bisham Stanford and at Dingley in the same county, in work

MATERIALS 295

of similar design, and in a few other places. The crescent type of hinge ornament was maintained on certain doors almost throughout the thirteenth century, as at Haddiscoe, Norfolk, and Rushden, Northants. At Oundle, Northants, the crescent of the straphinge is quite small, whilst at Spalding, Lincolnshire, it is yet more diminutive. Towards the close of the century, in Edward I's reign, the crescent dropped out, and the door ironwork dwindled down to a mere strap-hinge with a foliated end, as at Trotton, Sussex, in 1290.

Among the Early English doors with ornamental ironwork not hitherto mentioned, those of Reepham, Norfolk; North Ockendon, Essex; and Crowhurst and Merstham (tower), Surrey, are noteworthy.

Thomas de Laighton was the smith of the exquisite work, in 1293-94, of the grill over the tomb of Queen Eleanor in Westminster Abbey. The splendid hinge-work on the three Bedfordshire parish-church doors of Leighton Buzzard, Eaton Bray (Figs. 252, 253) and Turvey (Fig. 254) are undoubtedly due to the same artificer. His

252. EATON BRAY, BEDFORDSHIRE

work is also to be noticed in the masterly scroll-work on the parish-church doors of St. Mary's, Norwich, and St. Peter's, Colchester. The exceptional and singularly beautiful work on the south door of Tunstead, Norfolk, is also assigned by Mr. Gardner to his skill; in this case there are two plain narrow strap-hinges, but most graceful foliations branch out in all directions to the extent of 4 feet from a central cross. If this, however, is really Laighton's work it must have been re-affixed to a mid-fourteenth century door. The churches of Irstead and Stokesby in the same county have somewhat similar but less elaborate ironwork, foliated branchings from a central boss, but the doors themselves are certainly not thirteenth-century.

253. EATON BRAY, BEDFORDSHIRE

With the fourteenth century we come to the time when the application of elaborate ironwork to church doors, save for lock escutcheons and closing rings, nearly died out, and when the carving of the woodwork of the door began to come into fashion. The south door of the Decorated church of Dunsfold, Sussex, has long plain strap-hinges, closing ring, and key-escutcheon, and also an arched fillet of iron strengthening the

MATERIALS

top, unique, we believe, save in one or two Early Norman examples. The lock is original, and the key is 13½ inches long.

The upright boards of Decorated doors are not infrequently covered with panel-work and characteristic tracery. There is a beautiful example within the south porch of Harpley, Norfolk, which is well carved with ogee crocketed niches. Swineshead, Lincolnshire, has flowing tracery in the panel-work. The large vestry door of Halsall, Lancashire, has a succession of quatrefoils similar to wind tracery. Other examples of good Decorated wood-carving on doors may be noted at St. Cross, York; Holbeach and Boston, Lincolnshire; Milton, Kent; Arrow, Warwick; Buxton, Norfolk; Willesden, Middlesex; and Astbury, Cheshire (Fig. 255).

Now and again inscriptions appear on doors of this period. The south door of the nave of Castor, Northants, is a fine piece of fourteenth-century work, with an ornamental border bearing the inscription:

254. TURVEY, BEDS.

RICARDUS BEBY RECTOR ECCLECIE DE CASTRE FECIT.*

Across the centre of the Decorated south door of Balderton,

---

* Richard of Leicester appears among the fourteenth-century incumbents of Castor; this was probably the donor of the door, for there was a family of Beby resident in Leicester during that period : Vict. Co. Hist. of Northants, ii. 481. A strangely persistent series of blunders in a variety of books has hitherto maintained that this was a twelfth-century Norman door! Even Mr. Bond in his recent work assigns it to 1133.

Notts, on a handsome band, are the words "Jesu mercy Mary helpe."

In a few cases there is beautiful ironwork on fourteenth-century doors which is apparently of coeval workmanship, as at Hickling, Notts, and on both north and south doors of Hellesden, Norfolk.

255. THE SOUTH DOOR, ASTBURY, CHESHIRE

The appearance of church doorways changed considerably with the advent of the Perpendicular period and throughout the fifteenth century, but it was otherwise with the actual doors. The plainer examples usually made no more display of ironwork than in prolonged strap-hinges, plain save for cross hatching or vertical lines, and with the necessary closing and latch rings. These rings, when of unusual size or ornament, are frequently styled, in ignorance, "sanctuary rings." This is a fable of comparatively modern invention. The fact is that a fugitive was fully in sanctuary in mediæval England so soon as he had gained any consecrated churchyard. Every consecrated church or chapel and the surrounding graveyard formed an absolute sanctuary for forty days. A few special chartered sanctuaries, like Durham, Beverley, and Westminster, were life sanctuaries under certain conditions.*

The excellent door handle of Westcott Barton, Oxon, which is not of the ring form, has been several times engraved. A singularly graceful pierced ring escutcheon, of fifteenth-century date, which is attached to the lower rood-loft door of Stogumber, Somerset, has been engraved both in Parker's "Glossary" and Gardner's "Ironwork." The latter author considers it of Moslem type, and a proof of his contention as to the deep nature of Oriental influence. In Mr. Twopeny's work there are beautiful drawings of the fifteenth-century door handles and plates of Byarsh, Kent, and Bramham, W.R. Yorks.

256. BARKING, SUFFOLK

Traceried panels are somewhat oftener met with in fifteenth-century than in fourteenth-century doors. Winthorpe, Lincolnshire; Telaton, Devon; Maids Moreton, Bucks; Coates, Sussex; Send, Surrey; Thurlton, Sparham, Skeyton, and Sall, Norfolk; St. Peter Hungate and St. Michael-at-Plea, Norwich, may be cited as examples. A

* See Dr. Cox's "Sanctuaries and Sanctuary Seekers," 1911.

beautiful instance occurs at Martham, Norfolk, where the south door has a handsomely carved border of vine-leaves and grapes; the ironwork of the key-plate and the latch-ring is also good. Helmingham, Suffolk, has a singularly well-carved panelled door of late fifteenth century date; it is well illustrated in Mr. Twopeny's specimens of "Ancient Woodwork" (1859). Under the fine Tudor brick porch of Feering, Essex, is a notable original door with some good ironwork.

Several of the best Perpendicular doors bear inscriptions. The same legend —"Jesu mercy Mary helpe"— which we noted at Balderton, Notts, also occurs fully a hundred years later on the tower door of Hawton in the same county. At Worsborough, W.R. Yorks, is a very fine fifteenth-century south door; across it is the imperfect inscription " J. H. S. Nicolas Ge . . . Thomas Acott." The special feature of Sco-Ruston church is the well-carved fifteenth-century south door, which bears in the centre panel a raised inscription to the effect that it was the gift of Stephen Bolte and Eleanor his wife.

The larger and more cumbersome of the Perpendicular doors have occasionally wickets within them, as at Gedney, Lincolnshire. At St. Mullion, Cornwall, there is a unique diminutive wicket, only measuring 11 inches square, and nearly on the floor level; it was probably intended to permit the exit of dogs.

In the seventeenth century it became customary to date the principal panelled doors of a church. Thus at Poynings, Sussex, the west door is dated 1608, whilst the south doors of Botolphs and Wadhurst bear the respective years 1612 and 1682. South Collingham, Notts, is dated 1641, and Croft, Lincolnshire, 1631, etc.

256A. CLANFIELD, OXFORDSHIRE
[*Drawn by A. E. Newcombe*

CHAPTER V

WHAT TO NOTE IN AN OLD PARISH CHURCH

PROFESSOR FREEMAN, who was a most able exponent of a church, was in the habit of saying: "No one but a fool goes into a church without first inspecting the exterior." Let us follow this injunction. If there is a western tower, note carefully the size, also the condition of the basement masonry; Saxon work may be detected in such a position oftener than is generally supposed. Note the stages into which it is divided by string-courses or otherwise, west doorway, successive windows, corbel-table at summit or battlements, or both, and especially the buttresses. Also whether the tower was at one time external and afterwards incorporated. The east wall of a tower often bears the weather-moulds of former roof or roofs.

Proceed up the south side. Note the porch, its bench-tables (Fig. 258), roof, perhaps groined or slab-covered; holy-water stoup, saint-niche over entrance, upper room (in error called a "parvise"), battlements, and windows.

302   WHAT TO NOTE IN

On the jambs of the entrance or of the inner doorway small incised crosses (Fig. 259) may be noted, more or less roughly

257. MATERIAL FOR STUDY IN A VILLAGE CHURCH: STANTON-IN-THE-VALE, OXFORDSHIRE
[*Drawn by A. E. Newcombe*

cut. Do not call them "consecration crosses." They are nothing of the kind. The order in the Pontificals was that consecration crosses, marked by the bishop with chrism, were to be placed at such a height and in such a position (twelve outside and twelve inside) that the holy unction would not be easily rubbed off. These jamb crosses may have been devoutly marked with the general idea of the power of the cross to ward off evil influences, and afterwards carelessly imitated. Do not call them "pilgrim marks"; they occur just as frequently in districts where there is no trace of any known pilgrimage. The term "consecration cross"

258. SHOREHAM, KENT

is to be strictly reserved for those large-sized crosses which were anointed with chrism by the bishop at the time of dedication, or of reconstruction of the whole or part of the fabric. Such exterior crosses very rarely remain, save in certain large churches where they were elaborately sculptured, as at Salisbury Cathedral. At Edington, Wilts, consecrated in 1361, eight of the exterior crosses remain; at Uffington, Berks, consecrated in the previous century, there is an almost perfect set extant. They are also to be seen at Ottery St. Mary, Devon, and at Liskeard, Cornwall, whilst in Sussex external consecration crosses

259. MOOR, SOMERSET

304   WHAT TO NOTE IN

formed by black flints may be noted at Boxgrove, Broadwater, Seaham, and Westham.

The absurdity of calling any elaborate closing ring on an old door a "sanctuary ring" has been already pointed out (pp. 298-99).

Keep a careful eye for small incised sundials on the south buttresses, window jambs, quoins, or porch entrance. Note the number of the radii; this will usually indicate whether they are Saxon or of later date. A good example of an incised Saxon dial occurs in the interior of the south porch of the church of Holy Sepulchre, Northampton (Fig. 260). In a few cases these early dials bear inscriptions, as at Weaverthorpe,

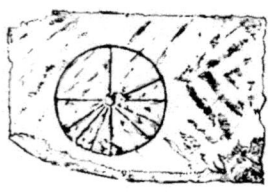

260. HOLY SEPULCHRE, NORTHAMPTON

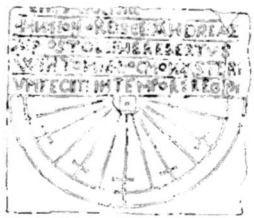

261. WEAVERTHORPE

E.R. Yorks (Fig. 261), where the tenth-century inscription is of great historical value. Be prepared to find these dials elsewhere than on the south side, and even in the interior, for stones on which they occur may have been used again in rebuilding.

It is well to look carefully for the original quoins or corner-stones of the nave, often left on the south side, even when there is an aisle, for in that position Saxon or early Norman work can be occasionally descried when there is no trace of it elsewhere.

It goes without saying that observation is made of the tracery, etc., of all old windows and their probable date and period, but there is one window now and again found, on the south side of either the nave or on the south side of the clere-

THE PARISH CHURCH

story of the south aisle (Fig. 262), which sometimes proves a puzzle. This is the rood window, specially designed in the fifteenth century to throw light upon the beautiful development of the rood, with its flanking saintly figures, over the chancel screen. Sometimes the window of the clerestory furthest to the east was much enlarged and renewed, as at Hemel

262. BOURN, CAMBRIDGESHIRE

Hempstead, Herts; Bourn, Cambs (Fig. 262); or Halsall, Lancashire. At the east end of the nave of Bedfont, Middlesex, is a late window of considerable size, evidently inserted with a like object. A single instance of a rood window on the north side of the nave has been noted at Great Abington, Cambs; there is also one high up in the nave wall of Pucklechurch, Gloucestershire. Pre-Reformation dormer windows in nave roofs are very rare. The few instances that occur seem to have a like origin. The highly interesting and often-cited parish accounts of Stratton, Cornwall, supply a detailed contract of 1531 for erecting an elaborate rood-screen, and providing, *inter alia*, for two dormer windows to be inserted in the nave roof above the crucifix, like those at St. Mary Week. At

WHAT TO NOTE IN

Welsh Newton, Hereford, there is an old dormer window which would very well serve for such a purpose.

The projecting turret or adjunct for the rood-stairs, of frequent occurrence in the south-west of England, should be noted; it is usually found in the last bay eastward on the south side, but sometimes on the north side, and sometimes on both.

Next comes the chancel with its priest's door; and here, too, on the south side may often be noted that *questio vexata* of ecclesiologists, the low-side window, usually on the south side and close to the west end, but sometimes on the north, when the chief village is there, and sometimes on both sides,

263. XIII-CENT. INDIVIDUALITY : THE EAST FRONT OF WYK RISSINGTON, GLOS.

when evidence will probably be found of two manor-houses, or two groups of dwellings. All such windows were originally shuttered, and the hinges were almost invariably on the east side, thus absolutely prohibiting the notion that they were "lychnoscopes" or "speculatories" (a word recently coined by a speculative antiquary) for outside viewing of the lights of the Sepulchre. The modern popular notion of "leper windows" is an absolute impossibility, for lepers might not

THE PARISH CHURCH

even enter a churchyard, and equally vain and easy of positive refutation are the confessional, offertory, or evil-spirit-scaring notions. It is best boldly to call them sacring windows. Matured opinion is surely but gradually concentrating on the opinion that these openings were for the ringing of the sanctus bell at the solemn periods of the Mass by the altar-clerk, before sanctus bell-cotes on the nave gable came into use. The shutter that closed the unglazed aperture would be opened in order that the sound of the hand-bell rung thereat might warn outsiders of the Holy Mysteries. It may suffice here to cite, without comment, two old passages in support of this view, which tell their own tale, the one in Latin, the other in English.

In the Constitutions of Archbishop Peckham, 1281, we read:

"*In elevatione vero ipsius corporis Domini pulsetur campana in uno latere, ut populares, quibus celebratio missarum non vacat quod idie interesse, ubicunque fuerint, seu in agris, seu in domibus flectant genua.*"

In Nicholas's "Narratives of the Days of the Reformation" it is stated that in the days of Queen Mary the Papists at Poole re-established the Mass, and built an altar "in olde Master Whyghts' howse, John Craddock, hys man being clarke to ring the bell and too help the priest to Mass, untyl he was threatened that yf he dyd use to putt hys hand owtt of the wyndow to ring the bell, that a hand goon sholde make hym too smartt, that he sholde not pull in hys hand agayne with ease."

This sacring window was afterwards often succeeded by the sanctus bell-cote, which forms an effective termination to the east gable of the nave. It may be noted at Bremhill, Wilts (Fig. 264), where the built-up Early English low side window and the later bell-cote both occur. In a few cases the old bell still remains *in situ*, as at Brailes, Long Compton, and Whichford, Warwickshire; Over, Cambridgeshire; Fordbury,

308   WHAT TO NOTE IN

Norfolk; Portishead and Weston-in-Gordano, Somersetshire; and Staveley, Derbyshire.

Occasionally a squint window or opening may be detected in the west wall of the nave, to enable a ringer within the belfry to sound a tower sanctus bell at the right moments; they occur at Brightstone, Isle of Wight, and at Fen Drayton, Cambridgeshire.

264. BREMHILL, WILTSHIRE

On the north side of the chancel, especially if there is a blocked-up doorway, look carefully for traces of a former vestry, or sacristy, or possibly of an anchorite's cell. On the north side of the nave note the north doorway, often closed up, and see if there are any remains of a porch.

Within the church, if there is no holy-water stoup in the porch, look for it immediately to the east of the south door. If there is an upper porch room, ascend the stairs, note the contents; also if there is a fireplace, or a squint into the church.

The font will be near the entrance; if there is any doubt as to its antiquity, look for the hinge or fastening marks of the cover on the rim; also note font covers, or, more rarely, pulleys to raise them in the beams above.

THE PARISH CHURCH

On the wall opposite the chief entrance, if there are any old mural paintings * there may be a large one in distemper of St. Christopher carrying the Holy Child ; anyone offering a prayer to St. Christopher on entering a church was considered safe from accidents for the day.

Sometimes at the west end, usually in the north wall, is a tall shallow recess, originally fitted with a door, for the storing of banner-staves, as at Kelshall, Herts, and fairly often in Northamptonshire and East Anglia.

Note the tower with possibly only a doorway instead of an arch; from the nave ascend the tower, carefully scrutinizing the masonry. Towers were frequently rebuilt, and often the

265. BURGH, LINCOLNSHIRE

* It is incorrect to call them "frescoes." A fresco is plasterwork stained when wet. There is not a single old one in English churches.

inner stones, secured from the weather, show their Norman origin by mouldings, or by the diagonal axing used by them prior to the mallet and chisel. Occasionally Saxon chevron tooling may be detected. Bells and bell inscriptions have probably been duly recorded in one of the many county monographs on campanology. But look carefully round belfries, for whole or parts of early sepulchral slabs are not infrequently found in such situations. The later mediæval builders, in a bad spirit, also used such early memorials, being of convenient shapes, in the lintels of their clerestory windows. Also note if the tower has a fireplace in one or more of its stages, and any other sign of occupation. At the basement is the probable modern place for an old parish chest ; note its salient points and probable age.

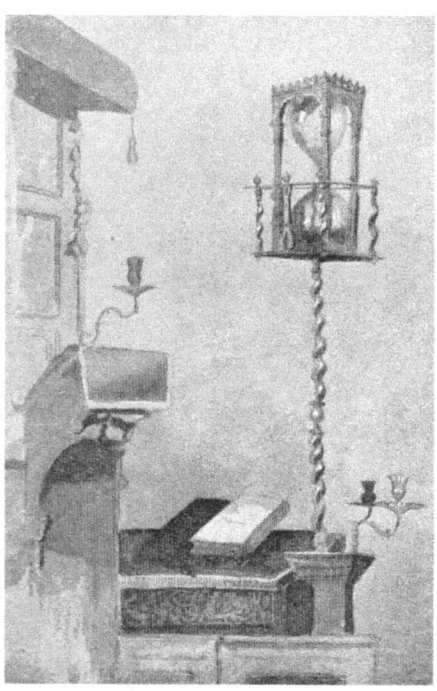

266. ST. ALBAN, WOOD STREET, ONDON
[*Drawn by John Wykeham Archer* (1850)]

With regard to the general stonework, both inside and out, look for signs in masonry of extensions, such as piercing old nave walls for aisles, corbel-tables left on walls afterwards covered by aisle roofs, or blocked-up Saxon or Norman windows over arcades. Also lengthenings both at east and west ends of naves. Do your very best to note the gradual growth of the fabric from early days. Look for traces of apse at east end of chancel or of transept chapels. Observe arches and piers of a central tower; whether north and south arches are of later piercing. Also if a central tower has fallen or been removed, to give way to later west tower. Especially note the character of arches, piers, and capitals of nave arcades, or of chancel arcades into chapels, and whether there is clerestory or not. Look also for bench-tables, or low stone seats, round nave piers or against the walls. Mark squints to the high altar, and don't call them "hagioscopes"; it is a clumsy Greek term invented to describe ritual openings in a Latin or Western church. Obtain, with care, dates and extents of "restorations."

267. UPWELL, NORFOLK

In the nave be ready to observe the old benches or bench-

312   WHAT TO NOTE IN

ends, and occasional well-carved pews, sometimes with testers

268. NORTH AISLE SCREEN AND PULPIT, ATHERINGTON, N. DEVON

over them. Also old alms-boxes, massive and curious, near the chief entrance. At the east end of the nave note the pulpit.

THE PARISH CHURCH

There are a fair number of survivals of mediæval stone pulpits, and more in wood. A few sixteenth-century oak pulpits remain, and a large number of the seventeenth century (Fig. 265). With regard to seventeenth-century woodwork, it is as well to abstain from the usual practice of calling it all Jacobean; it is surely better to confine the term "Jacobean" to the days of James I, and to use the word "Carolean" for the days of Charles I, when much good woodwork was introduced during the Laudian revival. Affixed to the pulpit or the wall close by, in upwards of one hundred instances the old Puritan hour-glass stand yet remains (Fig. 266).

Note, too, the lectern, for there are several survivals of mediæval examples, both in brass and wood, which used to be in the chancels, but now carry the Bible for the Lessons. Those in brass are usually in the form of an eagle, of which there is a beautiful fifteenth-century example at Upwell, Norfolk (Fig. 267). In this connexion it is well to note if there is a small stone Gospel lectern affixed to the north wall of the chancel near to the high altar, of which there are several instances in Derbyshire.

In the later mediæval church, almost peculiar to England, the chief feature of the interior was the rood-screen, with the rood-loft and rood and attendant figures. The stairway, or at least the doorways thereto, usually remain and are always of interest. This loft was not used, as often supposed, for the ceremonial reading of the Gospel at High Mass; this ritual was reserved for cathedral or collegiate churches. Its use in parish churches was chiefly for musical purposes, vocal or instrumental; in some churches where there was a wide rood-loft an altar stood in this position. This is chiefly to be recognized by a piscina or almery high up in the masonry on the south side of the chancel arch, as in at least a score of cases. Remains of the rood or chancel screen are frequent; if not, there are probably marks where it was fixed.

Altars were also almost invariably found at the east end of the aisles, with their piscinas. Look for traces of screens or

314 WHAT TO NOTE IN

269. SCREENS AND PULPIT AT HANDBOROUGH, OXFORDSHIRE

THE PARISH CHURCH 315

parcloses enclosing them. See if an old chancel arch has been removed.

Entering the chancel, there may be return stalls facing east, or other stalls for priests and choir. Note if arch existed by

270. SEDILIA AND PISCINA, CHERRY HINTON, CAMBRIDGESHIRE

traces in east face of screen. In the south wall note the sedilia or stone seats (Fig. 270) and piscina beyond. The sedilia may be of any of the periods, though very rarely Norman. Note their number and if graded. Most altars had one or more almeries, or recessed cupboards for altar vessels, &c., on the north side. Specially note such almeries if in the east wall. In the north wall there is often the Easter Sepulchre recess, sometimes combined with a founder's tomb. Look in the chancel or elsewhere for painted circular consecration crosses: upwards of two hundred English parish churches possess one or more of such crosses. On the chancel walls of Moorlinch, Somerset, ten of these crosses are extant, namely, four on each of the side walls and two at the east end. Observe if the chancel walls possess rings or other arrangements for supporting the Lenten Veil; it hung a little distance in front of the high altar, and not, as is sometimes said, at the chancel arch. Examine the roof for any trace of the pulley in front of, or rather over, the altar for the pyx, there suspended, containing the reserved Sacrament. Look, too, for old altar slabs or *mensæ*, especially on porch floor, where they may be found placed upside down. The remains or traces of a stone reredos behind an altar are more frequent than is usually supposed. A striking example of this occurs in the lovely Lady chapel of Patrington (Fig. 271), E.R. Yorks. The most exquisite gem of alabaster reredos work is in the south chapel of Drayton, Berks (Fig. 272); it was found buried in the churchyard. In woodwork observe, too, old altar rails, old altar tables, an occasional west gallery of pre-Reformation, Elizabethan, or even later date. Also note roofs in general, especially of the nave bay in front of the rood, which may be specially enriched to serve as a canopy over the rood.

271. THE LADY CHAPEL, PATRINGTON

THE PARISH CHURCH

This is not a book in any sense dealing with church furniture, but it may be well, in so many words, to remind the church visitor of old tiles, old painted glass, ironwork in connexion with tombs; also that there are such things as altar plate and pewter, old alms-boxes (Fig. 273), chained books, church libraries, and

272. ALABASTER REREDOS, DRAYTON, BERKSHIRE

old church embroidery; and that royal arms and even old boards of the Ten Commandments are not to be passed over. It is as well, too, not to forget to inquire after old parish documents and Churchwardens' Accounts, as well as parish registers.

As to monuments, all those of any age or interest should be fully noted. They are (1) early sepulchral slabs, often called coffin-lids, but many of them never covered a coffin; (2) recumbent effigies, successively of Purbeck marble, stone, and alabaster, or rarely wood; (3) incised effigies on alabaster slabs; (4) kneeling mural effigies of Elizabethan and later dates; and (5) later mural effigies, leaning on their elbows, or erect in classical dress. Brasses are a study in themselves; they are usually fully noted in Haines's general manual, or in a special county monograph. Ledger stones, of late seventeenth-century and eighteenth-century date, are also well worthy of

318 THE ENGLISH PARISH CHURCH

observation; the sculpture of heraldic bearings, with elaborate mantling, in medallions at the head, are often executed with much artistic effect.

DOMINE DILEXI DECORUM DOMUS TUAE.

273. ALMS-BOX, BLYTH, NOTTINGHAMSHIRE.

INDEX TO ILLUSTRATIONS ARRANGED UNDER COUNTIES

NOTE.—The numbers below refer to the figure numbers of the illustrations, not to the page on which they occur.

BEDFORDSHIRE
    Eaton Bray, 252, 253
    Luton, 85
    Marston Mortaine, 92, 93
    Turvey, 254

BERKSHIRE
    Didcot, 223
    Drayton, 272
    Great Coxwell, 35
    Stanton-in-the-Vale, 257
    Uffington, 41

BUCKINGHAMSHIRE
    North Crawley, 133
    Preston Bissett, 63
    Stewkley, 49, 50, 51

CAMBRIDGESHIRE
    Bourn, 262
    Cherry Hinton, 270
    Elm, 62
    Grantchester, 142, 215
    Madingley, 67
    Soham, 121, 151
    Sutton, 152

CHESHIRE
    Astbury, 255
    Marton, 226
    Nantwich, 195
    Warburton, 227

CORNWALL
    St. Columb Minor, 27
    St. Endellion, 236
    Kilkhampton, 188
    Lanteglos-by-Camelford, 237
    Launceston, St. Mary Magdalene, 71, 189
    Morwenstow, 7

DERBYSHIRE
    Ashbourne, 28
    Chesterfield, All Saints, 76
    Derby, All Saints, 10
    Melbourne, 119
    Steetley, 118
    Tideswell, 146

DEVON
    Atherington, 268
    Barnstaple, St. Peter, 246
    Branscombe, 15
    Brent Tor, 16
    Chulmleigh, 74
    Colebrooke, 75
    Combe Martin, 29
    Exeter, St. Petrock, 158
    Harberton, 164
    Kingsbridge, 9
    North Molton, 174
    Swimbridge, 32

DORSET
    Melbury Bubb, 91

DURHAM
    Escomb, 46, 109
    Jarrow, 182

ESSEX
    Blackmore, 218
    Bradwell-on-Sea, 105
    Buttsbury, 250
    Chipping Ongar, 103
    Colchester, Holy Trinity, 107
    Dedham, 24
    Feering, 208, 211
    Great Baddow, 209
    Great Bromley, 26
    Greensted, 216

INDEX TO ILLUSTRATIONS

ESSEX—*continued*
  Laindon, 217
  Little Braxted, 40
  St. Osyth, 212
  Sandon, 207, 210
  Shenfield, 219
  Woodham Walter, 170

GLOUCESTERSHIRE
  Cirencester, 65, 99
  Deerhurst, 86, 108
  Duntisbourne Rous, 248
  Fairford, 168
  Northleach, 153, 154
  Southrop, 117
  Wyk Rissington, 263
  Yate, 163

HAMPSHIRE
  Calbourne (I. of W.), 132
  Godshill (I. of W.), 2
  Nateley Scures, 112
  Odiham, 173
  Old Basing, 73, 214
  South Hayling, 220
  St. Mary Bourne, 186
  Wolverton, 177

HEREFORDSHIRE
  Kilpeck, 37, 38, 110, 113
  Ledbury, 140
  Pembridge, 225
  Pipe Aston, 111

HERTFORDSHIRE
  Flaunden, 228, 229
  Little Munden, 55
  St. Paul's, Walden, 175, 176

HUNTINGDONSHIRE
  St. Neots, 234

KENT
  Minster (Isle of Thanet), 193
  New Romney, 72
  Rolvenden, 17
  Shoreham, 258
  St. Margaret-at-Cliffe, 61
  Swanscombe, 102

LANCASHIRE
  Ormskirk, 159

LEICESTERSHIRE
  Leicester, St. Martin, 231

LINCOLNSHIRE
  Boston, 183
  Burgh, 265
  Donington, 87, 88
  Ewerby, 94, 95
  Frampton, 83
  Grantham, 135, 136, 137, 143
  Stamford, St. Mary, 184
  Stow, 114, 190

NORFOLK
  Acle, 242
  Blakeney, 239
  Bradfield, 200
  Castle Rising, 116
  Cley, 64
  Elsing, 52, 53
  Forncett St. Peter, 106A
  Haddiscoe, 198
  King's Lynn, St. Nicholas, 44, 45, 98, 162
  Norwich, St. Michael Coslany, 206
  Norwich, St. Peter Mancroft, 60
  Starston, 232
  Stow Bardolf, 230
  Thorpe-next-Haddiscoe, 197
  Tilney All Saints, 54
  Upwell, 267
  West Walton, 126, 127

NORTHAMPTONSHIRE
  Brixworth, 101
  Byfield, 139
  Castor, 79, 80
  Earl's Barton, 104
  Etton, 125, 131
  Higham Ferrers, 138
  Holdenby, 172
  Lowick, 161
  Northampton, St. Sepulchre, 36, 260
  Raunds, 69
  Rushden, 150
  Warmington, 128

NOTTINGHAMSHIRE
  Blyth, 273
  Hawton, 147, 148
  Newark, 100

OXFORDSHIRE
  Clanfield, 256A
  Ducklington, 144
  Ewelme, 31
  Handborough, 269
  Mapledurham, 213

INDEX TO ILLUSTRATIONS

OXFORDSHIRE—*continued*
    North Leigh, 196
    Witney, 42
    Yelford, 19

RUTLAND
    Ayston, 68
    Ketton, 129
    Oakham, *frontispiece*

SHROPSHIRE
    Church Stretton, 14
    Ludlow, St. Lawrence, 157
    Shrewsbury, St. Chad, 178
    ,,   St. Mary, 122
    Worfield, 12

SOMERSETSHIRE
    Bishop's Hull, 89, 90
    Bishop's Lydiard, 33
    Bristol, St. Mary Redcliffe, 194
    Brympton, 13
    Culbone, 4, 20, 21
    Doulting, 187
    Luccombe, 34
    Martock, 235
    Moor, 259
    Puxton, 6
    Taunton, St. Mary Magdalene, 3
    Wedmore, 82
    Winscombe, 166
    Wrington, 167

SUFFOLK
    Badingham, 181, 238
    Barking, 256
    Bramfield, 243
    Bramford, 245
    Earl Stonham, 205
    Eye, 201
    Framsden, 202
    Fritton, 244
    Herringfleet, 199
    Ixworth, 233
    Lavenham, 165, 169
    Lowestoft, St. Margaret, 156
    Needham Market, 240, 241
    Rickinghall Inferior, 134
    Southwold, 25, 204
    Ufford, 185
    Woolpit, 97
    Worlingworth, 203

SURREY
    Chaldon, 180
    Godalming, 247
    Guildford, St. Mary, 191
    Merstham, 70
    Newdigate, 222
    Ockham, 124

SUSSEX
    Amberley, 130
    Bersted, 249
    Bosham, 123
    Chithurst, 39
    Heyshott, 18
    Newhaven, 48
    New Shoreham, 120, 192
    Old Shoreham, 77, 78
    South Harting, 11
    Woolbeding, 106
    Worth, 47
    Yapton, 96

WARWICKSHIRE
    Coventry, Holy Trinity, 5
    ,,   St. Michael, 30, 66
    Stratford-on-Avon, 160

WESTMORLAND
    Crosthwaite, 23
    Wastdale, 22

WILTSHIRE
    Amesbury, 81
    Bremhill, 264

WORCESTERSHIRE
    Bredon, 179
    Crowle, 221
    Hanley, 171
    Warndon, 224

YORKSHIRE
    Adel, 115
    Hedon, 149
    Hull, Holy Trinity, 8
    Patrington, 84, 141, 271
    Skipwith, 251
    Tickhill, 155
    Weaverthorpe, 261

INDEX TO TEXT AND ILLUSTRATIONS

NOTE.—*The page numbers in thin type refer to references in the text; numbers in black type refer to illustrations, or to references accompanied by an illustration on the same page. The numbers are of pages in all cases; the figure numbers of illustrations are not referred to in this index.*

ABBREVIATIONS. E.E. = Early English; Trans. = Transitional; Dec. = Decorated; Geom. = Geometrical; Perp. = Perpendicular.

A

Abbeydore, Herefordshire : hinge-work, 29
Abbots Bickington, Devon : 100
Abbotsham, Devon : 100
Acle, Norfolk : thatched roof, **283**, 285
Acton Burnell, Salop : 102
Adderbury, Oxon : 275
Addington, Northants : Trans. work, 153
Adel, Yorkshire : Norman style, **147**, 272
Aidan, St., 282
Aisleless churches : **74**, 76, **78**
Aisles : addition of, 78–9, 87 ; lighting of,81; roofing of, 81–2 ; roofs of, **275**, 282
Alabaster : 46, 312
Alfred and Guthrune : laws of, 41
Alfriston, Sussex : timber spire, 264
Almeries : 315
Alms-box : 312, 317, **318**
Altar : accommodation for, 88, 315 ; slabs, 316
Amberley, Sussex : E.E. church, 160, **161**
Ambulatory, extension for : 130
Amesbury, Wilts : 104, **105**
Ancaster stone : 179, 223
Anchorite's cell : 308
Andrew, St,, cross : flint device, 240, 247
" Angel Choir," Lincoln : 161, 167
Apse : 65 ; pre-Norman, 71–4 ; Norman, **59**, 73, **150** ; Norman, **73**
Apsidal plan : **59**, **61**, 70–4
Arborfield, Berks : Trans. doors, 293
Arcade : 76, 78, **79** ; Dec., 183 ; Norman, 145, **146** ; Perp., **185**, **186** ; timber, 264, 267, 270
Arch : chancel, 144 ; pointed, 152–3
Arreton, Isle of Wight : Geom. work, 163
Ashbourne, Derby : 34, **35** ; Dec. tower, 104

Ashby St. Legers, Northants : Perp. work, 193
Ashford, Kent : pinnacles, 23
Astbury, Cheshire : carved doorway, 297, **298**
Asthall, Oxon : situation with regard to scenery, 16
Athelstan : 209
Atherington, Devon : screen, **312**
Augustine, St. : 71
Aumbry : *see* Almery
Axbridge : fan-vaulting, 233
Axminster : cruciform planning, 100, 105
Aylesbury, Bucks : 99, 128
Aymestry, Herefordshire : E.E. clerestory, 83
Ayston, Rutland : plan, 88 ; plan E.E. nave, **89**
Aythorpe Roothing, Essex : timber-work, 259

B

BABRAHAM : enclosed in park, 18
Bacton, Suffolk : flint-work, 240, 281
Badbury Camp, Berks : 56
Badingham, Suffolk : example of variety of material, **214** ; hammer-beam roof, **279**, 280
Bakewell : 34, 207
Balderton, Notts : Dec. door, 297, 300
Baldwin, Abbot : 219
Ball-flower moulding ornament : **139**, **140**, 170
Bamborough, Northumberland : E.E. vaulting, 230
Bampton, Oxon : 104
Banner-staves : 309

324 INDEX TO TEXT AND ILLUSTRATIONS

Banstead : E.E. roof, 273
Barfreston, Kent : Norman work, 147
Barking, Suffolk : door, **299**
Barnack, Northants : Saxon arch, 141 ; stone, 52, 168, 179, 216, 219
Barnstaple : St. Peter, broach lead spire, **286**, 288
Barrel vaults : 227
Barrington, Cambs : E.E. capitals, 157
Barton Mills, Suffolk : 28, 128
Barton-on-Humber, Lincs : 122 ; Saxon work, 139 ; Saxon windows, 140
Bases, Norman : 144
Basilican plan : 71
Basing, Old, Hants : plan, **94** ; XVII-century brickwork, **251**, 252
Bath : Lady Chapel of St. Michael, 11, 255 ; stone, 179, 220, 221
Baulking, Berks : Trans. doors, 293
Bede, Venerable : 215, 282, 287
Bedfont : Perp. roof, 277 ; window, 305
Beer, Devon : quarry, 219, 223
Belfries : timber, 258–9, **264** ; detached, 261, **268**
Bell-cote : **265** ; sanctus, 307, **308**
Bench : ends, 311 : tables, 301
Berkeley, Glos : 118 ; chamber over porch, 126
Bersted, Sussex : shingled spire, **290**
Beswick, near Driffield, Yorks : thatching, 287
Betley, Staffs : timber arcade, 270
Beverley Minster : E.E. style, 160 ; use of limestone, 221
Beverley, St. Mary's : 109 ; " Flemish Chapel " vaulting, 232
Biddenham, Kent : west tower, 23
Bideford, Devon : 100 ; Perp. work, 184
Billings, R. W. : 54
Billingshurst, Sussex : spire, 264 ; panelled ceiling, 276
Binstead, Isle of Wight : Norman chancel, 149
Biscop, Benedict : 137, 215
Bisham Stanford, Berks : 294
Bishop's Lydiard : tower, 52, **53**
Bishop's Hull, Somerset : 113 ; plan, **115** ; tower, **116**
Bishopstowe, Lincs : 122, 139
Black Death, the : 50, 171, 173, 179–81, 194
Blackmore, Essex : timber spire, **260**, 261
Blakeney, Norfolk : hammer-beam roof **280**
Blewbury, Berks : Trans. work, 154
Blount family : 250
Bloxam, Mr. : 203, 275
Bloxham, Oxon : Trans. work, 152 ; Dec. work, 176
Blyth, Notts : alms-box, **318**

Boarhunt, Hants : Saxon work, 139; Saxon windows, 140
Bodmin, Cornwall : 113 ; porch, 127 ; fan-vaulting, 233 ; St. Petrock, 11
Boldon, Durham : 55
Bolsover quarries : 221
Bosham, Sussex : 83, 111 ; E.E. windows, 154, **156** ; E.E. vaulting, 230 ; Saxon window, 141 ; timber spire, 264
Boston, Lincs : 87, 125, 300 ; Dec. woodwork, 297 ; stone building, 216, **217**
Bourn, Cambs : 85 ; rood window, **305**
Boxford, Suffolk : timber porch, 262
Boxgrove, Sussex : consecration cross, 303
Bradeston, Norfolk : fireplaces in tower, 113
Bradfield, Norfolk : flint-work, **236**, 237
Bradford-on-Avon, Wilts : Saxon church, 122
Bradwell-on-Sea, St. Peter : Saxon work, **138**, 139
Brailes, Warwickshire : 307
Bramfield, Suffolk : **284** ; thatching, 286, 287
Bramford, Suffolk : lead roof, **285**, 289
Brampton Ash, Northants : Perp. work, 192
Branscombe, Devon : scenery, **20**, 22 ; chapel, 102 ; chamber, 113
Brasses : 317
Breamore, Hants : Saxon central tower, 98, 139
Bredon, Worcs : 74 ; study of, 210, **211**, 213
Bremhill, Wilts : 307 ; bell-cote, **308**
Brentingham, Bishop of Exeter : 10
Brent Tor, Devon : **21**
Bricks : Roman, **141**, use of, 135 ; mediæval, 243–52 ; tracery, **247**
Brickwork : mediæval, 243–52, **244–51, 250**
Brighstone, Isle of Wight : squint window, **308**
Brigstock, Northants : 113, 128 ; Saxon " long-and-short," 141 ; Saxon head arch, 141
Bristol : St. Mary Redcliffe, 109, 130
Britford, Wilts : plaster, 253
Brixworth, Northants : 111, 138 ; Italian apse, 71 ; porch, 122 ; Roman bricks, **135** ; pre-Conquest crypt, 129 ; pre-Conquest masonry, 149 ; Saxon opening, **135**, 141
Broach spire : 159, **160**
Broads, Norfolk : 284, 285
Broadwater : use of Caen stone, 219 ; consecration crosses, 303 ; Trans. work, 152 ; Trans. vaulting, 229 ; porch, 123

INDEX TO TEXT AND ILLUSTRATIONS 325

Brookland, Kent: 118; timber porch, 262; detached timber belfry, 264
Broughton, Oxon: aisle windows, 87
Brumstead, Norfolk: 179
Bryant, Mr.: 236, 286
Brydges, Duke of Chandos: 203
Brympton, Somerset: situation, 16, **18**; Hall, domestic architecture, 16
Buildwas Abbey: pointed arch, 151
Bunwell, Norfolk: flushwork in porch, 239
Burford, Oxon: 127, 128, 210; "squint," 98; E.E. ironwork, 294; fan-vaulting, 233
Burgh, Lincs: pulpit, **309**
Burlingham St. Andrew, Norfolk: flint emblem, 240
Burpham, Sussex: E.E. vaulting, 230; E.E. roof, 272, 273
Bury St. Edmunds: 219, 257, 287; use of stone, 217
Buttresses: Norman, 146, 226; flying, 226
Buttsbury, Essex: ironwork on door, **292**
Byfield, Northants: 275; Dec. work, **168**, 170; porch, 174

C

CABOT, Sebastian: 38
Caen stone: 179, 217–219, 238
Caerwent, Monmouthshire: pre-Saxon work, 135
Caister, Lincs: 294
Calbourne, Isle of Wight: Geometric window, 163, **164**
Cambridge: All Saints, 119; St. Benet, Saxon tooling, 139; Great St. Mary, 11; King's College Chapel, fan-vaulting, 233
Canon estate, Edgware: 203
Canonical hours: 41–3
Canons: of Edgar, 41; Elfric, 41
Canterbury: Cathedral: 71, 288; choir, 229; basilican plan, 72. St. Martin, 252, 256; plaster-work, 252; masonry, 256; Roman walls, 135. St. Mildred, Saxon work, 139. St. Pancras, 122; basilican plan, 72; mortar, 256. St. Peter, groined vaulting, 229
Capitals: 154; foliage, 157–**158**; Norman, 145; E.E., 157–8; Perp., **184**
Carisbrooke, Isle of Wight: vaulting, 232
"Carolean" woodwork: 313
Cashel, Ireland: oratories, 71
Cassington, Oxon: Norman vaulting, 227

Castle Hedingham, Essex: 292; Norman ironwork, 291, 292; Trans. work, 152; brick clerestory, 247
Castle Rising, Norfolk: Norman work 147, **148**; ornamental arcade, 152
Castor, Northants: transeptal, **103**, **104**
Catesby, Antony: 198
Catesby, John de: 193
Ceda, St., Bishop: 73, 215
Chaldon, Surrey: description of, 210, **212**, 213
Chalvington, Sussex: timber belfry, 264
Chambers over porches: use of, 43, 125–6
Chancel: repairing of, 10; development of chancel aisles, 89: chapels of, Norman, **73**; plans, **89–91**, **94**; three-gabled, 93; arches of, 95; eastern extension, **129**, 130
Chantry chapels: 63, 96; founded by guilds, 97; position of, **97**
Chapels: chantry, in chancel, 89–95, **92–4**, 97; increase of, 96; influence of, on plan, 93
Charles: I, 313; II, 203
Charlton, Kent: 201; brick, 251
Checkendon, Oxon: Norman vaulting, 228
Chedgrave, Norfolk: 117
Chelmsford: 261; brick in tower, 249
Cheltenham stone: 179
Cherry Hinton, Cambs: sedilia, **315**
Chesterfield: twisted spire, 32, 288; Dec. tower, 104; chantry chapel, **97**; "squint," 97
Chester-le-Street, Durham: 55
Chests: 310
Chiddingfold, Surrey: 273
Chidham, Sussex: E.E. style, 159
Chignal St. James, Essex brick tracery, 247
Chignal Smealey, Essex: brick church, 247
Chilmark, Wilts: 223
Chipping Campden, Glos.: 87; crypt, 130
Chipping Norton, Oxon: 87, 128; flamboyant window, 173
Chipping Ongar, Essex: window, **136**
Chipstead, Surrey: 230; E.E. vaulting, 230
Chithurst, Sussex: square-ended plan, **60**, 61
Chittlehampton, Devon: 118; Perp. tower, 190
Chrishall, Essex: timber belfry, 261
Chrism: 302
Christopher, St.: 309
Chulmleigh, Devon: rood screen, **95**, 96
Church ales: 10, 12, 13
Church Stretton, Salop: **19**; cruciform plan, 20

Churches: harmony with surroundings, 15, 20–3, 27, 34, 51–2, 54; religious use of, 40, 44; the smallest, 2, 3, 4; secular use of, 13–4, 40
Churchwardens' accounts: 41, 198, 219, 242, 283, 291, 317
Churchyards: 13–5; uses of, 34
Cirencester, Glos: clerestory, **86**, 87; porches, 126, **127**; St. Catherine's Chapel, fan-vaulting, 233
Cistercian foundations: 151
Clanfield, Oxon: **301**
Clare, Suffolk: 249
Classic treatment: 205
Classical style in churches: 201–9
Clerestory: 63, **86**, **81–8**, 193; introduction of, 80–7; lighting problems, 80; continuous over nave and chancel, **82**; Norman, **83**; E.E., 83, **84**; Geometric, 83; Dec., 83, **85**
Clevedon, Somerset: Trans. work, 153
Cley, Norfolk: **85**, 123, 179
Cliffe, Kent: flintwork, 241
Clovelly, Devon: 100
Clunch stone: 179, 223
Clymping, Sussex: **115**; use of Caen stone, 219
Clyst St. George, Devon: cruciform planning, 100
Coddenham, Suffolk: flintwork, 240
Coggeshall, Essex: St. Nicholas' Chapel, brick arches, 246
Colchester: Holy Trinity, Saxon arch, **141**; St. Peter, 296
Colebrooke, Copplestone Chapel, Devon: **96**
Colley Weston, Northants: quarry, 289
Collumpton: Perp. chapel, 198
Columb, St.: Major, Cornwall, 31; Minor Cornwall, tower, 32, **33**
Colyton, Devon: cruciform planning, 100; upper chamber, 126; Perp. window, 189
Combe Martin, Devon: 34, **37**
Compton, Surrey: 151; vaulting, 227
Compton Wynyates, Warwicks: mixed styles, 202
Consecration crosses: 302, **303**, 316
Constable, John, painter: **29**, 30
Contrasts of English parish church: **2–7**; exteriors, **2–3**; interiors, **4–7**
Copdock, Suffolk: Perp. work, 185
Corbel tables: E.E., 159, 310
Corhampton, Hants: Saxon work, **139**; plaster, 253
Corinthian pillars: 205
Cornish granite: 225
Cotswolds: 290
Cotterstock, Northants: Dec. work, 169

Councils of: London and Westminster: 8
Mainz, 8
Coventry: 287; guilds, 38; St. Michael, **39**, **87**; characteristic features, 36; lantern tower, 36; screened enclosure, 97; guild chapels, 97: spire, 191: E.E. roofs, 273; Holy Trinity, **4**, 6; guild chapels, 97
Cowley, Middlesex: 265; Perp. roof, 277
Cranbrook, Kent: west tower, 23
Cransley, Northants: Dec. arcade, 170
Crécy: 179
Creed, St., Cornwall: groining in porch, 232
Crick, Northants: geometric spire, 164
Crockets: profusion of Dec., 174, **176**
Cromwell Bishop, Notts: 273
Crondal, Hants: brickwork in tower, 201; vaulting, 230; brickwork, 252
Consecration crosses: 302, 303, 316
Crosthwaite: size, **28**
Cross: churchyard, 26; incised, 302, **303**; on jamb, 303
Crowhurst, Surrey: 264, 295
Crowland, Lincs: use of stone, 216
Crowle, Worcs: timber porch, 262, **263**
Cruciform plan: 95, 98, **101**, 102; central towers, 98, **101**; mistaken idea of symbolism, 98–9; Norman plan in Cornish churches, 100; with Norman towers, **101**, **103**
Crypts: 129, 227; Norman, 130
Cuckfield, Sussex · timber spire, 264
Culbone, Somerset: **3**, 5; size, 25; early Saxon work, 26; windows, **26**, **27**; of timber, 267; Perp. rood screen, 26
Cullompton, Devon: 198; Lane aisle, fan-vaulting, 233
Curvilinear style: 172

D

Daglingworth, Glos: Roman altar, 137
Dale Abbey, Derbyshire: 255
Darenth, Kent: Norman vaulted chancel, 227
Darlington, Durham: 83
Decorated style: 168; roofs, 273; ball-flower, 170; ironwork, 296
Decuman's, St., Watchet, Somerset: wall-plate angels, 279
Dedham: 119; Vale of, **29**, 30
Deerhurst, Glos: tower interior, **111**; Saxon windows, **141**; pre-Conquest masonry, 149
Denison, William: 207
Derby: 38; All Saints tower, **12**, 197; restoration, 207

INDEX TO TEXT AND ILLUSTRATIONS 327

Despencer, Sir Hugh: 233
Development: of plan, 44; of parish churches, 45-6
De Vere family: Earl of Oxford, 193
Devizes: St. John, ornamental arcade, 152
Didcot, Berks: timber bell-cote, **265**, 266
Diddlebury, Salop: Saxon windows, 140; pre-Conquest masonry, 149
Dingley, Berks: 294
Distinguishing features of Saxon and Norman work: 138-42
Doddinghurst, Essex: timber-work, 259, 260, 266; timber porch, 262
Dog-tooth moulding: 170
Domestic architecture: early brickwork in, 246
Donington, Lincs: plan, **112**, 113; flank-in tower, **113**; use of stone, 216
Doors: 291; ironwork on, **291-6**; carving on, 296-300
Dorchester, Oxon: Geometric aisle, 164
Doulting, Somerset: 104, **223**; stone, 179
Dover: 38; Castle, 256; St. Mary-in-the-Castle, 71, 99, 116; Saxon work, 135
Downham Market, Norfolk: brick repairs, 249
Dubricius, St.: 26
Ducklington, Oxon: flamboyant window, **173**
Duddington, Northants: Trans. work, 153
Dundry stone: 179
Dunkery Beacon: 54
Dunsfold, Surrey: 264; fourteenth-century roof, 273; ironwork, 296
Dunstan, Archbishop: 41
Dunster, Somerset: 52, 128, 266
Duntisbourne Rous, Glos: Norman crypt, 130; slate roofing, **289**, 290
Durham Cathedral: 258, 288; sanctuary, 299

E

EADBERT, Bishop: 283
Eadmer: 71
Earl Stonham, Suffolk: flintwork, 240, **241**
Earls Barton, Northants: Saxon church, 76, **137**; tower, **137**, 139; belfry opening, 141
Early English: 154-60; capitals, 157, **158**; groined vaulting, 156; mouldings, 158, **159**; piers, 156, 158; problem of pointed arch, 151; windows, **156-7**

Easlington, Yorks E.E. work, 160
East Dereham, Norfolk: 117; Caen stone font, 219; flushwork in porch, 239
East Haddon, Northants: Dec. cornice 170
East Ham London: 74
East Hornden, Essex: brick church, 247
Easter sepulchre: 172, **176**, 177, 212, 315
Easthorpe, Essex: brick church, 247
Easton, Hants: Norman vaulting, 227
Eaton Bray, Beds: E.E. piers, 156; E.E. capitals, 158; ironwork, **295**, **296**
Edenhall, Cumb: enclosed-in park, 18
Edington, Wilts: exterior crosses, 303
Edmund, St.: 257-8
Edstaston, Salop: Norman ironwork, 292
Edwalton, Notts: diapered brickwork, 252
Edward: I, 295; II, 169; III, 169, 181, 237; IV, 237, 244; VI, 47, 198
Edward the Confessor: 48
Egloshayle, Cornwall: 31, 279; Caen stone pulpit, 220
Eleanor, Queen: 295
Ely Cathedral: 272, 288; Lichfield chapel, fan-vaulting, 233
Elizabeth, Queen: 47, 199
Elizabethan period: 199, 250, 281
Elkstone, Glos: Norman work, 75; Norman vaulting, 227
Elm, Cambs: E.E. clerestory, 83, **84**
Elsing, Norfolk: aisleless church, 76, **77**, **78**
Elstead, Surrey: timber porch, 262
Elsted, Sussex: pre-Conquest masonry, 149, 262
Emblems: in flint, 240
Endellion, St., Cornwall: wagonhead roof, **278**
English Gothic art: 50
Erith, Kent: ironwork, 292
Erpingham, Norfolk: flint emblems, 240
Escomb, Durham: **70**, 71, **142**; Roman brick, 135; plaster-work, 253; Saxon church, **142**; sculptured stones, 136; plaster-work, 253
Etton, Northants: E.E. windows, 156. **157**; Geometric windows, 162, **163**
Evesham, All Saints: fan-vaulting, 233
Ewelme, Oxon: craftsmanship, **47**
Ewerby, Lincs: 118, **120**, **121**, 128
Ewhurst, Surrey: timber porch, 262
Exeter: Dean and Chapter, 22; St. Petrock, Perp. work, 184, **187**
Exmoor, 52
Exning, Suffolk: 242
Eye, Suffolk: 31; flintwork **237**

F

FAIRFORD, Glos : Perp. work, 194, **195**
Fan-vaulting : 183, 232, **233**
Farly, Surrey : plaster-work, 253
Feering, Essex : brickwork, **245**, 247, **248**, 300
Felix, St., Bishop of East Anglia · 73, 235
Feltham, Surrey : Saxon work, 135
Fen Ditton, Cambs : Barnack stone, 216
Fen Drayton, Cambs : squint, 308
Filby, Norfolk ; 273
Filey, Yorks : 83 ; E.E. style, 160
Finan, Bishop : 282
Finedon, Northants : Dec. work, 169
Fireplaces : in porches, 126, 308 ; in towers 113
Fitzherbert family : 16
Flamboyant style : 4, 51 ; windows, 170, **172-3**
Flaunden, Herts : timber tower, **270**, **271**
" Flemish Chapel," St. Mary's, Beverley : 232
Flint : use of, in churches, 234-42 ; gauged or flushwork, **238-42** ; chequer-work, 241-2 ; clerestory, **241** ; emblems, **240** ; porches, **214**, **220** ; **238-9** ; round towers, **234**, **235** ; towers, **237**, **241** ; walling, 236
Flushwork in flint : **220**, **238-42**
Foliage : comparison of, 169, 174, 183 ; E.E. foliage, 157
Folkington, Sussex : 264
Fonts : 308
Ford, Suffolk : flushwork in porch, 239
Ford, Sussex : 251 ; use of Caen stone, 219
Fordingbridge, Hants : 116 ; Perp. roof, 276 (footnote)
Foremark, Derbys : St. Saviour, rebuilding of, 202, 203
Forncett St. Peter, Norfolk : Saxon flint tower, **140**, 236
Fowey, Cornwall : 31, 85 ; Perp. work, 184, **185** ; Perp. tower, 190
Frampton, Lincs : transeptal church, 106, **107**
Framsden, Suffolk : flushwork, **238**, 239
Franciscan building : 244
Freshwater, Isle of Wight : Geometric windows, 163
Freslingford, Suffolk : Dec. chapel, 89
Frittenden, Kent : crocketed spire, 23
Fritton, Suffolk : Norman apse, 73 ; thatched work, **284**, 286
Frosterly marble : 222
Fryerning, Essex : brick nave, 246

G

GABLES : timber, 268
Gabriel, Archangel : 257
" Galilee " : 123-4
Gedney, Lincs : use of stone, 216, 300
Geometrical work : 160-7 ; windows, 162, **165-7**
Georgian work : 204 *et seq.*
Gibbs, James, architect : 207
Glass, painted : 67, 87, 187, 212
Glastonbury, Somerset : use of timber, 256-7
Glendalough, Ireland : oratories, 71
Godalming, Surrey : lead spire, **287**, 288
Godshill, Isle of Wight : **1**, 5 ; situation, 15
Gosburton, Lincs : use of stone, 216
Granite, Cornish : 225
Grantchester, Cambs : Dec. windows, **171**, 172 ; plaster-work, **254**
Grantham, Lincs : 36, 38, 43, 118 ; Geometric style, 165, **166**, **167** ; curvilinear, **172**
Great Abington, Cambs : rood window, 305
Great Baddow, Essex : clerestory, brick, **246** ; porch, 247 ; lead spire, 288
Great Bookham, Surrey : timber-work, 263
Great Bromley, Essex : **32**
Great Coxwell, Berks : **55**, 56
Great Easton, Essex : timber towers, 260
Great Fire, the : 203, 245
Great Harwood, Bucks : flamboyant window, 173
Great Panton, Lincs : late Perp. church 198
Great Pestilence : 181
Great Plague : 169
Greenford, Middlesex : timber tower, 265
Greensted, Essex : use of split trunks, **257**
Gretton, Northants : 79, 118
Groombridge, Kent : 201 ; brickwork, 252
Grostete, Bishop of Lincoln : architectural efforts of, 50
Guild chapels : 94
Guildford, St. Mary : Saxon central tower, 98 ; Trans. vaulting, **228**, 230
Guildhall : City of London, 36 ; Coventry, 36
Guilds, work of : 42, 65 66, 96, 97, 98
Gwennap, Cornwall : 93, 117
Gwithian, St., Cornwall : oratories, 71

H

HACKET, Bishop : 202
Haddiscoe, Norfolk : **234**, 295 ; flintwork, 237 ; ironwork on door, 292

INDEX TO TEXT AND ILLUSTRATIONS 329

Hadleigh, Suffolk : lead spire, 288
Hales Owen, Salop : E.E. roof, 273
Halesworth, Suffolk : flushwork in porch, 239
Halsall, Lancs : 297, 305
Halvergate, Norfolk : flushwork in porch, 239
Ham Hill, Somerset : 266, 267 ; quarry, 222 ; stone, 26
Hammer-beam roofs : 280, **281, 282**
Hampnett, Glos : Norman work, 75
Hampton Poyle, Oxon : Geometric window, 164
Handborough, Oxon : screens and pulpit, **314**
Hanley, Worcs : Elizabethan repairs, **199**
Hanseatic League : 243, 244
Harberton, Devon : Perp. tower, **191**
Hargrave, Northants : clerestory, 83 ; Trans. work, 153 ; sixteenth-century brick tower, 250
Harleston, Northants : Geometric tower, 164 ; Dec. windows, 170
Harmony of churches with surroundings : 15–6, 20–4, 34–6
Harting, South Sussex : harmony with scenery, 16, **17**
Hartland, Devon : 100
Hartley Wespall, Hants : timber-work, 266
Hastings : St. Clement's, 232 ; All Saints, vaulting, 232
Hatch, Essex : brick church, 247
Hatton, Sir Christopher : 199
Hawton, Notts : 128, **175** ; Easter sepulchre, **176,** 177
Haydon, Lancs : hammer-beam roof, 281
Hayling, South, Hants : timber porch, **262**
Hazelbeach, Northants : 199
Heckington, Lincs : 36, 106, 128 ; Dec. style, 171, 172
Hedon, Yorks : 104 ; E.E. style, 160 ; fourteenth-century nave, **178**
Hemel Hempstead, Herts : 76,305 ; Norman vaulting, 227 ; lead spire, 288
Hereford Cathedral : 288
Henry : III, 48, 50, 161, 164, 209 ; VII, 197, 198, 246 ; VIII, 48, 182, 197, 246
Herringbone masonry : **149**
Herringfleet, Suffolk : Saxon window, 141 ; flint tower, **235,** 236
Heyshott, Sussex : 23, **24** ; windows, Dec. and Perp., 24 ; timber porch, 24
Hexham, Northumberland : sculptured stones in crypt, 136 ; stonework, 215 ; barrel-vaulting, 227
Higham Ferrers, Northants : 36, 127 ; Dec. work, **168,** 169 ; Dec. roof, 275 ; Lady Chapel, Geometric work, 164

Highworth, Wilts : fan-vaulting, 233
Hingham, Norfolk : 128
Hillesdon, Bucks : fan-vaulting, 233
Hitchin, Herts : charnel-house, 130
Hobhouse, Bishop : 9, 10
Holbeach, Lincs : 87 ; use of stone, 216, 297
Holdenby : Elizabethan work, 199 ; Renaissance screen, **200**
Hollingbourne : Culpeper chapel, 201
Holmer, Hereford : timber belfry, 267
Holton, Lincs : brick tower, 250
Holy-water stoups : 301–8
Honiton, Devon : cruciform planning, 100
Hood-moulds : 174
Horndon-on-the-Hill, Essex : timber-work, 260
Hormead, Herts : 293
Horsham, Sussex : 83 ; timber spire, 264 ; quarry, 289
Houghton-on-the-Hill, Lincs : 293
Hour-glass, **310**, 313
Huddington, Worcs : timber porch, 262;
Huish Episcopi, Somerset : 52, 190
Hull, Yorkshire, Holy Trinity : **7**, 240 ; brickwork, 244 ; Perp. arcade, 184
Hurstbourne Tarrant, Hants : timber tower, 266
Hythe, Kent : Sunday procession, 34, 120

I

ICHNOGRAPHY : 226
Ickenham, Middlesex : wooden belfry, 265
Icklesham, Sussex : Norman vaulting, 229
Iffley : 60 ; Norman mouldings, 143 ; Norman work, 147 ; Norman vaulting, 228
Ile Abbots, Somerset : 52
Ilkley, Yorks : sculptured stones, 136
Influence of scenery on builders : 52, 56
Ingatestone, Essex : brick tower, 246
Ingestre, Staffs : Charles II period, 203
Interdict : 50, 154
Ipswich : 38 ; St. Peter's, marble font, 221
Irchester, Northants : Geometric work, 164 ; Perp. spire, 181
Ironwork : on doors, **291–300** ; Norman, **292** ; Trans., **293** ; E.E., 294 ; Dec., 296
Irstead, Norfolk : 296 ; thatching, 286
Irthlingborough, Northants : 113
Isleham, Cambs : brick porch, 250
Islip, Northants : 128 ; Perp. work, 193
Ivinghoe, Bucks : 99 ; E.E. capitals, 158
Ives, St., Cornwall : 31 ; wagon roof, 278, 279

Ixworth, Suffolk: late fourteenth-century roofs, **275**, 276

J

JACOBEAN work: 313
James I: 291, 313
Jarrow, Durham: 137; stonework, 215, **216**
Jocelyn of Wells, Bishop architectural efforts of, 50
John, King: 50, 154
Joseph of Arimathea: 257
Juliot, St., Cornwall: groins in porch, 232
Just-in-Penwith, St., Cornwall: stripping of plaster, 254

K

KEDLESTON, Derbys: enclosed in park, 18
Kelshall, Herts: banner-staves, 309
Kelvedon, Essex: brick church, 247
Kenchester, Herefords: use of Roman piers, 137
Kentish rag: 219
Kesgrave, Suffolk: brick tower, 250
Kesteven Division, Lincs: 223
Kettering, Northants: 36; Perp. tower, 192; St. John Baptist, 199
Ketton, Rutland: 159; E.E. tower, **161**: stone, 217
Keyworth, Notts: 118
Kibworth, Leics: Geometric window, 162
Kiddington, Oxon: 273
Kilkhampton, Cornwall: 226; Perp. work, 51; granite piers, **224**
Kilpeck, Herefords: plan, **59**; Norman apse, 73; Norman door, **143**; Norman arch, 144, **145**; Norman vaulting, 228
King's Lynn, Norfolk: St. Nicholas, alteration of structure, 67; plan, **67**; interior, **68**; porch, **125**; Perp. window, **190**; Red Mount brick, 244
King's Sutton, Northants: 123; Perp. tower, 192
Kingsbury, Middlesex: timber belfry, 265
Kingsbridge, Devon: plan of town, **11**
Kingston-on-Sea, Sussex: E.E. vaulting, 230
Kippax, Yorks: Norman masonry, 149
Kirkby Stephen, Westmorland: 105
Kirton, Lincs: Barnack stone, 216
Knapton, Norfolk: double hammer-beam roof, 281

L

LADBROOK lithographs: 285
" Ladder of Salvation ": 212
Laighton, Thomas de: 295, 296
Laindon, Essex: timber-work, **259**, 260; timber porch, 262
Lakeland: churches, **27**, **28**
Landewednack, Cornwall: groining, 232
Landscape: effect of, on design, 20–32, 52–6
Landrake, Cornwall: quarries, 218
Lanfranc, Archbishop: 71
Langford, Essex: 71; Saxon work, 135
Langham, Essex: 30
Langport: lias, 222
Langton, Stephen: 50
Lanteglos, Camelford, Cornwall: wagonhead roofs, **278**, 279
Lastingham, York: 229; Trans. vaulting 215
Laud, Archbishop: 202
Laudian revival: 313
Launceston, Cornwall: St. Mary, 31; " three-gable " E. end, **92**, 93; Perp. clerestory, **192**, 193; Perp. arcade, **196**, 197; granite-work, **225**, 226; St. Stephen, 128
Lavenham, Suffolk: 31, 128, **192**, 193, **196**
Layer Marney, Essex: brick church, 247
Lead spires: **287–8**
Leatherhead, Surrey: chequer-work, 241
Leathley, Yorks: ironwork, 293
Lectern: **311**; Gospel lectern, 313
Ledbury, Herefords: St. Catherine's chapel, 117; Dec. windows, 168, **169**; reticulated tracery, 173
Leicester, St. Margaret's, Norman ironwork, 292; St. Martin's arched roof, **274**; St. Mary's, 275
Leighton Buzzard, Beds: 87, 295
Lenten veil: 316
" Leper " windows: 306
Leverington, Cambs: Barnack stone, 216
Lewes, Sussex: St. Anne, Trans. vaulting, 229
Libraries: 126; Radcliffe, Oxford, 207
Lichfield Cathedral: 225
Lierne vaulting: **231**, 232
Limington, Somerset: ribbed vaulting, 232
Limpsfield, Surrey: 273
Lincoln Cathedral: 221; " Angel Choir," 161; font, 221; spire, 288
Lindisfarne, Isle of: 215, 282–7
Linkoping, Sweden: 243
Little Addington, Northants: Geom. work, 164
Little Baddow, Essex: timber belfry, 261

INDEX TO TEXT AND ILLUSTRATIONS 331

Little Braxted : apsidal plan, **61** ; timber-work, 259
Little Bursted, Essex : brick tracery, 247
Little Casterton, Rutland : E.E. church, 159
Little Maplestead : circular plan, 59
Little Munden, Herts : plan, 78, **80**
Little Packington : Trans. work, 153
Littl《Wenham Hall : brickwork, 246
London : St. Alban, Wood Street, **310**, 313 ; Lincoln's Inn, 244 ; St. Mary Aldermary, Charles II period, 203 ; St. Mary-at-Hill, 43 ; St. Mary-le-Bow, Norman crypt, 130 ; St. Paul's, 288 ; St. Peter Cheap, 43 ; St. Sepulchre, chamber over porch, 126, 127 ; Templars' Church, circular plan, 59
Long Melford, Suffolk : flintwork, 237 ; parapet, 239
Longmynd, Salop : 20
Long Stanton, Cambs : trussed rafter roof, 273 ; thatching, 286
Long Sutton, Lincs : groining, 232 ; lead spire, 288
Long Sutton, Somerset : angel roof, 277
Lostwithiel, Cornwall : 85, 119 ; Perp. work, 185
Louth, Lincs : 36 ; Perp. tower, 191 ; steeple, 197
Lowestoft, Suffolk, St. Margaret's : Perp. work, 184, **185** ; east window, 188
Lowick, Northants : 122 ; Perp. work, **189**
Luccombe, Somerset : situation, 52, **54**
Ludlow, Salop : 11 ; Perp. work, 184, **186**
Lullingstone, Kent : enclosed in park, 18
Luna, Sweden : 243
Lurgashall, Sussex : timber porch, 263 ; timber spire, 264
Luton, Beds : 109 ; aisled transeptal plan, **110**, 128
"Lychnoscopes" : 306
Lydd, Kent : tower, 23, 38
Lyminge, Kent : Roman walls, 135
Lyminster, Sussex : E.E. roof, 264
Lynn, Norfolk : *see* King's Lynn

M

Madingley, Cambs : clerestory, 87, **88**
Maids Moreton, Bucks : 299 ; fan-vaulting, 233
Maldon, Essex : 122
Manor-court rolls : 9
Manor-house : proximity to church, 16 **18**, 19
Manton, Rutland : E.E. style, 159
Mapledurham, Oxon : brickwork, **250**

Marbles : Belgian, 221 ; Purbeck, 222 ; Frosterly marble, 222
March, Cambs : hammer-beam roof, 281
Margaret-at-Cliffe, St., Kent : Norman clerestory, **83**
Margaret Roothing, Essex : 291, 292
Margaretting, Essex : timber towers, 260 ; timber porches, 261
Market Overton, Rutland : Saxon work, 141
Martock, Somerset : Perp. roof, 276, **277**
Marston Moretaine, Beds : detached tower, **118, 119** ; Perp. roof, 276
Martham, Norfolk : flint pattern, 240, 300
Marton, Cheshire : timber-work, 268, **269**
Mary, St., of Quarr, Abbey of, Isle of Wight : 223
Mary Tudor, Queen : 252
Mary Week, St. : 305
Masonry : 256 ; Norman, 149
Masses, early : 43
Materials : 215–300
Mattingley, Hants : brickwork, 252 ; timber-work, 265
Medomsley, Durham : 54, 55
Meesden, Herts : brick porch, 250
Melbourn, Derbys : 34 ; Norman arcades, 78 ; Norman church, 150, **151**
Melbury Bubb, Dorset : tower, 115, **117**
Melton Mowbray, Leics : 109
Melverley, Salop : 267
Mendelsham, Suffolk : flushwork in porch, 239
Merrow, Surrey : timber porch, 262
Merstham, Surrey : E.E. chancel, **91** door, 295
Michaelmarsh, Hants : tower, 266
Mickleham, Surrey : chequer-work, 241
Middleton, Lancs : 95 ; Trans. work, 152
Midhurst, Sussex : 23
Milton, Kent : 297
Minehead, Somerset : 52, 266 ; timber arch, 267
Minster, Isle of Thanet : 230 ; E.E. vaulting, **229**, 230
Minster, Sheppey : lead spire, 288
Minster Lovell, Oxon : 105
Monastic : bodies, 71 ; churches, 73
Monkwearmouth, Durham : Saxon vaulting, 227
Montague, Bishop, of Norwich : 285
Monuments, study of : 317
Moor, Somerset : consecration crosses, **303**
Moorlinch, Somerset : 316
Morbourne, Hunts : Trans. work, 153 ; E.E. roof, 273
Morley, Derbys : passage from church to house, 18
Mornington, Herefords : Charles II's time, 203

332 INDEX TO TEXT AND ILLUSTRATIONS

" Morrow-mass priests " : 42
Mortar : 256 *et seq.*
Morwenstow, Cornwall : **6**, 291
Moulded brick : 248
Mouldings : 48, 143, 152, 158, 184, 185 ; Norman, **143**
Moulton, Lincs : Barnack stone, 216
Mount Bures, Essex : brick tracery, 247
Mountnessing, Essex : timber-work, 259–60
Mumby, Lincs : E.E. moulding, 159
Municipal churches : 36
Mural paintings : 253
Mylor, St., Cornwall : **117** ; Caen stone arcade, 220
Mystery plays : 13

N

NANTWICH, Cheshire : Sts. Mary and Nicholas, E.E. vaulting, **231**, 232
Nately Scures, Hants : Norman apse, 73 ; Norman windows, **144**
Navestock, Essex : timber towers, 260 ; timber arch, 262
Needham Market, Suffolk : hammer-beam roof, 281, **282**
Nene River : 52
Neot's, St., Hunts : **275**, 276 ; Perp. tower, 190, 197 ; Perp. roofing, 279
Net tracery : 173, **174**
Nether Peover, Cheshire : timber church, 270
Newark, Notts : 36, 43, 118, 179 ; chapels, **129**
Newdigate, Surrey : timber belfry, 263, **264**
Newhaven, Sussex : 60, **73**, 74
New Romney, Kent : 38, **93**
New Shoreham, Sussex : Trans. style, **152**, 153 ; use of Caen stone, 219 ; vaulting, 229
Nicholas, Earl of Scarsdale : 19
Nighton, St., Cornwall : wagon-roof in porch, 279
Norbury : covered way from house to church, 16
Norham, Northumberland : Norman arcades, 78
Norman : work, **134**, 143, **147** ; arches, **145** ; bases, 145 ; buttress, 146 ; capitals 145 ; ironwork, 291, **293** ; masonry, **149** ; mouldings, **143** ; roofs and vaulting, 146 ; tympanum, **144** ; walls, 145–6 ; windows, **144**
North Crawley, Bucks : Geometric window, 164, **165**
North Creak, Norfolk : hammer-beam roof, 280
North Flambridge, Essex : brick church 247

North Hill, Cornwall : groining, 232
North Leigh, Oxon : Wilcote chapel, fan-vaulting, **233**
Northleach, Glos : fireplace in porch, 126 ; Perp. windows, 182, **183**, **184**
North Molton, Devon : chancel panelling, **204**
Northborough, Northants : Geometric work, 164 ; Trans. work, 153
Northfield, Worcs : timber porch, 262
Northolt, Middlesex : timber tower, 277
Northwich, Cheshire : fireplace in porch, 126
Norton, Durham : Saxon central tower, 98
Norwich : use of stone, 216 ; Cathedral, 223, 288 ; St. Giles, 38 ; St. Gregory, procession path, 34 ; St. Mary, 296 ; St. Michael Coslany, flintwork, 240, **242** ; St. Michael-at-Plea, 299 ; St. Michael-at-Thorn, 294 ; St. Peter Hungate, ironwork, 299 ; St. Peter Mancroft, **82**, 83, 87, 128, 237 ; flintwork, 240 ; St. Stephen, 87
Nottingham : St. Mary, 95
Nottinghamshire : Norman herringbone work, 149

O

OAKHAM, Rutland : frontispiece, 109
Ockham, Surrey : E.E. windows, **156**
Odiham, Hants : late brick tower, **201** ; 95, 252 ; rectangular plan, 152
Ogee-heads : 169, 173
Old Basing, Hants : **94**, 95, **251**
Old Shoreham : 272 ; Caen stone, 219 ; cruciform, **101**, **102** ; Norman roof-beam, 272 ; square plan, 62
Ongar, Essex : brick window, 246 ; *v.* Chipping Ongar
Oolitic limestone : 216, 222
Oratories : converted into churches, 9
Orebro, Sweden : 243
Ormskirk : Perp. work, 185, **187**
Ornament : Norman, 143 ; E.E. (dog-tooth), 157, **159**, 160, 170 ; Dec., 174, **176**, 177 ; (ball-flower), **168**, **169**, 170 ; Perp. 183–5
Osiers, twisted : early use, 257
Osyth, St., Essex : brick arcading, 248, **249**
Othery, Somerset : 104
Ottery St. Mary, Devon : **115** ; E.E. vaulting, 232 ; fan-vaulting, 233 ; exterior crosses, 303
Oughton, Yorkshire : Perp. steeple, 198
Oundle, Northants : 36, 127, 295
Over, Cambs : Barnack stone, 216, 287, 307

INDEX TO TEXT AND ILLUSTRATIONS 333

Overton, Hants : E.E. roof, 273
Ovingdean, Sussex : Saxon work, 135
Oxbridge, Somerset : Perp. work, 193
Oxford : Cathedral, late fan-vaulting, 233 ; St. Peter-in-the-East, Norman crypt, 130 ; Norman vaulting, 227 ; St. Giles, Geometric window, 163

P

PAINTINGS, mural : 309
Pakefield, Suffolk : thatch, 286
Panelling : Perp., 183, 204
Pantiles : 289
Parapets : 193, **194**, **195** ; brick, **246**, **248**
Parclose screens : 14, **96**
Parish accounts of St. Andrew's, Holborn : 12*
Parish church centre for community life, 1, 13 ; enclosed in parks, 18 ; mystery plays, 13 ; religious devotion, 1, 13, 40 ; repositories for art work, 46–8, **47**, **49** ; sanctuaries, 15 ; store-house, 14, 38 ; chest, 310
" Parvise " (so-called) : 124–5
Patrington, York, 179, 232, 316 : aisled transeptal plan, 106, **108** ; Dec. work, **170**, 172, 176 ; E.E. vaulting, 232 ; Easter sepulchre, 172 ; lierne vaulting, **316** ; stone reredos, **316**
Paul of Caen : 255
Paul's Cathedral, St. : 245
Paul's Walden, St., Herts : Georgian work, 204, **205**, **206**
Peckham, Archbishop : Constitutions of, 307
Pembridge, Herefords : detached tower, 117, 267, **268**
Penkivel, Cornwall : 109, 113, 128
Periods : 132–213 ; Classical, 201–9 ; combination of styles, 210–3 ; Decorated, 123, 168–81 ; development of, 132–4 ; different nomenclature, 133-5 ; Early English, 133, 154–60 ; Elizabethan and Stuart, 199–201 ; Flamboyant, 51, 173 ; Geometrical, 134, 160–7 ; Norman, 133, 142–51 ; overlap of styles, 133–4 ; Perpendicular, 181–97 ; restorations, 208–10 ; Romanesque, 48 ; Saxon, 134–42 ; Transition, 151–4
Perpendicular : style (fifteenth century), 51, 173, 181–97 ; **185–7** ; arcades, **185–7** ; arches, 183, **186–7** ; capitals, 183, **184** ; clerestory, **87**, 192, 193 ; doorways, 298 ; moulding, 165, **184–7** ; painted glass in, **188** ; panelling, 183 ; parapets, **192–5**, 193 ; pillars, 183, **185–7** ; pinnacles, **189** 190, **194–5**

plinths, 183 ; rood screens, 232 ; roofs, **275**, 276, **277–82** ; towers, 190–2, **53**, **189**, **191–2**, **194–5** ; vaulting, 232, **233** ; windows, 174, **181–4**, **188–90**
Peterborough : use of Barnack stone, 216; Cathedral, whitewashing, 255, 272
Peter, St., Cheap : 43
Peter-on-the-Wall, St., Essex : Roman bricks, 135, **138** ; seventh-century apsidal plan, 72
Petersfield, Hants : Norman arcade, 145
Petworth, Sussex : 222
" Pilgrim " marks : 303
Pinchbeck, Lincs : Barnack stone, 216
Piers : 62 ; Norman, **79**, 145 ; E.E., 156–**158** ; Dec., **178** ; Perp., 183, **184–7**
Pilaster strips : **137**, **139**, 140
Pinnacles : **166**, **175** ; Perp., 190, **189**, **194–5**
Pipe Aston, Hereford : Norman tympanum, **144**
Piran, St., Cornwall : 71
Piscina : **313**
Pittledown, Dorset : Perp. church, 197
Plan : town, Kingsbridge, Devon, 10, **11**
Plans : 58–131 ; aisled, 87 et seq. ; apsidal, **61**, 70 ; basilican, 71 ; circular, **58**, 59 ; cruciform, 62, **100–109** ; development of, twelfth to thirteenth century, 65–6 ; nave and chancel, 61 ; parallelogram, 93–5, **94** ; Saxon, 60 ; square-ended, **60**, 61, **70**, **74** ; three-division Norman, **59**, **73–4** ; twelfth-century types, 58
Plaster : stripping of, 79–80, 139 ; use of, 252–5
Plastering : Saxon, 139, 252, 253
Plaxtole, Kent : Elizabethan roof, 202
Plough : Monday, 14 ; Light, 14
Polebrooke, Northants : Trans. work, 153, 273
Polyphant, Cornwall : quarry, 218
Ponsonby-Fane family . 16
Poore, Bishop of Salisbury and Durham, architectural efforts of : 50
Porches : brick, **245**, 288 ; double, 122–3 ; " Galilee," 123 ; gallery in, 124 ; " parvise," **124–5** ; position of, 122–3 ; Saxon, 122 ; three stages, 126 ; timber, **262**, **263**, **303** ; upper chambers in, 125, 308 ; use of, 122 ; western, 122, **123**
Potterne, Wilts : 99, 104
Poynings, Sussex : flintwork, 241, 300
Prestbury, Cheshire : 268, 270
Preston Bissett, Bucks : **84**, 85 ; flamboyant work, 173
Prideaux, Dr. John, Bishop of Worcester: 212

334 INDEX TO TEXT AND ILLUSTRATIONS

Problem of pointed arch : 151
Processions : Sunday, 34 ; at Hythe, Kent ; St. Gregory, Norwich ; Wrotham, Kent ; Wallaton, Notts, 34
Profusion of ornament in Dec. style : 174, **176**
Pucklechurch, Glos : rood window, 305
Pulham, Norfolk : flushwork in porch, 239
Pulpit : stone, 313 ; wood, **309, 313**
Purbeck marble : 46, 163, 222-30
Puxton, Somerset : **5, 6**
Pyrford, Surrey : timber porch, 262
Pyx, 316

Q

QUANTOCKS, architectural dividing-line, 52
Quarries, stone : 168, 217, 221, 222, 223, 224 225, 266, 289
" Queen of Holderness " (Patrington) : 171

R

RAMPTON, Cambs : thatched roof, 286
Ramsden Bellhouse, Essex : timber tower, 260
Ramsey, Hunts : use of stone, 216 ; Abbey, 98
Ramsey Pontifical : 258
Rattlesden, Norfolk : quarry, 219
Raunds, Northants : 89, **90**, 127, 128 ; Dec. chancel arch, 170
Rayleigh, Essex : timber arch, 262
" Reconciliation " : 15
" Rectilinear " : 182, 187
Reculver (2), Kent : basilican plan, 71 ; Roman work, 135
Redcliffe, St. Mary, Bristol : Dec. vaulting, **230**, 232
Reddenhall, Norfolk : flushwork in porch, 239
Reformation, the : 200
Reigate stone : 179
Renaissance : 4, 199, 200, 281
Repton, Derbys : 202 ; Saxon work, 139 ; vaulting crypt, 227
Reredos : stone, **316** ; alabaster, 316, **317**
Restoration : 202, 208-10
Reticulated tracery : 173, **174**
Ribblesford, Worcs : timber arcade, 267
Richard : Cœur de Lion, 50 ; II, 181, 182, 288
Rickinghall Inferior, Suffolk : Geometric window, 164, **165**
Ringstead, Northants : Dec. porch, 170
Ripon, Yorks : Minster, 221, 227 ; stonework, 215 ; crypt, barrel vaults, 227 ; lead spire, 288

Rissington, Wyck, Glos : **306**
Rocheford, Essex : brick tower, 246
Rochester : Cathedral, 288 ; St. Nicholas, classical building, 201
Rolvenden, Kent : **22** ; tower, 23
Roman Pharos : 256
Romanesque: 48, 134
Romney Marsh : 23
Romsey Abbey, Hants : 98
Rood screens : *see* Screens
Rood stairs : 236
Rood windows : **316**
Roofing materials : 282-90 ; lead, **285-7**, 288 ; pantiles, 289 ; shingles, **290**, 291 ; slates, **289**, 290 ; thatching, **282-4** ; tiling, 288-9
Roofs : 271-82, **272-82** ; aisle roofs, **275**, 282 ; angel supporters, **277**, **282** ; Dec. roofs, **274**, 275 ; E.E. roofs, **272**, 273, **274** ; flat, 273, **274**, **275**, 276 ; hammer-beam, **279, 280, 282** ; double hammer-beam, 281 ; Perp. roofs, **275**, 276-82, **277-82** ; stone, 226 (*see* Vaulting) ; thirteenth-century, 273 ; timber, 271-82 ; tie-beam roofs, **277** ; trussed rafter, 273 ; wagon-head (S.W. England type), **278-9**
Rotherfield, Sussex : timber-work, 264 ; Trans. work, 154, 199
Rothwell, Northants : charnel-house, 139
Round towers : **234, 235**, 236
Rubble : 146
Runwell, Essex : timber porch, 262
Rushbrooke, Suffolk : brickwork, 247
Rushden, Northants : 106, 127 ; Dec. cornice, 170 ; Geometric sedilia, 164 ; Perp. spire, **180**, 181
Rustington, Sussex : timber-work, 263
Rye, Sussex : E.E. vaulting, 230

S

SACRING window : 307
Sacheverell family : 18
St. Mary Bourne, Hants : marble font, **221**
St. Paul's Walden, Herts : 204, **205, 206**
Salisbury : Cathedral, 223, 303 ; St. Edmund's, 14, 38, " Morrowmasse " priests, 43
Sall, Norfolk : 31, 125, 299
Saltfleetby, All Saints, Lincs : E.E. vaulting, 231
Sanctuaries : 15, 88
" Sanctuary rings " : 298, 304
Sanctus bell : 306 ; bell-cote, **308**
Sandiacre, Derbys : 87 ; Saxon windows, 141
Sandon, Essex : brick porch, 247 ; brick tower, **244**, 246 ; brick window, **247**

INDEX TO TEXT AND ILLUSTRATIONS 335

Sandwich, St. Mary : 11, 38, 219
Saxmundham, Suffolk : flintwork, 237
Saxon : work, 48, 52, 70–3, 79–80, 99, 109–13, 122, **135–42**, 140–1, 301 ; arches, 141 ; masonry in Lincolnshire towers, 48 ; pilaster strip, **137**, 139–40 ; plans, **67**, **101** ; plastering, 139 ; pre-Saxon remains, 135 ; towers, 109, **111**, **137**, **140** ; triangular-headed windows, **141** ; walls, **138** ; windows, 136, 140, **141**
Scott, Sir Gilbert : 243, 271
Screens : rood, 14, **95–6**, 99, 305, **313** ; chancel, 205 ; Perp., 26, 95 ; plan, 65, 68, **97** ; Renaissance, **200**
Sculptured stones : 136
Seale, Surrey : timber porch, 262
Secular uses of churches : 36–8
Sedilia : **315**
Selmeston, Sussex : timber arcade, 264
Selsey, Sussex : bas-reliefs in Caen stone, 219
Sempringham, Lincs : ironwork, 294
Sepulchre : *see* Easter sepulchre
Shaddingfield, Suffolk : moulded brickwork porch, 249
Shenfield, Essex : brick church, 248 ; timber framing, 260 ; timber arcade, **261**, 262
Sherburn-in-Elmet, Yorks : Norman arcades, 78
Shillington, Beds : crypt, 130
Shingles : 290, **291**
Shoreham, Kent : timber porch, 303
Shorwell, Isle of Wight : vaulting, 232
Shrewsbury : St. Chad, classical design, **208** ; St. Mary, Trans. work, 154, **155**
Silchester, Hants : pre-Saxon work, 135 ; plaster-work, 252
Skelton, Yorks : E.E. church, 160
Skeyton, Norfolk : 299
Skipwith, Yorks : ironwork, **293**
Slates : 283, 288, **289**
Sleaford, Lincs : 36
Snettisham, Norfolk : Curvilinear window, 172
Soham, Cambs : Trans. work, **153**, 154 ; Perp. window, **181**
Somerby St. Margaret, Lincs : thatched church, 287
Sompting, Sussex : plaster, 253 ; Saxon tower, 139 ; Trans. vaulting, 229 ; use of Caen stone, 219
South Benfleet, Essex : 262
South Cerney, Glos : Trans. work, 153
South Elmham : seventh-century apsidal plan, 72
South Harting, Sussex : surroundings, **16** ; Elizabethan roof, 281

South Repps, Norfolk : St. James, flint emblems, 240
South Walsham, Norfolk : brickwork, 249
Southampton : St. Michael, marble font, 221
Southchurch, Essex : Norman ironwork, 29
Southminster, Essex : groins, 232
Southrop, Glos : Norman masonry, **149**
Southwell Minster : 221, 288
Southwold, Suffolk : surroundings, **31** ; flint flushwork, 237–**241** ; Perp. arcade, 184 ; porch groining, 232
Spalding, Lincs : use of stone, 216 ; fan-vaulting, 233
Spandrel : Perp., 185
Sparsholt, Bucks : 273, 292
" Speculatories " : 306
Spire : **35**, 55, **166**, 191–2 ; crocketed, 23 ; broach, **121**, **160**, **218** ; lead, **287**, 288 ; shingled, **260**, **290**
Spratton, Northants : Trans. tower, 153
Spring family : 193
Squint : **97**, 98 ; use of, 109, 308, 311
Stained glass : 86, 187–8
Stalls, choir : 315
Stamford, Lincs : St. Mary, use of stone, 217, **218**
Stanmore, Middlesex : brickwork, 202, 250 ; Parva (Whitchurch) rebuilding, 203
Stanton-in-the-Vale, Oxon : **302**
Staplehurst, Kent : ironwork, 293
Statham family : 18
Staunton Harold, Leics : Perp. traditions, 201
Staveley, Derbys : bell-cote, 308
Steeple : *see* Spire
Steetley, Derbys : Norman apse, 73, **150** ; Norman vaulting, 228
Stephen, King : 209
Stewkley, Bucks : Norman " threefold " planand central tower, 60, 73, **74**, **75**, **76**
Steyning, Sussex : use of Caen stone, 219 ; flintwork, 241
Stillingfleet, Yorks : ironwork, 293
Stock, Essex : timber tower, 260, 261
Stoke-by-Nayland, Suffolk : position of, 30
Stoke d'Abernon, Surrey : Saxon work, 135 ; E.E. vaulting, 230
Stoke Pero, Somerset : timber doorway, 267
Stondon Massey, Essex : timber-work, 259, 260
Stone : Ancaster, 223 ; Barnack, 216–7 ; Binstead quarries, Isle of Wight, 219 ; Caen, 217, 220 ; Doulting, 222; flushwork, 220, 239 ; Oolitic, 216

Stone slates (roofing): 288, **289**
Stonesfield, Oxon: quarry, 289
Stoups, holy-water: 301, 308
Stow, Lincs: 76; Norman vaulting in chancel, **227**; Norman work, 145, **146**; Saxon work, 139, 142, 144
Stowe Bardolf, Norfolk: roof, **272**
Stratford-on-Avon, Warwicks: Perp. windows, **188**, 189
Strawberry Hill: bastard Gothic, 208
String-course: Norman, 146, **150**
Stuart period: 201
Studying a parish church: 301
Sundials: 304; Saxon, **304**
Sutton, Cambs: 122, **182**
Sutton Hall: buildings attached to church, 19
Sutton-in-the-Dale, Derbys: enclosed in park, 19
Sutton St. Mary, Lincs (Long Sutton): detached tower, 117; lead spire, 288
Swanscombe, Kent: Saxon work, 135; Saxon window, **136**, 140
Swimbridge, Devon: interior, **49**; craftsmanship, 47
Swincombe, Oxon: Norman apse, 228

T

TADCASTER, Yorks: limestone, 221
Tandridge, Surrey: timber-work, 264
Tangmere, Sussex: timber-work, 264
Taunton, St. Mary Magdalene: **2**, **5**; Perp. tower, 52, 190
Tenterden, Kent: 191, 291
"Tenterden Steeple": 23
Tewkesbury Abbey church: 233
"Thack," to: 283
Thatching: 282–7, **283–5**
Thaxted, Essex: 31
Thomas, Earl of Essex: 199
Thornage, Norfolk: fireplace in tower, *115*
Thorney: use of stone, 216
Thorpe Abbots, Norfolk: fireplace in tower, 115
Thorpe, John, architect: 199
Thorpe-next-Haddiscoe, Norfolk: flintwork, **234**, 236
"Three-gable" east end: 81, **92**, **93**
Thundersleigh, Essex: timber-work, 259
Thursley, Surrey: timber-work, 264
Tickencote, Rutland: sexpartite vaulting, 229
Tickhill, Yorks: 87; Perp. capitals, 183, **184**
Tideswell, Derbys: 34, 126, 128; Dec. and Perp. windows, 173, **174**, 179

Tiles: Roman bonding, 136, **136**, 140, 288–9
Tiling: 288
Tilney All Saints, Norfolk: Norman arcade, 78, **79**, 145, 281
Timber: 256–71, **257**, **269**; arcade, 264, 267; belfries, **259**, 260, 261, **264**, **265**, 267, **269**; churches, **257**, **261**, **270**; porches, **262–3**, **303**; roofs, **272–82**; spires with wooden frame, 261; split trunks, 257; towers, 260, **266**; with shingled spires, 264
Tisbury, Wilts: sixteenth-century roof, 282
Tithes: 8, 9; "Goddes Portion," 8
Tollerton Hall, Notts: cloister, 18
Topsfield, Essex: brick church, 247
Torbrian, Devon: fan-vaulting, 233
Tottenham, Middlesex: brick porch, 250
Totternhoe quarries, Beds: 225
Tournay marble: 221
Towers: 22–3, 30–2, 52–4; belfry towers, 117; Dec., 62, 104; defensive, 111; detached, 117, **118**, **119**; engaged, 118–9, **121**; fireplaces in, 113; flanking, 113–17; flint, **235–7**, 236, **241**; inhabited, 111–3; Norman, **101**, **103**; octagonal, 122; on external piers, 119–20; Perp., **191–5**; position of, **112–4**, 115, 117; primary use of, 119; Saxon, 98; study of, 309; unusual form, 122; windows in, 111
Tracery, window: 133; brick, 247; Dec., **168–75**; E.E., 162–3; flamboyant, 173; flowing, **172**, **175**, **181**; Geometrical, **163**, **165–7**, 164; net, 173, **174**; origin of, 162; plate, 162; Perp., **183–9**; reticulated, 173
Transeptal: chapels, **62**, 93–4, 100, 102, **108**, **110**; plan, disadvantages of, 63; mistaken idea of symbolism, 98; reversion to aisled type, 63, 93, **94**; wide distribution of, 99, 100; towers, 115, 117
Transepts: 58, 62–3, 98–109; aisles added to, 106, **108**, 109, **110**; chapels of, **62**, **103**; connexion with central tower, 62, 104–6; development of, 63, 102, 106, 109; E.E., 104; Dec., 104; Perp., 105
Transition (the twelfth to thirteenth centuries): 151–3, **152–5**; doors, 293; vaulting, **229–30**
Transition periods: 151, 161
Tredington, Worcs: Trans. work, 154
Trotton, Sussex: 295; fourteenth-century roof, 273
Tudor rose: 185, 193.
Tunstead, Norfolk: flintwork, 240, 296

INDEX TO TEXT AND ILLUSTRATIONS 337

Turvey, Beds : ironwork, 295, **297**
Tympanum, Norman : **144**

U

UFFINGTON, Berks : 104, 122, 294 ; cruciform plan, **62** ; exterior cross, 303
Ufford, Suffolk : flint porch, **220**
Upleadon, Glos : ironwork, 294
Upper chambers : in porches 125 ; uses of, 125–6 ; fireplaces in, 126 ; porch chamber, 126 **127** squint in, 126
Upper Deal, Kent : red brick tower, 252
Upsala Cathedral, Sweden : 243
Upwell, Norfolk : 276 ; lectern, **311**, 313

V

VAULTING : 146, 152–6, 226–33 ; Saxon, 227 ; Norman, 146, **227** ; Trans., 152, 183, 225, **229** ; E.E., **229**, 230 ; barrel-vault, 146, 226 ; cross-vaulting, 227 ; fan-vaulting, 183, 232, **233** ; groined vaulting, 156 ; lierne, **230**, 231 ; quadripartite, 227, 230 ; ribbed vaulting, 227 ; sexpartite, 229
Vestry : 127–8, 308 ; altar in, 128 ; position of, 127
Viking ship in door ironwork : 293
Vine-leaf moulding ornament : 185

W

WAKERLEY, Northants : Norman arch, 144
Walberswick, Suffolk : 237 ; flintwork, 239
Waldringfield, Suffolk : brick tower, 250
Wall-paintings : 253
Walls, Saxon : 139
Walpole, Horace : 208
Walpole St. Peter, Norfolk : 120
Walsoken, Norfolk : Trans. work, 152
Walton Priory, Yorkshire : 255
Waltham Abbey, Essex : ironwork on door, 292
Wansford, Northants : Saxon tooling, 139
Warbledon : timber porch, 262
Warburton, Cheshire : timber-work, **269**, 270
Wareham, Dorset : Saxon windows, 140
Warkworth, Northumberland : Norman vaulting, 227
Warmington, Northants : clerestory, 83 ; E.E. work, **159**
Warndon, Worcs : timber tower, **266**
Wars of Roses : 51

Warwick : St. John's, 119
Wastdale, Westmorland : 25, **27**
Watchet, Somerset : wall-plate angels, 279
" Water-holding " moulding : 158
Weald, churches of the : 23
Wearmouth, Durham : stonework, 113, 137, 215
Weaverthorpe, Yorks : sundial, **304**
Wedmore, Somerset : 105, **106**
Weekley, Northants : E.E. and Dec. arches, 89
Wells Cathedral : west front, 222 ; St. Cuthbert, tower, 52 ; Perp. roof, 276
West Chiltington, Sussex : 272 ; timberwork, 263
West Hanningfield, Essex : timber towers, 260, 261
West Mersey, Essex : use of Roman piers, 137
West Theddlethorpe, Lincs : brickwork, 249
West Walton, Norfolk : 117 ; E.E. capitals, **158**
West Wittering, Sussex : use of Caen stone, 219
Westcott Barton, Oxon : 292–9
Westhall, Suffolk : Dec. window, 172
Westham, Sussex : consecration crosses, 303
Westminster Abbey : Romanesque work, 48, 161 ; grill, 295 ; sanctuary, 299
Weston-in-Gordano, Somerset : 124 ; bellcote, 308
Wetherden, Suffolk : flintwork, 237
Whaplode, Lincs : 115 ; Barnack stone, 216
Whiston, Northants : Perp. church, 198 199
Whitchurch (Stanmore Parva), Middlesex : 203
White Roothing, Essex : 294
Whitewashing : 255–6
Whittlesford, Cambs : 128
Wicket in door : 300
Wicklewood, Norfolk : fireplace in tower 113
Widdicombe, Devon : Perp. tower, 190
Wilby, Northants : 122
Wilfrid, St. : 255, 287
Wilfrid, Bishop of York : 215
William of Malmesbury : 257
William the Conqueror : 48
Willingale Spain : 292
Willingham, Cambs : 128 ; vaulting, 232, 287
Wimborne : E.E. window, 156
Winchcombe, Glos : 87
Winchester Cathedral : 98, 223 ; marble font, 221
Winchfield, Hants : Norman arch, 144

338 INDEX TO TEXT AND ILLUSTRATIONS

Windows : Saxon, **136**, 140, **141** ; Norman, **144**, **146** ; E.E., **156**, **157** ; Geometric, **163**, **165**, **167** ; Dec., **171–5** ; Perp., **181–92** ; dormer, 305 ; " low-side," 306 ; rood, **395**–6 ; sacring, 306 ; square-headed, 173, **174**
Windrush, River : 24
Wing, Bucks : Italian apse, 71 ; pre-Conquest crypt, 129
Wingerworth : enclosed in park, 19
Wingham, Kent : timber arcade, 264
Winkburn, Notts : enclosed in park, 19
Winkfield, Berks : wooden arcade, 267
Winscombe, Somerset : Perp. work, 193, **194**
Witham, Essex : timber spire, 261
Witley, Surrey : timber porch, 262
Witney, Oxon : 63, **64**, 99, 130 ; E.E. work, 159
Wittering, Northants : Trans. work, 153
Wittlewood : chequer-work, 241
Wolds, Yorkshire : 75
Wollaton, Notts : 34
Wolstenham, Sir John : 202
Wolverton, Hants : rebuilding, 205, brickwork, **207**, 252
Woodbury, Devon : 100
Woodford, Northants : Geometric work, 164
Woodham Walter, Essex : brick Elizabethan church, **197**, 199, 247
Woodstock, Oxon : E.E. capitals, 158 ; Geometric aisle, 164
Woolbeding, Sussex : Saxon, **139**

Woolpit, Suffolk : hammer-beam roof, 281 ; porch, **124**, 125
Worbstow, Cornwall : quarries, 218
Worfield, Salop : harmony with scenery, 16, **17**
Worlingworth, Suffolk : hammer-beam roof, 281
Worstead, Norfolk : 128 ; vaulting, 232
Worth, Sussex : pre-Conquest apsidal plan, 71, **72**
Wren, Sir Christopher : 203, 245
Wrington, Somerset : Perp. work, 193 tower, **194** ; fan-vaulting, 233
Wrotham, Kent : 34, 119, 291
Wykeham, William of : 194
Wymondham, Norfolk : 31 ; hammer-beam roof, 28
Wysall, Notts : Dec. roof, 275
Wythburn, Cumb : 25, 27

Y

YAPTON, Sussex : **123**, 264
Yardley Hastings, Northants : Geometric work, 164
Yarmouth, Norfolk : 179
Yarpole, Herefords : 267
Yate, Glos : Perp. tower, 190, **191**
Yedding, Suffolk : brick tower, 250
Yelford, Oxon : **25** ; Perp. work, 24
York : Minster, 179, 221, 255 ; St. Cross, 297 ; St. Michael-le-Belfry, Perp. work, 198 ; St. Peter, 287
Yorkshire millstone grit : 179

www.ingramcontent.com/pod-product-compliance
Ingram Content Group UK Ltd.
Pitfield, Milton Keynes, MK11 3LW, UK
UKHW021257180426
11947UKWH00015B/897